FRANK BISHOP

ULTIMATE DIY SELF-SUFFIC...

OFF GRID
SURVIVAL PROJECTS

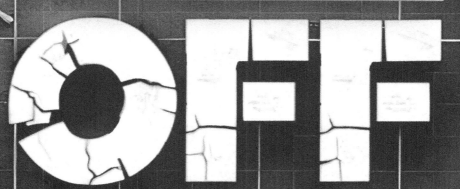

80+ PROJECTS

EXCLUSIVE BONUSES

PROTECT YOUR FAMILY & HOME
BEFORE DISASTER STRIKES

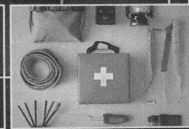

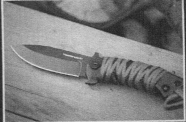

TABLE OF CONTENTS

BONUS GUIDE

What You'll Get:

1. **The Survival Vault: 20 Bonus Videos on Off-Grid Survival**
   - Gain access to **over 8 hours of expert-led video tutorials** covering **water filtration, solar power setup, food preservation, and home security strategies**. These hands-on demonstrations bring the projects in this book to life, ensuring you can apply every skill with confidence.
2. **The Blackout-Proof Kitchen**
   - A **survival cookbook** designed for **grid-down scenarios**, featuring **fuel-efficient, long-lasting meals** using preserved foods and off-grid cooking methods.
3. **The 4-Season Survival Planner**
   - A **month-by-month guide** to **off-grid maintenance, prepping tasks, and seasonal survival strategies**, ensuring your home and resources remain secure year-round.
4. **The Forever Food Secrets**
   - A **detailed guide to food preservation**, covering **canning, bottling, and long-term storage techniques** to keep your food supply stocked for any crisis.

How to Access Your Bonuses:

There are two easy ways to access your bonuses:

1. **Scan the QR Code:**

   - **Step 1:** Open your smartphone's camera.
   - **Step 2:** Point it at the QR code shown on this page.
   - **Step 3:** Click the notification to access your bonuses.

2. **Visit the Web Address:**

   - **Step 1:** Open your web browser.
   - **Step 2:** Type in the following URL: (inkworks.site/off-grid-frank-bishop)
   - **Step 3:** Press Enter to unlock your digital bonuses.

These bonuses are designed to enhance your learning experience, giving you the tools and knowledge to thrive in any off-grid situation. Take the next step toward self-reliance today!

1. OFF-GRID SURVIVAL FUNDAMENTALS

1.1 INTRODUCTION

In a world marked by uncertainty—be it climate change, economic instability, or other unforeseen challenges—having the skills to thrive independently is more important than ever. This chapter lays the groundwork for understanding the fundamentals of off-grid living, achieving self-sufficiency and resilience through practical off-grid projects, and setting you up for success as you delve deeper into each project throughout the book.

Off-grid living isn't just about survival; it's about embracing a lifestyle that empowers you. As you turn these pages, you'll discover how to reclaim control over your resources, reduce your carbon footprint, and cultivate a harmonious relationship with nature. Each sub-chapter within this book will equip you with the essential knowledge and tools needed to face global challenges head-on. You will learn how to build, create, and innovate, transforming your living space into a sustainable haven.

The journey begins with a proactive and confident mindset. You need to approach these projects with determination, ready to embrace both the challenges and the rewards that come with off-grid living. Each task you undertake will enhance your skills, build your confidence, and deepen your connection to the land. You may encounter obstacles along the way, but remember that every problem has a solution. The key lies in your willingness to learn and adapt.

As you embark on this path, you will explore a range of projects that are both practical and impactful. From setting up a worm composting system to constructing a rainwater harvesting setup, each project not only serves a functional purpose but also contributes to a broader vision of sustainability. These initiatives vary in terms of investment, from minimal to significant, yet many can typically be accomplished using easily obtainable materials, ensuring they are within reach for everyone, no matter their level of experience.

This chapter will introduce you to the principles of off-grid living, helping you to understand the underlying concepts that make each project successful. You'll learn about the importance of resource management, waste reduction, and energy efficiency. These fundamentals will provide a solid foundation for the more complex projects that lie ahead. By the end of this chapter, you will feel empowered and ready to take the first steps toward building a self-reliant future.

You will also gain insight into the mindset necessary for successful off-grid living. It requires a willingness to experiment and a readiness to think outside the box. There may be moments of trial and error, but these experiences will sharpen your problem-solving skills and foster a sense of accomplishment. You'll discover that each project not only enhances your physical environment but also enriches your mental resilience.

As you read through the projects, pay close attention to the safety guidelines and material specifications. They are there to ensure your well-being as you navigate through potentially hazardous tasks. Remember, safety is paramount, especially when working with tools or engaging in tasks that involve electricity or heavy lifting. Following the instructions closely will keep you safe and help you achieve the desired results.

In addition to safety, consider the environmental impact of each project. Many of the techniques you'll learn are designed to reduce waste and conserve resources, contributing to a healthier planet. By adopting sustainable practices, you not only enhance your own quality of life but also play a part in the larger effort to protect the Earth for future generations.

This chapter serves as your launchpad into the world of off-grid living. It's a place to gather your thoughts, prepare your mindset, and get acquainted with the tools and techniques that will follow. You will find that each project is designed with clarity and precision, providing you with step-by-step instructions that are easy to follow. Whether you are a seasoned DIY enthusiast or just starting out, you will find value in the information presented.

As you progress through this book, remember that the journey to self-sufficiency is not a race. Take your time to absorb the information, practice the skills, and appreciate the small victories along the way. Every project completed is a step toward greater independence and self-reliance.

With this foundational knowledge in hand, you are ready to embark on the exciting projects that await. Let's dive into the first steps of your off-grid survival journey. Your adventure toward a more sustainable, resilient, and fulfilling life begins now.

1.2 UNDERSTANDING OFF-GRID SURVIVAL PROJECTS

Off-grid survival projects are practical, hands-on initiatives designed to help you reclaim your independence and self-sufficiency. They represent a vital pathway to a lifestyle where you can thrive without being overly reliant on public utilities and modern conveniences. In a world where disruptions can occur at any moment, mastering these projects equips you with the skills and knowledge to navigate challenges with confidence.

By engaging in off-grid projects, you gain control over your life. You learn to harvest water from the environment, produce your own food, and create renewable energy sources. These skills empower you, transforming you from a passive consumer into an active participant in your own survival. You discover that the ability to manage resources, even in difficult circumstances, can significantly enhance your security and peace of mind.

As you delve into this journey, you will explore a variety of projects that address critical aspects of off-grid living. These projects encompass Water Harvesting, Collection, Purification, and Storage, allowing you to ensure a consistent and safe water supply. You will learn how to capture rainwater, filter it, and store it efficiently, enabling you to live sustainably.

Energy and Power Sources projects will teach you how to harness renewable energy. You'll gain insight into solar panel installations, wind turbines, and other alternative energy methods that reduce your reliance on the grid. By generating your own electricity, you take a significant step toward autonomy.

Food Production and Preservation is another essential area you'll explore. You'll discover how to grow your own vegetables, fruits, and herbs, and learn preservation techniques to store your harvest for later use. This knowledge not only enhances your diet but also reduces your dependency on grocery stores.

First Aid, Hygiene, and Health projects prepare you to handle medical emergencies and maintain personal wellness without the immediate support of healthcare systems. You'll learn to create basic first aid kits, understand essential medical procedures, and promote hygiene practices that protect your health.

Infrastructure, Communication, and Safety projects will help you develop a secure living environment. You'll learn how to create shelters, set up reliable communication systems, and establish safety protocols. These elements are critical for ensuring your well-being in an off-grid lifestyle.

Waste Management and Recycling are crucial for maintaining a clean and sustainable living space. You will explore composting methods, recycling techniques, and strategies for minimizing waste. Understanding how to manage your waste effectively contributes to a healthier environment.

Finally, you'll familiarize yourself with essential Tools and Equipment. You'll learn which tools are necessary for various projects and how to maintain them, ensuring you have the right resources to succeed in your off-grid endeavors.

With the right knowledge and a positive attitude, you can embark on this rewarding journey toward off-grid living. Each project you undertake not only enhances your skill set but also builds your confidence. You'll find that with determination and practice, you can master these techniques and create a sustainable lifestyle that meets your needs.

As you begin this journey, keep in mind that the process may involve trial and error. You might face challenges, but each obstacle presents an opportunity for learning and growth. Embrace the mindset of a problem solver. Celebrate small victories along the way, and don't hesitate to seek out resources, whether it's books, online forums, or local workshops, to deepen your understanding.

Remember, the goal is not perfection but progress. Each project completed brings you one step closer to a life of independence and security. By taking the initiative to learn and implement these skills, you're investing in your future and the environment. You have the power to shape your destiny, reduce your environmental footprint, and contribute positively to the world around you.

So gather your materials, roll up your sleeves, and prepare to dive into the world of off-grid survival projects. The skills you acquire will serve you well, providing you with the tools to thrive in any situation. With each step, you're not just building a more sustainable lifestyle; you're forging a path to greater resilience and empowerment.

1.3 THE IMPORTANCE OF SELF-SUFFICIENCY IN AN UNCERTAIN WORLD

In today's uncertain world, self-sufficiency emerges as a vital skill set. Global events, from natural disasters to economic downturns, highlight the importance of taking control of your resources. You face challenges that can disrupt daily life, whether due to hurricanes, wildfires, or even supply chain shortages. By engaging in off-grid survival projects, you equip yourself with the tools necessary to weather these storms.

Imagine a scenario where a severe weather event strikes your area, causing widespread power outages and disruption of services. In such times, your ability to produce your own food, harvest water, and generate energy becomes paramount. Each off-grid project you undertake builds a buffer against the unpredictability of life. You gain confidence knowing that you can rely on your skills and resources, rather than waiting for external assistance that may be delayed or unavailable.

Climate change exacerbates these challenges, bringing extreme weather patterns and shifting agricultural zones. The increasing frequency of droughts, floods, and storms pushes the need for self-reliance further to the forefront. Off-grid projects, such as rainwater harvesting or solar energy systems, offer solutions to adapt to these changes. They empower you to create a resilient lifestyle that mitigates the impacts of environmental shifts.

Economic instability also poses a significant threat. Fluctuating prices for food and fuel can strain your budget and limit your access to essentials. By growing your own vegetables or producing energy through solar panels, you reduce your reliance on the volatile market. You transform your living space into a source of stability, allowing you to weather financial uncertainties with greater ease.

During the COVID-19 pandemic, many individuals experienced the stark reality of supply shortages. Grocery store shelves emptied quickly, leaving families scrambling for basic necessities. Those who had previously invested time in off-grid projects found themselves in a more secure position. They had homegrown produce, stored food, and alternative energy sources that allowed them to thrive despite the chaos. This experience serves as a powerful reminder of the benefits of preparation.

Consider the lessons learned from recent natural disasters, such as hurricanes or wildfires. Communities affected by these events often find themselves isolated, cut off from external help. Residents with off-grid capabilities can sustain themselves, accessing food and water independently. This level of preparedness not only supports individual families but can also foster community resilience. When more people engage in self-sufficient practices, entire neighborhoods become less vulnerable to crises.

Reflect on your current level of preparedness. Are you equipped to handle an emergency? How would you fare if your access to basic resources was suddenly cut off? Off-grid projects provide you with the means to enhance your resilience. Whether it's constructing a rainwater collection system, establishing a vegetable garden, or learning to preserve food, each step you take brings you closer to independence.

Start by evaluating your immediate needs. Assess your water supply, energy sources, and food production capabilities. Consider where you currently rely on external systems and how you can transition to more self-sufficient practices. For instance, if you depend on municipal water, explore the feasibility of a rainwater harvesting system. If you buy produce weekly, think about creating a small garden or joining a local cooperative to source food directly from farmers.

Embrace the idea of incremental progress. You don't have to overhaul your entire lifestyle overnight. Begin with small, manageable projects that fit your skills and resources. Perhaps you start by composting kitchen scraps or installing a few solar lights in your garden. As you gain confidence, expand your efforts to include more complex projects like building a greenhouse or a full-scale solar power system.

The journey toward self-sufficiency is not merely about survival; it's about empowerment. Each project you complete instills a sense of accomplishment and control. You learn valuable skills, gain practical knowledge, and develop a deeper connection to your environment. This process fosters a mindset of resilience, equipping you to handle future challenges with a proactive attitude.

By thinking critically about your lifestyle and preparedness, you take the first step toward building a secure and independent future. Off-grid survival projects provide practical solutions to address the uncertainties of modern life. The skills you acquire through these endeavors create a foundation for resilience, ensuring that you can navigate whatever comes your way. Each project not only enhances your self-sufficiency but also contributes to a broader movement towards sustainability and environmental stewardship.

You are not just preparing for the unexpected; you are cultivating a lifestyle that aligns with your values and goals. As you delve into these projects, keep your eyes open to the possibilities. Each task completed brings you closer to a more resilient and empowered self, capable of thriving in an ever-changing world.

1.4 PREPARING FOR CLIMATE CHANGE AND ECONOMIC INSTABILITY

In today's world, the impacts of climate change and economic instability are increasingly evident. You see it in erratic weather patterns, devastating wildfires, floods, and rising food prices. The urgency to prepare for these challenges cannot be overstated. By adopting an off-grid lifestyle, you empower yourself to face these uncertainties head-on, ensuring that your basic needs are met, even when external systems falter.

Imagine the stress of a sudden supply chain disruption. Grocery store shelves empty overnight, leaving you scrambling for essentials. You have a choice: panic or prepare. When you invest in off-grid projects, you take control of your situation. Growing your own food, collecting rainwater, and generating energy through solar panels not only fulfill your needs but also shield you from the volatility of commercial systems.

As climate change progresses, extreme weather events will become more common. Communities may find themselves without power for days or even weeks. In such instances, those who have established alternative energy sources, like solar or wind, remain unaffected. You can continue to cook, stay warm, and maintain your daily routine while others are left in the dark. This independence fosters resilience, enabling you to adapt to sudden changes in your environment.

Furthermore, economic instability often leads to rising prices for goods and services. When the economy takes a hit, you may find yourself grappling with higher costs for food and energy. By producing your own food and harnessing renewable energy, you create a buffer against these financial pressures. You reduce your reliance on the market, allowing you to allocate resources elsewhere, such as savings or emergency funds.

Consider the long-term implications of adopting an off-grid lifestyle. Each project you undertake is a step towards sustainability and security. Establishing a vegetable garden today means fresh produce for your family tomorrow. Creating a rainwater collection system provides you with a reliable water source, regardless of external conditions. These are not just short-term fixes; they are investments in your future.

Moreover, living off-grid allows you to mitigate risks associated with global supply chains. The more self-sufficient you become, the less vulnerable you are to outside forces. If a natural disaster strikes or a political crisis unfolds, you are better equipped to weather the storm. Your ability to meet your own needs reduces the panic that often accompanies such events, leading to a calmer, more controlled response.

Beyond practical advantages, engaging in off-grid projects cultivates a mindset of resourcefulness and innovation. You learn to troubleshoot problems, think critically, and develop skills that extend beyond mere survival. This self-sufficiency fosters confidence. You become a problem solver, equipped to handle challenges that arise in everyday life and emergencies alike.

Consider how empowering it feels to provide for yourself and your loved ones. You know exactly where your food comes from and how it is produced. You take pride in the effort you put into growing vegetables or raising chickens. This connection to your food source enhances your appreciation for what you consume and fosters a sense of responsibility toward the environment.

Each off-grid project is a building block in your journey toward sustainability. You start with simple tasks—perhaps building a compost bin or starting a herb garden. As your skills develop, you can tackle more complex projects, like constructing a solar water heater or a chicken coop. With each completed project, you reinforce your capacity to provide for yourself while deepening your understanding of the systems that sustain you.

Moreover, these projects offer an opportunity to connect with your community. As you embark on your off-grid journey, share your experiences and knowledge with neighbors. Organize workshops or skill-sharing sessions. When you engage with others, you not only expand your own capabilities but also foster a spirit of cooperation and support. Communities that work together are more resilient, and this collaboration becomes invaluable in times of crisis.

You also cultivate a sense of environmental stewardship through off-grid living. By minimizing waste, conserving resources, and prioritizing renewable energy, you actively contribute to the health of the planet. Your actions create a ripple effect, inspiring others to consider their own environmental impact. Each small step you take contributes to a larger movement toward sustainability, reinforcing the idea that individual actions matter.

You may encounter challenges as you embrace this lifestyle. Not every project will go smoothly, and you might face setbacks along the way. However, view these obstacles as opportunities for growth. Each failure teaches you valuable lessons and strengthens your resolve. You learn to adapt, pivot, and find alternative solutions, honing your skills in the process.

As you embark on your off-grid journey, consider setting clear goals. Identify which projects align with your immediate needs and long-term aspirations. Focus on creating a diverse skill set that encompasses food production, energy generation, and waste management. By establishing a roadmap for your journey, you maintain motivation and ensure that each project builds upon the last.

Remember, becoming off-grid is not just about surviving; it's about thriving in an uncertain world. By taking control of your resources and honing essential skills, you lay the foundation for a more secure, sustainable future. Embrace the process, celebrate your achievements, and remain open to learning. Each step you take brings you closer to a life of independence and resilience.

1.5 THE BENEFITS OF LIVING OFF THE GRID

Going off the grid offers a transformative journey that fosters independence, cost savings, and enhanced security. This lifestyle change isn't just about disconnecting from utilities; it's about taking control of your life and resources. You harness the power of nature, using it to meet your needs while creating a more sustainable future.

Independence is one of the most compelling benefits of off-grid living. When you cultivate your own food, produce your own energy, and manage your water supply, you free yourself from the fluctuations of the market and the demands of utility companies. You choose what you grow, when to harvest, and how to live. This self-reliance instills a sense of empowerment that resonates deeply. You no longer depend on grocery stores or power grids for survival. Instead, you develop skills that serve you for a lifetime, whether it's gardening, raising livestock, or installing solar panels.

Imagine the satisfaction of walking into your garden and picking fresh vegetables for dinner. You know exactly where your food comes from, and you've eliminated the middleman. This not only saves you money but also guarantees that you're consuming organic, chemical-free produce. You can grow seasonal crops, ensuring a diverse diet while also preserving the harvest for the winter months. You might even barter with neighbors, trading surplus vegetables for eggs or homemade goods, further enhancing your independence.

Cost savings play a significant role in the appeal of off-grid living. While the initial investment in systems like solar panels, wind turbines, or water collection might seem daunting, the long-term savings far outweigh these costs. Once you install your renewable energy systems, your electricity bills drop dramatically, often disappearing entirely. You gain the ability to generate your own power, reducing reliance on commercial energy sources that can hike prices unexpectedly.

Moreover, by growing your own food, you significantly cut grocery bills. A well-planned garden can yield a bountiful harvest, providing fresh produce throughout the growing season and beyond. With careful planning, you can produce enough to last through the winter, further decreasing your food expenses. For example, you can preserve fruits and vegetables through canning, freezing, or dehydrating, creating a stockpile that keeps you well-fed and financially stable.

Greater security is another key advantage of living off the grid. In uncertain times—whether due to economic fluctuations, natural disasters, or global crises—being self-sufficient offers peace of mind. You can ride out storms without fear of power outages or food shortages. With your own systems in place, you maintain a steady supply of energy and food, providing a safety net for your family.

When you rely on public utilities, you become vulnerable to disruptions. Power outages, water shortages, and supply chain issues can leave you scrambling for basic necessities. By contrast, off-grid living fortifies your resilience. You can store water, generate electricity, and have food on hand, reducing stress during emergencies. You create a stable environment for yourself and your loved ones, which contributes to an overall sense of well-being.

Beyond the immediate benefits, living off-grid significantly improves your quality of life in both the short term and the long term. The autonomy you experience fosters a deep connection to your environment. You become more aware of natural cycles and develop a profound appreciation for the land that sustains you. Each project you undertake—whether it's building a chicken coop or setting up a rainwater collection system—deepens your relationship with your surroundings and instills a sense of accomplishment.

Moreover, off-grid living promotes a simpler lifestyle that encourages mindfulness. Without the distractions of constant connectivity, you find more time to enjoy the little things—savoring a home-cooked meal, spending evenings under the stars, or reading a book by candlelight. This shift leads to improved mental health, as you cultivate gratitude and presence in your daily life.

The long-term gains of this lifestyle extend beyond personal benefits. By living sustainably, you contribute to environmental health. You reduce waste, conserve resources, and minimize your carbon footprint. Each step toward self-sufficiency has a positive ripple effect, encouraging others to consider their impact on the planet. This sense of community—whether through local farmers' markets, shared workshops, or online forums—creates a network of like-minded individuals who support each other in their off-grid journeys.

In embracing an off-grid lifestyle, you cultivate not only skills but also resilience and adaptability. You learn to troubleshoot problems and innovate solutions, qualities that are invaluable in any aspect of life. Each challenge you face—be it fixing a broken solar panel or dealing with pest issues in the garden—builds confidence and resourcefulness. These traits carry over into everyday situations, enhancing your ability to navigate life's uncertainties.

In conclusion, going off the grid offers a pathway to independence, cost savings, and greater security. Each project you undertake empowers you to take control of your resources, enhances your quality of life, and fosters a sustainable future. As you embark on this journey, remember that every step, no matter how small, contributes to a more resilient and fulfilling existence.

1.6 COMMON MISCONCEPTIONS ABOUT OFF-GRID LIVING

Many misconceptions surround off-grid living, leading potential enthusiasts to hesitate before taking the plunge. One common myth suggests that off-grid living requires complete isolation from society. In reality, individuals can enjoy a connected lifestyle while embracing self-sufficiency. Many off-grid communities thrive on collaboration and mutual support. Neighbors often share resources, tools, and knowledge, fostering a sense of camaraderie that enriches the experience. Regular gatherings, local markets, and shared projects ensure that residents maintain social connections while living independently.

Another misconception is the belief that going off-grid necessitates a hefty financial investment. While some initial costs—like solar panels or rainwater collection systems—can seem daunting, there are various ways to minimize expenses. Many off-grid dwellers start small, implementing simple systems that gradually expand as they gain experience. For instance, one can begin with a modest garden and a few solar lights before scaling up to a larger solar array and more complex systems. Utilizing reclaimed materials for building projects and sourcing second-hand tools can also drastically reduce costs. By prioritizing budget-friendly solutions, anyone can embark on an off-grid journey without breaking the bank.

Additionally, the idea that off-grid living means abandoning modern technology is another prevalent myth. While some individuals choose to disconnect completely, many others find a balance between self-sufficiency and technology. For example, solar-powered devices and energy-efficient appliances allow off-grid residents to enjoy conveniences like refrigeration, heating, and communication without relying on the grid. Internet access is also possible through satellite or mobile connections, enabling individuals to work remotely or stay connected with loved ones. This integration of technology allows for a more comfortable lifestyle while still embracing the principles of sustainability.

Moreover, off-grid living encourages innovation and creativity. Many individuals find joy in problem-solving and experimenting with various systems that enhance their quality of life. DIY projects, like building a solar oven or setting up a composting toilet, not only reduce dependence on commercial products but also foster a sense of accomplishment and self-reliance.

By addressing these misconceptions, potential off-grid dwellers can see that this lifestyle is accessible, affordable, and compatible with modern conveniences. With the right mindset and resources, anyone can embark on an off-grid journey that aligns with their values and aspirations.

1.7 ASSESSING NEEDS AND GOALS

Assessing your needs and goals is the cornerstone of embarking on a journey towards off-grid living. It involves a clear-eyed evaluation of what you and your family require to live comfortably and safely without reliance on public utilities and services. This step is not just about dreaming big but grounding those dreams in practicality and achievable steps. Start by considering the essentials: water, food, shelter, and energy. How much water do you use daily? What are your dietary needs and how can they be met through gardening, foraging, or raising animals? What kind of shelter will protect you from the elements and at what temperature do you feel comfortable? How much energy do you need to power necessary appliances and tools? These questions form the foundation of your off-grid survival plan.

Next, think about your goals. Are you looking to be completely self-sufficient, or are you aiming to reduce your reliance on certain utilities? Do you want to live off-grid temporarily or make it a permanent lifestyle? Goals can range from building a fully sustainable home that generates its own power and collects rainwater to simply starting a vegetable garden to supplement your food supply. Your goals will guide the projects you prioritize and the skills you need to develop.

It's also important to assess your current skills and knowledge. What do you already know how to do, and what do you need to learn? If you're a beginner gardener, for example, you might start with a small, manageable plot before expanding. If you're unfamiliar with solar panel installation, seeking out workshops or online tutorials could be a good first step. Identifying these gaps early on allows you to plan for learning and improvement.

Consider, too, your financial resources. Many off-grid projects require an initial investment, whether it's buying tools, seeds, or materials for a rainwater collection system. By assessing your budget, you can plan projects that are financially feasible and look for ways to save money, such as repurposing materials or doing the work yourself.

Finally, think about your timeline. Some projects can be completed in a weekend, while others might take months or even years. Setting realistic deadlines for each goal will help you maintain momentum and measure your progress. Remember, transitioning to a off-grid lifestyle is a marathon, not a sprint. It's about making consistent, sustainable changes that align with your long-term vision for self-sufficiency.

By taking the time to assess your needs and goals, you're laying the groundwork for a successful transition to off-grid living. This process not only helps you prioritize and plan but also ensures that your journey is tailored to your unique situation and aspirations. With a clear understanding of where you're starting from and where you want to go, you're ready to take the next steps toward a more independent and resilient lifestyle.

1.8 CREATING A PERSONALIZED OFF-GRID SURVIVAL PLAN

To embark on the journey of off-grid living, the first step involves creating a personalized Off-Grid Survival Plan. This plan reflects individual circumstances, preferences, and aspirations. The process begins with a thorough evaluation of daily routines.

Evaluate Daily Routines:

Start by examining your current daily life. What activities are essential? How much water do you consume each day? Consider not just drinking water, but also what is used for cooking, cleaning, and gardening. Document the frequency and quantity of your water use. Next, analyze your food consumption patterns. What types of meals do you prepare? Do you rely heavily on processed foods, or do you incorporate fresh fruits and vegetables? Take note of your dietary needs and preferences, as these will shape your gardening and food preservation efforts.

Additionally, assess energy usage. Identify which appliances are vital for daily operations. List out items like refrigerators, lights, computers, and tools. Calculate how much electricity they consume and consider alternatives. Understanding your energy needs will guide you in selecting appropriate off-grid energy solutions, whether it be solar panels, wind turbines, or a combination.

Map Out Available Space:

Once you have a clear picture of daily routines, the next step is to map out available space. This can be done using graph paper or digital design tools. Sketch your property, marking existing structures, gardens, and areas suitable for new projects. Pay attention to sunlight exposure, as this will impact solar energy collection and gardening efforts.

Determine how much space you can dedicate to various projects. If gardening is a priority, allocate a section of land for growing vegetables and herbs. Consider building a composting area, a chicken coop for eggs, or even a rainwater collection system. Understanding the layout of your property allows you to optimize space and plan for future expansion.

Plan the Budget:

With a clear evaluation of daily routines and space mapping, the next step is planning the budget. Begin by identifying the costs associated with your essential projects. Make a list of materials and tools required for each task. For example, if you're planning to build a raised garden bed, you'll need lumber, soil, and seeds. Research prices from local suppliers and estimate total costs for each project.

Factor in potential hidden costs as well. Some projects may require additional permits, equipment, or maintenance supplies. Establish a budget range for each project and prioritize based on urgency and feasibility. It's essential to remain realistic about what can be accomplished within your financial means.

Prioritize Projects Based on Goals, Resources, and Timeline:

Now, it's time to prioritize projects according to your goals, available resources, and timelines. Review the initial goals you set for your off-grid lifestyle. For example, if your primary goal is food self-sufficiency, focus on establishing a garden and composting system first.

Consider the resources you have at hand. Do you possess tools that can aid in construction? Are there existing materials that can be repurposed? Use these assets to inform your project selection. Projects that require fewer resources should be tackled first, building confidence and skills as you progress.

Establish a realistic timeline for each project. For instance, a simple task like starting a small herb garden may take only a week, while constructing a rainwater collection system could require several weeks of planning and installation. Break larger projects into smaller, manageable tasks with specific deadlines. This method helps maintain motivation and a sense of accomplishment as you check items off your list.

Create a Visual Project Timeline:

A visual project timeline can serve as a useful tool to keep track of progress. Use a calendar or project management software to mark deadlines for each project. Include milestones for significant tasks, such as planting seeds or completing construction. This timeline not only organizes your efforts but also offers a clear view of what lies ahead.

Assess and Adjust:

As you implement your Off-Grid Survival Plan, remain open to reassessment. Life circumstances, resource availability, and personal goals can shift over time. Schedule regular check-ins to evaluate your progress. Are you meeting your targets? Are there areas where adjustments are necessary?

Flexibility is vital in off-grid living. Embrace the learning curve and be willing to adapt. If a particular gardening method proves unsuccessful, explore alternatives. If energy needs change, revisit your energy solutions. Staying responsive to challenges and successes keeps the momentum alive in your journey.

Engage the Community:

Lastly, don't underestimate the power of community. Engage with local groups or online forums dedicated to off-grid living. Sharing experiences and gathering insights from others can provide invaluable guidance and support. Collaborating on projects or participating in workshops helps expand knowledge and resources.

By evaluating daily routines, mapping out available space, planning the budget, and prioritizing projects, individuals set the stage for a successful transition to off-grid living. This personalized plan serves as a dynamic blueprint, guiding each step towards a self-sufficient lifestyle.

1.9 OFF-GRID RESILIENCE & ADAPTATION

Cultivating Resilience and Adaptability in Off-Grid Living

Embracing an off-grid lifestyle requires more than just a change in living conditions; it demands a mindset shift towards resilience and adaptability. To thrive in this environment, individuals must equip themselves with the skills and knowledge to face unpredictable challenges. Here's how to cultivate these essential traits.

Continuous Learning:

First and foremost, committing to continuous learning is vital. Off-grid living encompasses various skills—farming, construction, renewable energy, and more. Start by identifying areas of interest or necessity. For instance, if you plan to grow your own food, delve into gardening techniques suited for your climate. Research companion planting, pest management, and soil health. Books, online courses, and local workshops serve as excellent resources.

Engage with experienced off-grid dwellers. Their insights can reveal practical tips and techniques not found in books. For example, learning about seasonal planting can drastically improve crop yields, while understanding local wildlife helps prevent garden losses. Regularly update your knowledge base to adapt to new challenges, such as changing weather patterns or pest infestations.

Building Robust Systems:

Next, focus on building robust systems. This means creating self-sustaining processes that reduce reliance on external resources. For instance, establish a water collection system that gathers rainwater. Use gutters to channel rain into storage barrels, ensuring a steady supply for gardening and household needs.

Create a composting system that transforms kitchen scraps into valuable soil amendments. By reducing waste and enriching soil, this practice not only supports gardening efforts but also fosters a circular economy on your property. When systems are interconnected, they create a buffer against disruptions. If the garden struggles, compost can improve soil quality, while excess produce can feed livestock or be preserved for later use.

Fostering Community Support:

Community support plays a crucial role in navigating the challenges of off-grid living. Seek out like-minded individuals who share similar goals and values. This can include local gardening clubs, off-grid forums, or homesteading groups. Establishing relationships within this community provides a network for sharing resources, skills, and advice.

Participating in group activities fosters a sense of belonging and collaboration. Consider organizing skill-sharing workshops where individuals can teach others how to build, grow, or craft. These gatherings not only enhance personal skills but also strengthen community bonds. When faced with adversity, such as natural disasters or economic fluctuations, a supportive community can offer assistance, whether through shared resources or moral support.

Embracing Flexibility:

Resilience also hinges on the ability to embrace flexibility. Off-grid living is inherently unpredictable. Weather can change plans overnight, crops may fail, or equipment might malfunction. Instead of viewing these setbacks as failures, approach them as opportunities to learn and adapt.

For example, if a drought affects your garden, consider implementing drought-resistant planting techniques. Experiment with new crops better suited to changing conditions or explore alternative watering methods, such as drip irrigation. Adaptability involves a willingness to pivot and explore new strategies that align with current circumstances.

Regular Reflection and Adjustment:

Set aside time for regular reflection. Evaluate what works and what doesn't in your off-grid lifestyle. Journaling can be an effective tool for this process. Document successes, challenges, and lessons learned. By tracking experiences over time, you can identify patterns and adjust strategies accordingly.

When a particular system or approach fails, analyze the reasons behind it. Was it due to a lack of resources, improper planning, or unforeseen circumstances? This reflective practice cultivates a growth mindset, allowing for continual improvement and innovation in daily routines.

Practicing Patience and Persistence:

Finally, cultivate patience and persistence. Off-grid living often involves trial and error. Projects may not yield immediate results, and setbacks are inevitable. Recognize that resilience is built over time. Celebrate small victories, such as successfully preserving food or generating enough energy from solar panels to power your home.

Adopting a long-term perspective allows you to remain motivated during challenging times. Understand that each obstacle is an opportunity for growth. By staying committed to your off-grid journey, you develop the tenacity needed to thrive in a self-sufficient lifestyle.

In summary, cultivating resilience and adaptability in an off-grid lifestyle involves a multifaceted approach. Embrace continuous learning, build robust systems, foster community support, and remain flexible in the face of challenges. Through regular reflection, patience, and persistence, individuals can navigate the unpredictable landscape of off-grid living with confidence and strength.

1.10 Adopting a No-Grid Mindset

To fully embrace the off-grid lifestyle, you need to adopt a no-grid mindset. This perspective transforms how you interact with the world, urging you to prioritize sustainability, resilience, and a profound connection to the natural environment. Each choice you make—from the food you consume to the energy you harness—reflects your commitment to living in harmony with the earth.

Sustainability as a Guiding Principle:

At the core of this mindset lies sustainability. You begin by examining your daily habits. Consider your consumption patterns. Are you relying on single-use plastics or convenience foods that contribute to waste and environmental degradation? Shift your focus to reusable items and whole foods. Invest in glass containers, cloth bags, and bulk purchasing to minimize waste. This conscious decision not only reduces your ecological footprint but also fosters a sense of responsibility toward the planet.

Your food choices further embody sustainability. Grow your own vegetables and herbs, selecting varieties suited to your climate. Companion planting enhances yields and naturally deters pests, reducing the need for harmful chemicals. Embrace seasonal eating—this not only supports local farmers but also reconnects you with the rhythms of nature. As you learn to work with the land, you gain a deeper appreciation for the resources it provides.

Resilience Through Resourcefulness:

Resourcefulness emerges as a crucial aspect of the no-grid mindset. Instead of viewing limitations as obstacles, you see opportunities for creativity and innovation. When faced with a shortage of resources, you brainstorm alternative solutions. For instance, if your garden produces a surplus of zucchini, you might experiment with preserving it through canning or dehydrating. This not only extends the life of your harvest but also minimizes food waste.

Embrace DIY projects that promote self-sufficiency. Build your own solar oven for cooking or create a simple rainwater collection system to irrigate your garden. Each project cultivates skills that enhance your resilience, allowing you to adapt to changing circumstances. If a power outage occurs, you'll rely on your solar oven instead of conventional appliances. When a drought hits, your rainwater collection system becomes invaluable.

Connection to Nature:

The no-grid mindset fosters a deep connection to nature. Spend time outdoors, immersing yourself in the environment. Observe the patterns of wildlife and the changing seasons. This connection nurtures respect for the ecosystems that sustain life. Engage in practices such as foraging or herbal medicine to deepen your understanding of local flora and fauna. Learning to identify edible plants and medicinal herbs empowers you to use nature's resources responsibly.

Incorporate nature into your daily routine. Create outdoor spaces that invite you to spend time outside, whether it's a cozy reading nook in the garden or a shaded area for relaxation. This connection enhances your well-being and reinforces the importance of living in harmony with the earth.

Guiding Daily Actions:

The no-grid mindset shapes daily actions, encouraging mindful choices that reflect your values. Start each day with intention. For example, plan your meals around what's available in your garden or at local farmers' markets. This not only reduces reliance on industrial agriculture but also supports local economies.

When shopping, prioritize products with minimal packaging and those made from sustainable materials. Each purchase becomes a vote for the kind of world you want to create. Educate yourself about the companies you support. Seek out brands committed to ethical practices and environmental stewardship. Your consumer choices contribute to a larger movement toward sustainability.

In your home, embrace energy efficiency. Utilize natural light during the day, and opt for LED bulbs in the evening. Insulate your living spaces to reduce heating and cooling needs. Small changes accumulate over time, leading to significant energy savings and a reduced carbon footprint.

Long-Term Goals:

Your long-term goals reflect the principles of the no-grid mindset. Set objectives that align with sustainability, resilience, and connection to nature. This could include achieving energy independence through solar panels, building a food forest, or participating in local conservation efforts.

As you envision these goals, break them down into manageable steps. For instance, if you aim to create a food forest, start by planting a few fruit trees and companion plants. Over time, expand this area, nurturing biodiversity and creating a self-sustaining ecosystem.

Regularly reassess your progress. Reflect on what you've accomplished and adjust your goals as needed. Life is dynamic, and flexibility is key to thriving in an off-grid lifestyle. Celebrate milestones, no matter how small. Each step forward reinforces your commitment to a sustainable future.

In essence, the no-grid mindset empowers you to view the world through a lens of sustainability and resilience. By prioritizing responsible resource use and fostering a deep connection to the natural environment, you transform daily actions and long-term aspirations into meaningful practices that contribute to a more harmonious existence.

2. WATER HARVESTING, COLLECTION, PURIFICATION, AND STORAGE

2.1 INTRODUCTION

Water is the most essential resource for sustaining life, and securing a reliable source of clean water is one of the foremost priorities when living off the grid. In off-grid scenarios, where access to municipal water supplies is unavailable or unreliable, the ability to harvest, collect, purify, and store water becomes vital for survival. Without a consistent and safe water supply, even the most well-prepared off-grid homestead can face significant challenges.

This chapter is dedicated to the comprehensive management of water in an off-grid environment. From capturing and storing rainwater to filtering and purifying water from natural sources, we will cover the entire spectrum of off-grid water systems. Understanding how to effectively manage water resources not only ensures your survival but also contributes to your overall self-sufficiency and resilience.

We begin with water harvesting and collection, focusing on techniques like rainwater collection systems and well construction. These methods provide the foundation for creating a dependable water supply, regardless of your location or climate. By capturing rainwater or accessing groundwater, you can create a sustainable source of water that meets your daily needs.

Next, we delve into water purification, a critical aspect of off-grid living. Even if you have access to water, ensuring that it is safe to drink and use is paramount. We will explore various purification methods, from simple DIY filters to more advanced systems like bio-filters and solar stills, giving you the tools to make any water source potable.

Finally, we address water storage, which is essential for maintaining a stable water supply over time. Proper storage solutions allow you to preserve water during times of abundance and rely on it during dry spells or emergencies. This section will guide you through setting up large-capacity storage systems and maintaining them to ensure long-term reliability.

By the end of this chapter, you will have a thorough understanding of how to manage water resources effectively in an off-grid setting. You will be equipped with practical skills and knowledge to build, maintain, and optimize a complete water system, ensuring that you and your household have access to clean, safe water at all times.

2.2 HARVESTING AND COLLECTION

2.2.1 RAINWATER COLLECTION SYSTEM

A rainwater collection system harnesses the natural resource of precipitation, allowing you to capture, store, and use rainwater for various purposes. This project is crucial for off-grid living, as it provides a sustainable and often free water source, reducing reliance on external supplies. By collecting rainwater, you conserve municipal resources, minimize your environmental footprint, and ensure access to water even during dry spells. The benefits extend beyond personal use; they also contribute to groundwater recharge and help prevent soil erosion. A well-designed rainwater system can supply water for gardening, irrigation, and even household use when properly filtered and purified. This guide outlines the steps to build an efficient rainwater collection system, ensuring you can manage water resources effectively in an off-grid lifestyle.

Materials and Tools:

- Food-grade barrels, 55-gallon - 2 units (or more as needed)

- Roof gutters (PVC or metal) - Length depends on roof perimeter

- Downspouts (PVC or metal) - Length depends on the height of the house

- Hose spigots with ¾-inch pipe threads - 2 units (1 per barrel)

- ¾-inch x ¾-inch couplings - 2 units (1 per barrel)

- ¾-inch x ¾-inch bushings - 2 units (1 per barrel)
- Pipe threads with 1-inch hose adapters - 2 units (1 per barrel)
- Lock nuts, ¾-inch - 2 units (1 per barrel)
- Metal washers - 8 units (4 per barrel)
- Silicone caulk - 1 tube
- Aluminum downspout elbows, "S"-shaped - 2 units (1 per downspout/barrel)
- Aluminum window screens - 2 pieces (1 per barrel)
- Concrete blocks - 4-6 units (2-3 per barrel)
- Drill with ¾-inch hole saw - 1 unit
- Tape measure - 1 unit
- Box cutter - 1 unit
- Hacksaw - 1 unit
- Teflon tape - 1 roll

Step-by-Step Guide:

1. **Measure Roof Perimeter:** Measure the total linear distance around the roof's edge where gutters will be installed, taking into account the roof's slope and orientation. Install gutters only along the edges where water will naturally flow off the roof, as determined by the roof's pitch and design. Use a tape measure to calculate this distance, and ensure you purchase sufficient gutter material to cover the entire length.

2. **Measure House Height:** Measure the height from the roof edge down to the ground where the downspouts will be installed. This measurement will determine the length of the downspouts required. Measure at multiple points around the house if the ground is uneven to ensure accurate downspout lengths.

3. **Gutter Installation:** Mark where the gutters will be attached to the roof. Install gutter brackets along the roof edge, spacing them about 24-36 inches apart to support the gutters. Attach the gutters to the brackets, ensuring they are sloped slightly toward the downspout locations (about 1/4 inch drop per 10 feet) to facilitate water flow.

4. **Choose a Location**: Select an area next to your downspout that receives direct rainfall. Ensure the location is accessible and allows for easy maintenance.

5. **Level the Ground**: Clear the chosen area of debris and rocks. Use a shovel to level the ground, creating a flat surface large enough to accommodate your rain barrels.

6. **Create a Drainage Base**: Dig a rectangle approximately 5 inches deep and fill it with ½ inch of pea gravel to promote drainage. This prevents water pooling around the barrels.

7. **Stack Concrete Blocks**: Position 4-6 concrete blocks to create a sturdy platform for the barrels. Arrange them side by side to ensure stability and support for the barrels.

8. **Prepare the Downspout**: Determine the height where the downspout will connect to the barrel. Use a hacksaw to cut the downspout at the appropriate length, ensuring it aligns with the rain barrel.

9. **Attach Downspout Elbow**: Connect the aluminum downspout elbow to the cut end of the downspout, securing it with screws. Ensure the elbow directs water into the rain barrel.

10. **Prepare the Rain Barrel**: Use a drill with a ¾-inch hole saw to create a spigot hole on the side of each barrel, placing it high enough to allow buckets to fit underneath.

11. **Seal the Spigot Hole**: Apply a circle of silicon caulk around the hole on both the inside and outside of the barrel to prevent leaks.

12. **Attach the Spigot**: Insert the spigot through the hole from the outside, adding a washer to the threaded end. Secure it with a bushing, ensuring a tight fit to prevent leakage.

13. **Create an Overflow Hole**: Drill a second hole a few inches from the top of the barrel for overflow. Repeat the sealing process with silicone caulk and washers.

14. **Connect the Hose Adapter**: Insert a 1-inch hose adapter through the overflow hole, securing it with washers and a lock nut on the inside.

15. **Cut Collection Hole in Barrel Lid**: Use a box cutter to create a hole in the lid of the rain barrel, positioning it near the edge to allow for the downspout elbow to fit.

16. **Install Metal Screen Filter**: Cover the hole in the lid with an aluminum window screen to prevent debris from entering the barrel while allowing rainwater to flow in.

17. **Cover with Landscaping Fabric**: Place a large piece of landscaping fabric over the top of the barrel, securing it to keep out pests and debris while allowing water to pass through.

18. **Connect Additional Barrels**: If using multiple barrels, connect them using hoses from the overflow valves of the first barrel to the inlet of the second barrel.

19. **Set Up First Flush Diverter**: Install a first flush diverter if desired, which directs the initial dirty runoff away from the barrels. This can be achieved with a simple setup of additional piping.

20. **Test the System**: Once everything is connected, check for leaks by running water through the system. Ensure that all joints and connections are secure.

Maintenance:

- **Monthly**: Inspect the rain barrels for any debris or algae buildup. Clean the metal screens and check the integrity of the seals and connections.

- **Seasonally**: Flush out the barrels with clean water to remove sediment. Inspect the gutters and downspouts for clogs and ensure they are clear.

- **Annually**: Perform a thorough check of the entire system. Replace any worn or damaged components, and clean the barrels with a mild soap solution to prevent algae growth.

Complexity:

The rainwater collection system project is moderate in complexity. It requires basic construction skills, including measuring, cutting, and securing fittings. Challenges may arise in ensuring proper alignment and sealing of connections, particularly with plumbing components. Attention to detail is crucial in preventing leaks and ensuring the system operates efficiently.

Estimated Time:

- **Preparation and Setup**: 2-3 hours to gather materials, level the ground, and set up the platform.

- **Barrel Preparation**: 1-2 hours to drill holes, attach spigots, and prepare the barrels.

- **Gutter and Downspout Installation**: 2-3 hours to install gutters, downspouts, and make connections.

- **Final Assembly and Testing**: 1 hour to connect everything, test for leaks, and make adjustments.

- **Total estimated time:** Approximately 6-9 hours, depending on your experience and the number of barrels used.

2.2.2 WELL POINT INSTALLATION

Installing a well point is an essential project for off-grid living, providing a reliable source of water. This system allows individuals to access groundwater, making it a crucial step toward self-sufficiency. A well point system uses a driven well to extract water from shallow aquifers, offering numerous benefits such as independence from municipal water supplies, reduced utility costs, and a sustainable water source for irrigation, drinking, and other household needs. This guide will walk you through the entire installation process, ensuring you understand each step required to successfully set up a well point system. By the end, you will have the knowledge to provide your own water supply, enhancing your off-grid lifestyle and promoting environmental stewardship.

Materials and Tools:

- Well point - 1 unit (standard 2-inch diameter)

- Drive pipe - 10 feet (2-inch diameter, galvanized steel)

- Drive cap - 1 unit (2-inch)

- Sledgehammer - 1 unit (10-12 pounds)

- Water well drilling auger - 1 unit (manual or powered)

- Teflon tape - 1 roll

- Hose clamp - 1 unit (2-inch)

- Gravel - 5 gallons (for drainage)

- Bucket - 1 unit (for water removal)

- Water level gauge (measuring tape) - 1 unit

- PVC pipe (optional) - 10 feet (2-inch diameter, for additional depth)

- Well pump (manual or electric) - 1 unit (as needed)

- Safety glasses - 1 unit

- Gloves - 1 pair

Step-by-Step Guide:

1. **Select a Site**: Choose a location for the well point that is at least 50 feet from septic systems or other potential contaminants. Ensure the area has good drainage and is accessible for equipment.

2. **Gather Tools and Materials**: Assemble all tools and materials listed above. Ensure everything is in good condition and ready for use.

3. **Mark Well Point Location**: Use stakes to mark the precise location of the well point. Clear any debris, vegetation, or obstacles from the area to ensure a clean working space.

4. **Install the Well Point**: Attach the drive cap to the top of the drive pipe. Place the well point on the bottom of the drive pipe and secure it. Ensure it fits tightly.

5. **Drive the Pipe**: Position the drive pipe vertically above the marked location. Use a sledgehammer to drive the pipe into the ground. Strike firmly but avoid excessive force that could bend the pipe.

6. **Check Depth**: Periodically check the depth of the drive pipe as you drive it into the ground. Use the water level gauge to measure how deep you are going. Aim for a depth of 10-15 feet, depending on your local groundwater level.

7. **Remove Obstructions**: If you encounter rocks or hard soil, use the water well drilling auger to bore through these obstacles. Clear the area around the well point as necessary to ensure it remains unobstructed.

8. **Monitor Water Flow**: Once the well point reaches the desired depth, pour a small amount of water into the pipe. This action helps prime the well point and facilitates the flow of water. If water begins to flow, you are on the right track.

9. **Add Gravel for Drainage**: After confirming water flow, remove the drive pipe and insert a bucket to catch any excess water. Add gravel around the well point to enhance drainage and prevent clogging.

10. **Install Pump**: If you plan to use a pump, connect the well point to the pump system. Secure all connections with Teflon tape to prevent leaks. Use a hose clamp for additional security.

11. **Test the System**: Turn on the pump and check for water flow. Monitor the system for leaks or pressure issues. Ensure the water is clear and free from contaminants.

12. **Adjust as Necessary**: If water flow is insufficient, consider extending the drive pipe or using a longer well point. Assess the local groundwater levels to determine the optimal depth for water extraction.

Maintenance:

- **Monthly**: Inspect the well point and pump for signs of wear or damage. Tighten any loose fittings or connections. Clear debris from the surrounding area to prevent clogging.

- **Yearly**: Test the water quality for contaminants, particularly if the water is used for drinking. Use a water testing kit or send samples to a lab for analysis. Clean the well point and surrounding gravel to ensure optimal water flow.

Complexity:

The complexity of installing a well point is moderate. Basic skills in measuring and manual labor are required. Challenges may arise when driving the pipe through hard soil or encountering rock formations. It is crucial to have patience and the right tools to manage these obstacles effectively.

Estimated Time:

- **Setup**: 3-5 hours for site preparation, gathering materials, and installing the well point.

- **Monitoring**: 1-2 hours for testing the system and making necessary adjustments.

- **Maintenance**: 30 minutes monthly for inspections and cleaning; 1 hour yearly for water testing.

2.2.3 AUGER DRILLING

Auger drilling is a method used to create holes in the ground for various purposes, such as installing water wells, setting posts, or establishing garden beds. This project holds particular importance for individuals pursuing off-grid living or DIY sustainability. Auger drilling allows for the efficient extraction of soil and rocks, enabling you to access groundwater or prepare sites for planting. With the right equipment, you can control the depth and diameter of the hole, ensuring that it meets your specific needs. This method is not only practical but also empowers you to take charge of your land and resources, significantly contributing to self-sufficiency.

The benefits of auger drilling extend beyond simple hole creation. For off-grid enthusiasts, accessing groundwater through well installation can provide a reliable water source for drinking, irrigation, and livestock. Furthermore, auger drilling is versatile; it can be used for various applications, including creating holes for fence posts, planting trees, or installing structures. By mastering auger drilling techniques, you equip yourself with a valuable skill set that enhances your capability to live sustainably and independently.

Materials and Tools:

- Auger drill (manual or powered) - 1 unit

- Auger bit (choose size based on project needs, e.g., 6-inch diameter) - 1 unit

- Water source (for dust control and soil lubrication) - As needed

- Measuring tape - 1 unit

- Safety goggles - 1 pair

- Work gloves - 1 pair

- Ear protection (if using a powered auger) - 1 unit
- Marking paint or stakes - 1 unit
- Shovel (for clearing the site) - 1 unit
- Trowel (for finishing edges) - 1 unit
- Bucket (for soil removal) - 1 unit

Step-by-Step Guide:

1. **Select a Location**: Identify a suitable spot for drilling based on your project requirements (e.g., near water source for wells, clear of utility lines).

2. **Mark the Spot**: Use marking paint or stakes to clearly indicate where you will drill, ensuring it is visible from all angles.

3. **Clear the Area**: Remove any debris, rocks, or vegetation within a 3-foot radius of the marked spot using a shovel.

4. **Put on Safety Gear**: Don safety goggles, work gloves, and ear protection if using a powered auger to protect against debris and noise.

5. **Assemble the Auger**: If using a powered auger, follow the manufacturer's instructions to assemble the auger drill and attach the appropriate auger bit.

6. **Position the Auger**: Stand the auger upright above the marked spot, ensuring that the bit is perpendicular to the ground.

7. **Start Drilling**: Engage the auger drill, applying consistent downward pressure while allowing the auger to penetrate the soil. For manual augers, turn the handle steadily.

8. **Monitor Depth**: Use a measuring tape to check the depth of the hole periodically, ensuring you reach the desired depth (typically 10-15 feet for water wells).

9. **Remove Soil**: Periodically pull the auger out of the hole to remove the collected soil, depositing it in a bucket for later disposal or use.

10. **Adjust as Necessary**: If encountering rocks or hard soil, back out the auger, clear the obstruction, and resume drilling. Consider using water to lubricate the auger bit if the soil is particularly dry or compact.

11. **Finish the Hole**: Once you reach the desired depth, carefully withdraw the auger and inspect the hole for consistency. Use a trowel to smooth the edges if necessary.

12. **Clean Up**: Remove any remaining soil from the site, ensuring that the area is safe and tidy.

Maintenance:

- **Weekly**: Inspect the auger for any wear or damage. Clean the auger bit after each use to prevent rust and build-up.

- **Monthly**: Check the power source (if applicable) for the auger, ensuring that it is functioning correctly. Lubricate moving parts to maintain efficiency.

- **Yearly**: Conduct a thorough inspection of the auger and its components. Replace any worn-out bits or parts as needed to ensure optimal performance for future projects.

Complexity:

The complexity of auger drilling is moderate. While the physical act of drilling is straightforward, challenges may arise depending on soil conditions, depth, and the presence of rocks. Familiarity with using power tools is beneficial, particularly for powered augers. Those who are physically fit and comfortable handling equipment will find this project manageable, but beginners may require practice to develop the necessary skills.

Estimated Time:

- **Setup**: 30 minutes to gather materials, clear the area, and mark the drilling spot.

- **Drilling**: 1-3 hours, depending on soil conditions and desired depth.

- **Cleanup**: 30 minutes to remove debris and ensure the area is tidy.

- **Total estimated time**: 2-4 hours, with additional time required for complex or deep drilling projects.

2.3 PURIFICATION

2.3.1 3-BUCKET DIY BIO-FILTER

The 3-Bucket DIY Bio-Filter is an innovative water purification system that allows individuals to create clean, safe drinking water using readily available materials. This project is essential for those living off-grid or pursuing a sustainable lifestyle, as it provides a reliable means to filter and purify water from natural sources. With increasing concerns about water quality, especially in remote areas, having a DIY bio-filter offers peace of mind. The system utilizes a series of filtration layers to remove impurities, sediments, and harmful microorganisms, resulting in water that is safe for consumption. The 3-Bucket Bio-Filter is not only practical but also empowers you to take control of your water supply, significantly reducing reliance on store-bought bottled water.

By engaging in this project, you contribute to environmental sustainability while enhancing self-sufficiency. The bio-filter can be customized to fit specific needs and is easily maintainable. Whether you're gathering rainwater or sourcing water from a nearby stream, this filtration system equips you with the tools to ensure your water is clean and safe.

Materials and Tools:

- Plastic buckets with lids - 3 units - 5 gallons each

- Drill with a ¼ inch drill bit - 1 unit

- Activated carbon - 1 bag - 5 pounds

- Gravel - 1 bag - 5 pounds

- Sand - 1 bag - 5 pounds

- Fine mesh screen or cloth - 1 unit - 1 square yard

- Hose or PVC pipe - 1 unit - 3 feet

- Bucket spigot - 1 unit

- Marker - 1 unit

- Water source (rainwater or stream water) - As needed

Step-by-Step Guide:

1. **Prepare the Buckets**: Take three plastic buckets and ensure they are clean and free of any chemicals. Remove any labels for easier identification.

2. **Drill Drainage Holes**: Use the drill with a ¼ inch bit to create small drainage holes in the bottom of the first bucket. Space the holes evenly, allowing water to flow through without letting sediment escape.

3. **Create a Lid for the First Bucket**: Cut a piece of fine mesh screen or cloth to fit the diameter of the first bucket's lid. This will act as a barrier to prevent larger debris from entering while allowing water to pass through.

4. **Assemble the First Bucket**: Place the mesh screen on the lid of the first bucket. Secure it with the lid to hold the screen in place. This bucket will serve as the primary filtration unit.

5. **Layer the Filtration Materials**: In the first bucket, add 2 inches of gravel at the bottom, followed by 2 inches of sand, and finally 2 inches of activated carbon. This layered approach maximizes filtration efficiency.

6. **Prepare the Second Bucket**: Repeat the process by drilling holes in the bottom of the second bucket. This bucket will catch the filtered water from the first bucket.

7. **Connect the Buckets**: Place the first bucket (with filtration layers) on top of the second bucket. Ensure that the drainage holes align directly above the second bucket.

8. **Install the Spigot**: Drill a hole near the bottom of the second bucket and insert the bucket spigot. This will allow for easy dispensing of the filtered water.

9. **Set Up the Third Bucket**: The third bucket will act as a storage container for the filtered water. Place it beneath the second bucket to catch the clean water dispensed through the spigot.

10. **Test the System**: Pour water into the top bucket. Observe how the water filters through the layers, collecting in the second bucket. Check for any leaks around the spigot and ensure proper flow.

11. **Adjust the Filter Layers**: If the water flow is slow, ensure that the layers are not compacted. Gently stir the sand and gravel to allow better water movement.

12. **Final Inspection**: Check all connections and ensure the system is stable. Place the lids on the buckets to keep out debris and insects.

Maintenance:

- **Monthly**: Inspect the filter layers in the first bucket. If they appear clogged, replace the sand and activated carbon to maintain effective filtration. Clean the spigot and ensure there are no blockages.

- **Annually**: Replace the gravel, sand, and activated carbon in the first bucket to ensure optimal filtration performance. Inspect the buckets for any cracks or damage, replacing as necessary to prevent leaks.

Complexity:

The complexity of the 3-Bucket DIY Bio-Filter is moderate. While the construction involves basic drilling and layering techniques, understanding how to properly set up and maintain the filtration system requires attention to detail. Challenges may include ensuring that the filter layers are correctly installed and that the water flow remains consistent. Basic DIY skills and familiarity with tools are beneficial but not mandatory.

Estimated Time:

- **Setup**: Approximately 2-3 hours to gather materials, drill holes, layer the filtration materials, and assemble the buckets.

- **Ongoing maintenance**: 15-30 minutes monthly for checking filter condition and cleaning the spigot.

- **Annual maintenance**: 1-2 hours to replace filtration materials and inspect the system.

2.3.2 DIY BERKEY WATER FILTRATION SYSTEM

The DIY Berkey Water Filtration System is a highly effective, gravity-fed water filtration solution that removes impurities and contaminants from water sources. This system is particularly vital for individuals pursuing off-grid living, emergency preparedness, or those who want to ensure access to clean drinking water in any situation. The Berkey system excels at filtering out bacteria, viruses, heavy metals, and other harmful substances, providing you with safe water without relying on electricity or complicated setups.

By constructing your own Berkey-style filter, you gain the ability to purify water from various sources, such as lakes, rivers, or even municipal supplies that may contain chemicals or sediments. This project promotes self-sufficiency, allowing you to control your water quality and reduce dependency on commercial bottled water. It is an economical and practical approach to ensuring that you and your family have access to clean, safe drinking water.

Materials and Tools:

- Stainless steel container (upper and lower) - 2 units (each 5-gallon)
- Berkey filter elements - 2 units (or more, depending on your needs)
- Spigot (food-grade plastic or stainless steel) - 1 unit
- Drill with ½ inch drill bit - 1 unit
- Food-safe silicone sealant - 1 tube
- Measuring tape - 1 unit
- Marker - 1 unit
- Bucket for collecting filtered water - 1 unit (5-gallon)
- Cleaning cloth - 1 unit
- Gloves - 1 pair

Step-by-Step Guide:

1. **Prepare the Containers**: Begin with two stainless steel containers, one for the upper chamber and one for the lower chamber. Ensure both containers are clean and free of debris.

2. **Mark the Spigot Hole**: Measure approximately 3 inches from the bottom of the lower container. Use a marker to indicate where the spigot will be installed.

3. **Drill the Spigot Hole**: Use a drill with a ½ inch drill bit to create a hole at the marked spot on the lower container. Ensure the hole is smooth and free of sharp edges.

4. **Install the Spigot**: Insert the spigot into the drilled hole. Apply food-safe silicone sealant around the edges of the hole on the inside of the container to create a watertight seal. Allow the sealant to cure as per the manufacturer's instructions.

5. **Prepare the Upper Chamber**: Place the upper container upside down on a clean surface. This chamber will hold the filter elements.

6. **Mark Filter Element Holes**: Depending on the number of Berkey filter elements used, measure and mark two holes on the bottom of the upper container. Space the holes evenly, approximately 4 inches apart.

7. **Drill Filter Element Holes**: Using the ½ inch drill bit, drill through the marked spots on the upper container to create holes for the filter elements.

8. **Install the Filter Elements**: Insert the Berkey filter elements into the holes from the inside of the upper container. Ensure that they fit snugly and seal properly.

9. **Assemble the System**: Stack the upper container onto the lower container, ensuring that the filter elements sit directly above the lower chamber.

10. **Add Water**: Fill the upper chamber with water from your chosen source. Avoid overfilling; leave some space to prevent overflow.

11. **Allow Water to Filter**: Wait for the water to filter through the Berkey elements into the lower chamber. This process may take several minutes to hours, depending on the water quality and filter elements used.

12. **Collect Filtered Water**: Once the water has filtered into the lower chamber, open the spigot to dispense the clean water into a bucket or other container for use.

Maintenance:

- **Weekly**: Check the water flow rate. If it slows significantly, it may indicate that the filter elements need cleaning.

- **Monthly**: Clean the exterior of the stainless steel containers with a soft cloth to remove any stains or marks. Ensure that the spigot remains clean and free of blockages.

- **Every 6 Months**: Remove the filter elements and scrub them gently with a soft brush and clean water to remove any buildup. This process rejuvenates the filters and maintains their effectiveness.

- **Annually**: Replace the Berkey filter elements according to the manufacturer's guidelines or when the flow rate significantly decreases. Regular replacement ensures optimal filtration performance.

Complexity:

This project is rated as moderate in complexity. It requires basic drilling and assembly skills. Challenges may arise when ensuring watertight seals and aligning components correctly. However, following the step-by-step instructions carefully will lead to successful assembly and function.

Estimated Time:

- **Setup**: 2-3 hours for gathering materials, drilling holes, and assembling the system.

- **Ongoing maintenance**: 15-30 minutes monthly for cleaning and inspecting the system.

- **Filter cleaning**: 15 minutes every six months for scrubbing and maintaining the filter elements.

- **Annual replacement of filters**: 30 minutes for removal and installation of new elements.

2.3.3 LifeStraw

The LifeStraw is a portable water filter designed for individual use, providing a simple and immediate way to filter water. Originally developed for humanitarian crises, the LifeStraw has gained popularity among outdoor enthusiasts, travelers, and survivalists. It can filter out bacteria, parasites, and microplastics, making it safe to drink from streams, lakes, and other questionable water sources.

While not a DIY project, the LifeStraw is an essential tool to have in your off-grid arsenal, particularly for emergencies. Its ease of use and portability make it invaluable when quick access to clean drinking water is crucial. It requires no electricity, batteries, or complex setup, making it an ideal tool for those in remote areas or during natural disasters. This guide will explain how to use and maintain the LifeStraw to ensure you always have access to clean drinking water.

Materials and Tools:

- LifeStraw filter (commercially available) - 1 unit

Step-by-Step Guide:

1. **Preparation**: Remove the caps from both ends of the LifeStraw. Inspect the filter to ensure it is clean and free from any visible damage.

2. **Drinking**: Place the straw end into the water source. The LifeStraw is designed to be used directly in the water, so you can drink from streams, lakes, or any other water source. Suck water through the mouthpiece to drink. The filter will remove bacteria, parasites, and microplastics as the water passes through.

3. **Post-Use Cleaning**: After each use, blow air back through the LifeStraw to expel any remaining water and debris from the filter. This helps to keep the filter clean and prevents clogging.

4. **Storage**: Store the LifeStraw in a clean, dry place when not in use. Avoid exposing the filter to extreme temperatures or direct sunlight, as this can degrade the filter material.

Maintenance:

- **Filter Replacement**: Replace the LifeStraw after filtering approximately 1000 liters of water. The LifeStraw is designed for limited use, and the filter will become less effective over time.

- **Regular Inspection**: Periodically inspect the LifeStraw for any signs of wear or damage. Replace the filter if it shows signs of cracking or if the flow rate decreases significantly.

- **Cost**: Approximately $20

- **Complexity**: Very Easy. The LifeStraw requires no setup or technical skills to use. It is ready to use out of the box and can be used directly in the water source. Its maintenance is simple and straightforward.

- **Estimated Time**: 5-10 minutes. The LifeStraw is portable and requires no installation, making it quick to use and clean.

2.3.4 SOLAR STILL

A solar still is a simple, effective device that harnesses the power of the sun to purify water. This method is particularly valuable for off-grid living, survival situations, or any scenario where clean water is scarce. The solar still operates on the principle of evaporation and condensation, transforming dirty or saline water into fresh drinking water. By capturing solar energy, the still heats water, causing it to evaporate. The vapor then condenses on a cooler surface, dripping into a collection container as purified water. This project is essential for those seeking self-sufficiency, as it provides a sustainable solution to water purification without the need for electricity or complex equipment. Building a solar still requires minimal materials and offers an eco-friendly approach to ensuring a safe water supply.

Materials and Tools:

- Plastic sheet (clear) - 1 unit - 6 feet x 6 feet

- Shallow container (like a bowl or pan) - 1 unit - 1-gallon capacity

- Rocks or small weights - 4-6 units - for holding the plastic sheet down

- Dirty or saline water - As needed - for distillation

- Small collection container - 1 unit - for the purified water

- Scissors - 1 unit

- Measuring tape - 1 unit

Step-by-Step Guide:

1. **Choose a Location**: Select a sunny spot with minimal shade to maximize solar exposure throughout the day.

2. **Dig a Hole**: Dig a shallow hole in the ground, approximately 2 feet wide and 1 foot deep. This will house the collection container and facilitate the condensation process.

3. **Place the Collection Container**: Position the shallow container in the center of the hole. Ensure it is stable and level to collect the distilled water efficiently.

4. **Add Dirty Water**: Pour dirty or saline water into the hole, surrounding the collection container. Fill the hole until the water level is about 1-2 inches deep, but do not let it overflow into the collection container.

5. **Cut the Plastic Sheet**: Use scissors to cut the clear plastic sheet into a square that is at least 6 feet by 6 feet. This size provides ample surface area for condensation.

6. **Cover the Hole**: Stretch the plastic sheet over the hole, ensuring it covers the collection container completely. Secure the edges of the plastic sheet with rocks or small weights to prevent it from blowing away.

7. **Create a Dip**: Adjust the plastic sheet so that it forms a slight dip above the collection container. This dip allows condensed water to drip directly into the container. Ensure that the plastic sheet is tight but not overly taut, which may cause it to tear.

8. **Monitor the Still**: Check the solar still periodically throughout the day. Observe the condensation process; you should start seeing water droplets forming on the underside of the plastic sheet.

9. **Collect Purified Water**: After several hours of sunlight, check the collection container for purified water. Carefully remove the plastic sheet, taking care not to let any of the dirty water mix with the distilled water.

10. **Repeat as Needed**: If additional purification is necessary, refill the hole with dirty water and cover it with the plastic sheet again. Continue the process until sufficient clean water is collected.

Maintenance:

- **Weekly**: Inspect the plastic sheet for any tears or damage. Replace it if necessary to maintain effectiveness.

- **After Heavy Rain**: Ensure that no water from rainfall contaminates the collection container. Adjust the setup if needed to prevent contamination.

- **Monthly**: Clean the collection container to remove any residual impurities and ensure optimal hygiene for drinking water.

Complexity:

The solar still project is straightforward and suitable for beginners. The primary challenges include selecting an appropriate location with adequate sunlight and ensuring the setup is secure against wind or rain. Attention to detail during assembly is essential for effective water purification.

Estimated Time:

- **Setup**: 30-45 minutes to gather materials, dig the hole, and assemble the solar still.

- **Ongoing monitoring**: 5-10 minutes throughout the day to check for condensation and collect water.

- **Water collection**: 10-15 minutes to carefully remove the plastic sheet and gather the purified water.

- Overall, expect to spend a few hours throughout the day to fully utilize the solar still for maximum water purification.

2.3.5 PLANT TRANSPIRATION BAGS

Plant transpiration bags are an innovative and effective method for collecting moisture from plants through the natural process of transpiration. This project is essential for off-grid living and DIY enthusiasts, as it harnesses the sun's energy and plant biology to create a sustainable water source. Transpiration occurs when plants absorb water through their roots and release moisture into the atmosphere through small openings in their leaves. By using transpiration bags, you can capture this moisture, condense it, and collect it for drinking or irrigation.

This method is particularly beneficial in arid environments where water scarcity is a concern. Not only does it provide a way to gather fresh water, but it also promotes a deeper understanding of plant ecology and sustainable practices. By implementing plant transpiration bags, you actively engage in water conservation while supporting the growth and health of local vegetation. This project is simple to set up, requires minimal materials, and offers an ongoing source of water, making it an invaluable tool for self-sufficient living.

Materials and Tools:

- Plastic bags (gallon-sized, clear) - 5 units

- Twine or string - 10 feet

- Small rocks or weights - 5 units

- Scissors - 1 unit

- Marker - 1 unit

- Funnel - 1 unit

- Water (for initial setup) - As needed

- Tape (optional, for securing bags) - 1 roll

Step-by-Step Guide:

1. **Select the Plants**: Choose healthy plants with significant leaf coverage, such as fruit trees or large shrubs, as they will produce more moisture through transpiration.

2. **Prepare the Plastic Bags**: Take a gallon-sized clear plastic bag and ensure it is clean and free from any holes.

3. **Label the Bags**: Use a marker to label each bag with the plant name and the date of setup to keep track of the collection process.

4. **Wrap the Bags**: Gently wrap the plastic bag around a cluster of leaves on the chosen plant. Ensure that the bag covers the leaves without damaging them.

5. **Secure the Bags**: Use twine or string to tie the bag around the plant, ensuring it stays in place. Leave the top of the bag open to allow for air circulation.

6. **Add Weights**: Place small rocks or weights at the bottom of the bag to help it maintain its shape and keep it secure against the wind.

7. **Check for Condensation**: After a sunny day, check the inside of the bag for condensation. This moisture collects as the plant releases water vapor.

8. **Collect the Water**: After several days, use a funnel to pour the collected water into a clean container for storage or use.

9. **Monitor the Plants**: Regularly check the bags for condensation and ensure they remain securely attached to the plants. Adjust the bags if necessary to maintain proper positioning.

10. **Maintain the Bags**: If any bags become damaged or start leaking, replace them immediately to continue the collection process.

Maintenance:

- **Weekly**: Inspect each bag for signs of wear and tear. Replace any damaged bags to maintain water collection efficiency. Check for condensation levels inside the bags and ensure they are functioning properly.

- **Monthly**: Remove and clean the bags thoroughly if they show signs of algae or dirt buildup. Reinstall them on the plants after cleaning. Adjust the placement of bags if the plant grows significantly or if weather conditions change.

- **Annually**: Evaluate the effectiveness of the transpiration bags. Consider relocating them to new plants if certain areas yield better results or if the original plants have died or become less productive.

Complexity:

This project is low to moderate in complexity, making it accessible for beginners. The primary challenge lies in selecting the right plants and ensuring the bags are correctly positioned to maximize moisture collection. Participants need to be mindful of the plants' health and avoid damaging leaves during setup. Basic gardening skills are beneficial, but no advanced technical knowledge is required.

Estimated Time:

- **Setup**: 1-2 hours to gather materials, select plants, prepare bags, and install them properly.

- **Ongoing monitoring**: 5-10 minutes weekly to check the condition of the bags and the moisture levels.
- **Water collection**: 15-30 minutes every few days to gather the collected water, depending on the number of bags and the volume of condensation.

2.4 STORAGE AND TREATMENT

2.4.1 LARGE CAPACITY WATER STORAGE SYSTEM

A large capacity water storage system is essential for anyone pursuing off-grid living or seeking self-sufficiency. This system allows individuals to collect, store, and utilize water efficiently, providing a reliable water source for drinking, irrigation, and household needs. The importance of such a system cannot be overstated; it not only ensures access to water during dry spells or emergencies but also promotes conservation by collecting rainwater or reusing greywater.

The project encompasses various methods of water storage, including above-ground tanks, underground cisterns, and rainwater harvesting systems. By implementing a large capacity water storage solution, you can significantly reduce your dependence on external water sources and improve your resilience against droughts or water shortages. Additionally, this system can enhance your gardening efforts, allowing you to maintain healthy plants and crops without relying solely on municipal water.

Materials and Tools:

- Rainwater collection tank - 1 unit - 1,000 to 2,500 gallons
- PVC piping - 1 roll - 2 inches in diameter
- Downspout diverter - 1 unit
- Hose bib - 1 unit
- Water filter - 1 unit
- Gravel - 1 bag - 50 pounds
- Leveling tool - 1 unit
- Shovel - 1 unit
- Drill with a hole saw attachment - 1 unit
- Teflon tape - 1 roll
- Concrete blocks or bricks - Quantity as needed for support
- Optional: Water level indicator - 1 unit

Step-by-Step Guide:

1. **Select the Location**: Choose a flat area for the tank installation, preferably close to the roof downspouts to maximize rainwater collection.
2. **Prepare the Ground**: Clear the area of debris and vegetation. Use a leveling tool to ensure the ground is even. If needed, excavate to create a level surface.
3. **Set the Foundation**: Arrange concrete blocks or bricks in a square shape to support the tank. Ensure the foundation is level and sturdy to hold the tank's weight when full.
4. **Install the Rainwater Collection Tank**: Position the rainwater tank on the prepared foundation. Ensure the inlet is facing the downspouts for easy connection.

5. **Attach the Downspout Diverter**: Cut the existing downspout to install the diverter. Ensure the diverter aligns with the tank inlet, directing rainwater into the tank while allowing overflow to exit through the original downspout.

6. **Connect PVC Piping**: Measure and cut the PVC piping to connect the downspout diverter to the tank inlet. Use a drill with a hole saw attachment to create an inlet hole if the tank does not have one.

7. **Seal Connections**: Apply Teflon tape to the threaded connections of the diverter and hose bib to ensure a watertight seal. Tighten connections securely to prevent leaks.

8. **Add a Filter**: Install a water filter at the inlet of the tank to keep debris and sediment out of the stored water. Ensure the filter is easily accessible for maintenance.

9. **Create a Drainage System**: If the tank has a drainage outlet, connect a hose or PVC piping to direct excess water away from the tank area. This prevents water pooling around the foundation.

10. **Monitor Water Levels**: If using a water level indicator, install it according to the manufacturer's instructions to keep track of water levels in the tank.

11. **Maintain the System**: Regularly inspect the system for leaks or blockages. Clean the filter and ensure the diverter operates smoothly.

Maintenance:

- **Monthly**: Inspect the rainwater collection tank for any signs of leaks or wear. Check the diverter and filter for blockages, cleaning as necessary.

- **Seasonally**: Clean the roof gutters to ensure they are free of debris, allowing for maximum water collection. Test the water quality for contaminants if used for drinking.

- **Annually**: Inspect and clean the entire system, including the tank, diverter, and filters, to maintain optimal function. Replace any worn or damaged components as needed.

Complexity:

The project presents a moderate complexity level. While basic skills such as measuring, cutting, and sealing connections are necessary, the project may involve physical labor, especially when preparing the ground and moving materials. Understanding plumbing basics and water management will also help mitigate potential challenges. Familiarity with local building codes may be required, particularly for large installations.

Estimated Time:

- **Preparation and Groundwork**: 2-4 hours to clear, level, and set the foundation.

- **Tank Installation and Setup**: 3-5 hours for connecting the diverter, piping, and testing for leaks.

- **Ongoing Maintenance**: 15-30 minutes monthly for inspections and cleaning.

2.4.2 GREYWATER RECYCLING SYSTEM

A greywater recycling system captures and reuses water from household activities like bathing, laundry, and dishwashing. This system is crucial for off-grid living or DIY sustainability, providing a practical solution for water conservation in areas where water resources are limited. By recycling greywater, you reduce water waste, lower utility costs, and create a sustainable loop in your household. This project not only minimizes the burden on septic systems but also enhances irrigation efforts for gardens and landscaping, leading to healthier plants and reduced reliance on external water sources. Understanding how to implement a greywater recycling system empowers you to take control of your water usage while promoting environmental responsibility.

Materials and Tools:

- Greywater collection tank - 1 unit - 50 gallons

- PVC pipes (1.5 inches in diameter) - Length depends on the layout

- PVC elbows and connectors - 10 units

- Hose bib or valve - 1 unit

- Pump (if gravity flow isn't feasible) - 1 unit

- Filter (mesh or sand) - 1 unit

- Level - 1 unit

- Shovel - 1 unit

- Drill with appropriate bits - 1 unit

- Saw (for cutting PVC) - 1 unit

- Teflon tape - 1 roll

- Garden hose - 1 unit - 50 feet

- Plastic storage container (for filtration) - 1 unit - 5 gallons

- Pipe insulation - As needed

- Gloves - 1 pair

Step-by-Step Guide:

1. **Select a Location**: Choose a site for the greywater collection tank that is easily accessible and within proximity to the sources of greywater (i.e., laundry, sink, shower). Ensure the area allows for proper drainage and does not accumulate standing water.

2. **Excavate the Ground**: Use a shovel to dig a hole for the greywater collection tank, ensuring it is deep enough to accommodate the tank with at least 6 inches of space around it for drainage. A depth of 2-3 feet typically suffices.

3. **Install the Tank**: Place the 50-gallon greywater collection tank into the hole. Ensure it is level by checking with a level tool. Backfill the hole with soil, compacting it around the tank to secure it in place.

4. **Connect PVC Pipes**: Measure and cut PVC pipes to connect the greywater sources (e.g., laundry machine drain, sink drain) to the collection tank. Ensure that all cuts are clean and straight.

5. **Assemble Connections**: Use PVC elbows and connectors to create a system that directs greywater into the tank. Apply Teflon tape on all threaded connections to ensure they are watertight.

6. **Install Filter**: Position a filter (mesh or sand) at the entrance of the collection tank to prevent debris from entering the tank. This filter is crucial for maintaining water quality and prolonging the system's lifespan.

7. **Attach Hose Bib or Valve**: Install a hose bib or valve on the collection tank for easy access to the recycled water. Ensure it is positioned at the lowest point of the tank to allow for complete drainage.

8. **Set Up Pump (if needed)**: If gravity flow isn't feasible, install a pump to facilitate water movement from the tank to your irrigation system or garden. Follow the manufacturer's instructions for proper installation.

9. **Insulate Pipes**: Use pipe insulation on exposed PVC pipes to protect against temperature fluctuations, particularly in colder climates. This helps prevent freezing and ensures optimal flow.

10. **Direct Recycled Water**: Connect a garden hose to the hose bib or valve, leading it to your garden or irrigation area. Ensure that the hose is long enough to reach the desired locations without kinking.

11. **Test the System**: Once all connections are secure, run water through the system to check for leaks and ensure everything is functioning properly. Monitor the flow and adjust as necessary.

Maintenance:

- **Weekly**: Inspect the collection tank for any signs of leaks or cracks. Ensure that the tank remains clean and free from debris. Check the filter for blockages and clean it as needed to maintain optimal flow.

- **Monthly**: Examine all PVC connections and joints for signs of wear or leaks. Tighten any loose fittings and replace any damaged parts. Monitor the pump (if used) for proper operation, cleaning the intake if necessary.

- **Yearly**: Clean the greywater collection tank by draining it completely and scrubbing the interior with a non-toxic cleaner. Inspect the entire system for structural integrity and make any repairs or replacements as needed.

Complexity:

The greywater recycling system project is moderate in complexity. It requires basic plumbing skills, including cutting and assembling PVC pipes. Familiarity with water flow and drainage principles is beneficial. Challenges may arise from ensuring proper filtration and avoiding contamination, so attention to detail during setup is crucial.

Estimated Time:

- **Setup**: 3-5 hours to gather materials, excavate the site, and assemble the system components.

- **Ongoing maintenance**: 10-15 minutes weekly for inspecting the tank, checking filters, and ensuring proper operation.

- **Annual maintenance**: 1-2 hours to clean the tank and inspect the entire system thoroughly.

2.4.3 CONSTRUCTED WETLANDS FOR WASTEWATER TREATMENT

Constructed wetlands for wastewater treatment represent an innovative and sustainable solution for managing domestic wastewater, particularly in off-grid living scenarios. These systems mimic natural wetland processes to filter and purify water, providing a practical method for treating greywater and blackwater. The importance of constructed wetlands lies in their ability to reduce environmental impact, conserve water resources, and support self-sufficiency. By employing a constructed wetland, you not only address waste management needs but also contribute positively to local ecosystems.

This project aims to construct a simple, effective constructed wetland system that can treat wastewater generated from household activities. The benefits are significant: reduced reliance on traditional sewage systems, lower operational costs, and improved soil and water quality in the surrounding environment. This guide provides detailed steps to create your own constructed wetland, ensuring a cleaner, more sustainable way to manage wastewater.

Materials and Tools:

- Excavator or shovel - 1 unit

- PVC piping (4 inches in diameter) - Length depends on the design

- Geotextile fabric - 1 roll (approximately 15 feet by 10 feet)

- Gravel (pea-sized) - 1 cubic yard

- Sand - 1 cubic yard

- Activated carbon - 1 cubic yard

- Native wetland plants (e.g., cattails, bulrushes) - 10-20 plants

- Water level gauge (PVC pipe) - 1 unit

- Hose for water input - 1 unit

- Rake - 1 unit

- Leveling tool - 1 unit

Step-by-Step Guide:

1. **Site Selection**: Choose a flat area with good drainage and away from structures, at least 10 feet from the property line. Ensure the location receives sufficient sunlight.

2. **Excavate the Wetland Area**: Use an excavator or shovel to dig a basin about 1-2 feet deep, with a surface area of at least 100 square feet. The shape can be rectangular or circular, depending on available space.

3. **Create a Shallow Sloping Edge**: Gradually slope the edges of the excavation to a depth of about 6 inches, allowing for easier access and planting of wetland vegetation.

4. **Install a Drainage Pipe**: Place a PVC pipe at one end of the wetland basin to serve as an outlet for treated water. Ensure it is slightly elevated above the bottom of the basin to avoid clogging.

5. **Add Geotextile Fabric**: Line the bottom and sides of the excavation with geotextile fabric to prevent soil from mixing with gravel and to allow for water filtration.

6. **Layer with Gravel**: Pour a layer of pea-sized gravel, about 6 inches deep, on top of the geotextile fabric. This layer will act as the main filtration medium.

7. **Add Sand Layer**: Place a layer of sand, about 6 inches deep, on top of the gravel. This layer will help filter finer particles from the wastewater.

8. **Incorporate Activated Carbon**: Add a 2-inch layer of activated carbon on top of the sand to enhance the adsorption of contaminants and odors.

9. **Plant Wetland Vegetation**: Arrange native wetland plants evenly across the surface. Space them about 1-2 feet apart to allow for growth. These plants will absorb nutrients and help maintain the ecosystem.

10. **Set Up Water Input System**: Connect a hose to your water source and direct it into the constructed wetland. This system will allow you to control the flow of wastewater into the wetland for treatment.

11. **Install Water Level Gauge**: Place a piece of PVC pipe vertically in the wetland to serve as a water level gauge. This allows you to monitor the water levels and adjust the input as needed.

12. **Maintain Water Levels**: Ensure that the wetland maintains a consistent water level, ideally between 6-12 inches deep. Adjust the flow of wastewater as necessary.

13. **Regular Monitoring**: Check the system regularly for clogs, plant health, and overall function. Clear any debris that may block the drainage pipe or water input.

Maintenance:

- **Weekly**: Inspect the water levels and adjust the input hose as needed. Check for clogs in the drainage pipe.

- **Monthly**: Trim any overgrown plants and remove dead vegetation. This keeps the system healthy and promotes new growth.

- **Yearly**: Replace any depleted activated carbon and refresh the gravel and sand layers if necessary. Assess the overall condition of the wetland and make adjustments based on performance.

Complexity:

This project is of moderate complexity. It requires basic excavation and landscaping skills, along with some knowledge of wetland ecology. Challenges may include ensuring proper drainage and plant growth, as well as managing wastewater input to avoid overwhelming the system. With attention to detail and careful monitoring, these challenges can be effectively managed.

Estimated Time:

- **Setup**: 1-2 days for excavation, layering, and planting.

- **Ongoing maintenance**: 15-30 minutes weekly for inspections and adjustments.

- **Annual maintenance**: 2-3 hours for a thorough check and replacement of materials as needed.

3. ENERGY AND POWER SOURCES

3.1 INTRODUCTION

In the modern world, energy is an essential resource that powers nearly every aspect of daily life. From lighting our homes to cooking food, charging devices, and operating essential equipment, reliable access to energy is critical. However, when living off the grid or in scenarios where traditional power sources are unavailable or unreliable, the ability to generate and manage your own energy becomes not just a luxury but a necessity.

This chapter is dedicated to exploring various off-grid energy solutions, providing the knowledge and tools needed to set up and maintain reliable power sources in remote or emergency situations. Whether you're preparing for a future where energy independence is crucial or simply looking to reduce your reliance on the grid, understanding how to harness and manage alternative energy sources is key to long-term self-sufficiency.

We begin with an in-depth exploration of solar power, the most popular and widely available renewable energy source. Solar power systems offer a scalable and sustainable way to generate electricity, and when paired with battery storage, can provide continuous power even when the sun isn't shining. This section will guide you through every aspect of setting up an off-grid solar power system, from determining your energy needs to choosing the right components and installing them.

Following solar power, we'll dive into wind energy, another powerful renewable resource that can complement solar power or serve as a primary energy source in areas with consistent wind. We'll cover the different types of small wind turbines, how to set up a DIY wind turbine kit, and the steps for installing a small wind turbine.

In addition to renewable energy sources, we'll discuss the importance of protecting your off-grid energy system from electromagnetic pulses (EMPs), which can be devastating to electronic equipment. We'll provide practical strategies for safeguarding your power systems and electronics from potential EMP damage.

Finally, we'll explore a variety of DIY energy projects that can serve as alternative or supplementary power sources. These projects, ranging from pedal-powered generators to hand crank chargers and DIY candle making, offer practical solutions for generating and storing energy in low-tech, resource-scarce environments.

By the end of this chapter, you will have a comprehensive understanding of how to establish and maintain a robust, off-grid energy system. You'll be equipped with the knowledge to choose the right power sources, protect your systems from potential threats, and ensure that you have the energy needed to sustain an independent, off-grid lifestyle.

3.2 OFF-GRID SOLAR POWER

Off-grid solar power systems harness solar energy to provide electricity independently from traditional utilities. This project is crucial for those seeking self-sufficiency, especially in remote areas or for those wanting to reduce their environmental impact. By establishing a solar power system, one can generate clean energy, lessen fossil fuel dependence, and achieve energy independence.

The significance of off-grid solar power lies in its sustainable energy solutions. With rising energy costs and the visible effects of climate change, renewable sources like solar power present a practical alternative. Generating electricity from abundant sunlight addresses energy scarcity and promotes a cleaner planet.

Implementing an off-grid solar power system offers benefits beyond environmental impact. Financially, it reduces long-term energy costs. Although initial setup requires investment, savings on utility bills and potential tax incentives enhance the return on investment, often bringing electricity costs close to zero, allowing for better budgeting.

Moreover, off-grid solar systems empower individuals to control their energy production. In a world increasingly affected by disasters and instability, an independent power source ensures resilience. Concerns about outages or fluctuating grid prices diminish, enabling essential appliances to run and maintaining comfort even in tough situations.

Beyond practicality, off-grid solar power fosters a deeper connection with nature. It encourages appreciation for the sun's cycles, mindfulness of energy consumption, and awareness of environmental impacts. This mindset nurtures a sustainable lifestyle and a harmonious relationship with the earth.

This project encompasses assessing energy needs, selecting components, installing systems, and ongoing maintenance. You will explore solar panels, inverters, batteries, charge controllers, and mounting systems, gaining insights into their interconnectivity. Additionally, the guide addresses local regulations, challenges, and strategies for maximizing energy efficiency.

As you engage in this project, prepare for hands-on work that may involve basic electrical skills, physical labor, and critical thinking. While the process may be complex, it offers a rewarding chance to create a self-sufficient energy source tailored to your needs. With determination and understanding of the components, you can successfully install an off-grid solar power system that enhances your lifestyle and benefits the environment.

This introduction lays the foundation for understanding off-grid solar power, highlighting its significance and transformative potential for your life and the planet. As you progress, you will acquire the knowledge to implement a solar power system that meets your energy needs and aligns with your values.

3.2.1 DETERMINING SOLAR POWER NEEDS

Planning an off-grid solar power system begins with a thorough understanding of your energy consumption and the potential solar energy available at your location. This step is crucial to ensure that your system is correctly sized to meet your needs year-round, providing reliable and sustainable power. To achieve this, you'll need to calculate how much energy you use, assess your local solar potential, and determine the appropriate size and number of solar panels required for your setup.

Materials and Tools:

- Tape measure - 1 unit
- Solar irradiance map or app or calculator

Step-by-Step Guide:

1. **Assessing Your Energy Consumption**:
   a. **Understanding Your Power Usage**: Begin by listing every appliance and device that you plan to run on solar power. This includes everything from lighting and refrigerators to electronics and water pumps. For each item, note its power rating in watts and estimate how many hours it operates daily.
   b. **Calculating Daily Energy Needs**: Multiply each device's wattage by the number of hours it's used per day to find the daily energy consumption in watt-hours. Adding up these values will give you the total amount of energy your household consumes in a typical day.

2. **Sizing Your Solar Panels**:
   a. **Energy Needs and Efficiency**: To determine how much solar energy you need to generate, divide your total daily energy consumption by your expected system efficiency. This accounts for energy losses that occur during the conversion and storage of solar power.
   b. **Considering Sunlight Availability**: The amount of sunlight your location receives plays a significant role in determining the size of your solar panel array. Locations with more sunlight will require fewer panels. Use local solar insolation data to find out how many hours of peak sunlight your area gets each day.

3. **Calculating Panel Capacity**:

a. **Solar Panel Capacity**: Divide your adjusted daily energy needs by the number of peak sunlight hours to find the necessary solar panel capacity in kilowatts (kW). This tells you how much energy your panels need to produce daily to meet your consumption.

b. **Example**: If your household uses 20 kWh of electricity per day, and your system operates at 85% efficiency, you would need: Adjusted Daily Energy Needs = 20 kWh / 0.85 = 23.53 kWh In a location with an average of 6 hours of peak sunlight daily, the required panel capacity would be: Solar Panel Capacity = 23.53 kWh / 6 hours = 3.92 kW

4. **Determining Number of Panels**:

   a. **Panel Specifications**: Check the specifications of the solar panels you plan to use, specifically their wattage rating. To find out how many panels you need, divide your total required capacity by the wattage of a single panel.

   b. **Example**: If each panel produces 320 watts (0.32 kW), you would need: Number of Panels = 3.92 kW / 0.32 kW = 12.25 panels (rounded up to 13 panels)

5. **Estimating Solar Panel Output**:

   a. **Real-World Output Considerations**: Solar panels typically have a rated output based on optimal conditions, but actual output depends on several factors, including panel orientation, shading, and geographic location. To estimate how much energy your panels will produce daily, multiply the number of peak sunlight hours by the panel's wattage and adjust for real-world efficiency losses.

   b. **Example**: A 300-watt panel in an area with 5 hours of peak sunlight might realistically generate: Estimated Daily Output = 5 hours × 300 watts × 0.8 (adjusting for losses) = 1200 watt-hours (Wh)

6. **Understanding Solar Panel Efficiency**:

   a. **Efficiency Metrics**: Solar panel efficiency measures how effectively a panel converts sunlight into electricity. Panels with higher efficiency generate more power for the same surface area. To calculate efficiency, divide the panel's maximum power output by its surface area and convert this into a percentage.

   b. **Example**: A panel with a surface area of 1.5 square meters and a maximum output of 300 watts has an efficiency of: Efficiency = (300 watts / 1.5 m²) ÷ 1000 × 100% = 20%

Maintenance:

- **Regular Energy Audits**: Annually review your energy consumption and adjust your solar setup to account for any changes in your needs.

- **Monitoring Solar Output**: Periodically check your panels to ensure they're receiving adequate sunlight and aren't obstructed by new shading or debris.

Complexity:

Moderate. This process involves several calculations and a good understanding of solar energy systems.

Estimated Time:

- 2-3 hours for assessing your energy needs and calculating the required system size.

3.2.2 TYPES OF SOLAR PANELS

Choosing the right type of solar panel is crucial for maximizing efficiency and cost-effectiveness in your off-grid solar power system. Solar panels come in different types, each with its own advantages and disadvantages. Understanding these differences will help you select the best panels for your specific needs and environment.

Monocrystalline Solar Panels:

- **Overview**: Monocrystalline panels are made from a single crystal structure, making them the most efficient and space-saving option available. These panels are highly efficient, often reaching efficiencies between 15-22%, and are particularly effective in low-light conditions.

- **Space and Efficiency**: Because of their high efficiency, monocrystalline panels require less space to produce the same amount of energy as other panel types, making them ideal for areas with limited space.

- **Durability**: Monocrystalline panels have a long lifespan, often exceeding 25 years, and perform well in a wide range of environmental conditions.

Polycrystalline Solar Panels:

- **Overview**: Polycrystalline panels are made from multiple silicon crystals, which makes them slightly less efficient than monocrystalline panels, with efficiencies ranging from 13-16%. However, they are more affordable and still provide a good balance between cost and performance.

- **Cost-Effectiveness**: These panels are a cost-effective choice for larger installations where space is not a limiting factor. They offer a lower price per watt compared to monocrystalline panels.

- **Installation Considerations**: Polycrystalline panels require more space to generate the same amount of power as monocrystalline panels, so they are better suited for installations with ample space.

Thin-Film Solar Panels:

- **Overview**: Thin-film panels are made by depositing one or more layers of photovoltaic material onto a substrate. These panels are lightweight, flexible, and can be used in a variety of applications, including on rooftops, windows, or even vehicles.

- **Efficiency and Space Requirements**: Thin-film panels have lower efficiencies (typically 7-13%) compared to crystalline panels, which means they require more space to produce the same amount of energy. However, their flexibility and light weight make them suitable for installations where traditional panels might not fit.

- **Temperature Tolerance**: Thin-film panels perform better in high temperatures and partial shading than crystalline panels, making them a good choice for certain climates and installation scenarios.

Choosing the Right Panels:

- **Space Constraints**: If space is limited, monocrystalline panels are usually the best choice due to their high efficiency.

- **Budget Constraints**: For those with a tighter budget, polycrystalline panels offer a good balance of cost and efficiency.

- **Unique Applications**: If you need a lightweight, flexible panel for a non-traditional installation, thin-film might be the best option.

Maintenance:

- **Regular Cleaning**: Dust, dirt, and debris can accumulate on the panels, reducing their efficiency. Regular cleaning, especially in dusty or rainy climates, is essential to maintaining optimal performance.

- **Annual Inspection**: Inspect the panels and their mounting hardware annually to check for any physical damage, wear, or corrosion.

Complexity:

Easy. Understanding the types of panels and their pros and cons requires basic knowledge of solar technology.

Estimated Time:

- 1-2 hours for selection and decision-making.

3.2.3 BATTERY STORAGE

Battery storage is an essential component of an off-grid solar power system. It allows you to store the energy generated by your solar panels during the day for use at night or during periods of low sunlight. Choosing the right battery type and capacity is crucial for ensuring that your system meets your energy needs reliably and efficiently.

Types of Batteries:

- **Lead-Acid Batteries**: Lead-acid batteries are the most common and affordable option for off-grid solar power systems. They come in two main types: flooded and sealed (AGM or gel). Flooded batteries require regular maintenance, including checking electrolyte levels and performing equalization charges, while sealed batteries are maintenance-free. Lead-acid batteries typically have a shorter lifespan and lower depth of discharge (DoD) compared to other types, meaning you can only use a portion of their total capacity before needing to recharge.

- **Lithium-Ion Batteries**: Lithium-ion batteries are more expensive but offer several advantages over lead-acid batteries, including a longer lifespan, higher efficiency, and deeper depth of discharge (up to 90%). They are also lighter and more compact, making them easier to install and maintain. Lithium-ion batteries require little to no maintenance, but their higher initial cost can be a barrier for some users.

- **Saltwater Batteries**: A newer technology, saltwater batteries are environmentally friendly and non-toxic. They offer good safety and longevity, but have a lower energy density and are less common than lead-acid or lithium-ion batteries. Saltwater batteries are a good option for those looking for a sustainable, low-maintenance energy storage solution.

Battery Capacity:

- **Calculating Capacity**: To determine your battery capacity needs, start by calculating your daily energy usage in watt-hours. Multiply this by the number of days you want your system to operate without sunlight (usually 2-3 days for safety). Divide this figure by the voltage of your battery bank (12V, 24V, or 48V) to determine the total amp-hours required.

- **Depth of Discharge (DoD)**: Consider the depth of discharge for the type of battery you are using. Lead-acid batteries typically have a DoD of 50%, meaning you can only use half of their total capacity before needing to recharge. Lithium-ion batteries have a higher DoD (up to 90%), which allows you to use more of their total capacity without damaging the battery.

Battery Bank Sizing:

- **Series vs. Parallel Connections**: Decide whether to connect your batteries in series or parallel, depending on your voltage and capacity needs. Connecting batteries in series increases the voltage, while connecting them in parallel increases the capacity. The choice between series and parallel connections will depend on your system's overall design and the voltage of your other components (e.g., charge controller, inverter).

- **Location and Ventilation**: Choose a cool, dry, and well-ventilated location for your battery bank. Proper ventilation is essential to prevent overheating and to dissipate gasses that may be released by certain types of batteries. Ensure that the battery bank is easily accessible for maintenance but protected from extreme temperatures and moisture.

Maintenance:

- **Regular Inspection**: Check the battery terminals and connections regularly for corrosion or loose connections. Clean and tighten as necessary to ensure a secure and efficient connection.

- **Equalization Charging (Lead-Acid Only)**: Perform an equalization charge every few months to balance the charge in all cells and extend the battery life. This is especially important for flooded lead-acid batteries.

- **Temperature Monitoring**: Monitor the temperature of your battery bank, especially during extreme weather conditions. High temperatures can reduce battery life, while low temperatures can reduce performance.

Complexity:

Moderate to Hard. Requires understanding battery technology, calculating capacity, and proper installation and maintenance.

Estimated Time:

- 2-3 days for selecting, purchasing, and installing batteries.

3.2.4 SOLAR CHARGE CONTROLLERS AND INVERTERS

Solar charge controllers and inverters are crucial components in an off-grid solar power system. The charge controller regulates the flow of electricity from the solar panels to the batteries, ensuring that the batteries are not overcharged and that they charge efficiently. The inverter converts the DC electricity stored in the batteries into AC electricity, which is used to power household appliances. Understanding these components and choosing the right ones for your system is essential for a successful off-grid solar installation.

Materials and Tools:

- Charge controller (PWM or MPPT) - 1 unit

- Inverter (pure sine wave or modified sine wave) - 1 unit

- Wiring and fuses - As needed

- Multimeter - 1 unit

Step-by-Step Guide:

1. **Choosing a Charge Controller**:

    a. **PWM vs. MPPT**: The two main types of charge controllers are PWM (Pulse Width Modulation) and MPPT (Maximum Power Point Tracking). PWM controllers are more affordable and work well in small systems with a consistent sunlight profile. They regulate the charging process by gradually reducing the current to the batteries as they reach full charge. MPPT controllers are more efficient, especially in larger systems or areas with varying sunlight conditions. They optimize the power output from the solar panels by constantly adjusting the voltage and current to match the battery's charging requirements.

    b. **Sizing the Controller**: The charge controller should be rated to handle the total current output of your solar panels. To calculate the required current rating, divide the total wattage of your solar panels by the system voltage (e.g., 12V, 24V, or 48V). For example, if you have a 2 kW solar array and a 24V battery bank, you would need a charge controller rated for at least 83 amps (2000W ÷ 24V = 83.33A).

2. **Choosing an Inverter**:

    a. **Pure Sine Wave vs. Modified Sine Wave**: Pure sine wave inverters produce clean, smooth AC power that is compatible with all types of household appliances, including sensitive electronics like computers and medical equipment. Modified sine wave inverters are cheaper but produce a rougher power output, which may not work well with all appliances and can cause issues with certain devices. Pure sine wave inverters are recommended for most off-grid solar systems due to their reliability and compatibility.

    b. **Sizing the Inverter**: The inverter should be rated for your peak power needs, which is the total wattage of all devices you plan to run simultaneously. Add a 20-30% buffer to this figure to ensure reliable operation. For example, if your peak power needs are 3000 watts, you should choose an inverter rated for at least 3600-4000 watts.

3. **Wiring and Installation**:

   a. **Wire Sizing**: Use appropriately sized wires to connect your solar panels, batteries, charge controller, and inverter. The wire gauge depends on the current and distance between components. Undersized wires can cause overheating, reduce system efficiency, and pose a fire risk.

   b. **Fuse Protection**: Install fuses or circuit breakers between the panels and charge controller, and between the charge controller and batteries, to protect your system from overloads. Ensure that the fuses are rated for the maximum current that could flow through the circuit.

4. **Installation**:

   a. **Mounting the Charge Controller**: Install the charge controller in a cool, dry, and well-ventilated location, away from direct sunlight and moisture. Ensure that it is easily accessible for monitoring and maintenance.

   b. **Connecting the Inverter**: Place the inverter in a location close to the battery bank to minimize power losses in the DC cables. Use thick, short cables to connect the inverter to the battery bank, and ensure that all connections are tight and secure.

Maintenance:

- **Controller and Inverter Checks**: Regularly inspect the charge controller and inverter for signs of wear or malfunction. Ensure they are operating within their specified ranges and that all connections are secure.

- **Firmware Updates**: If your charge controller or inverter supports firmware updates, check for and install any updates periodically to improve performance and reliability.

Complexity:

Moderate. Requires understanding electrical specifications and proper installation procedures.

Estimated Time:

- 1-2 days for installation and testing.

3.2.5 SOLAR BATTERY CHARGERS

Solar battery chargers are essential for maintaining the charge in your off-grid batteries. These chargers are designed to work with the specific type of battery you are using, ensuring that it is charged efficiently and safely. Understanding how to choose the right solar charger and how to integrate it into your system is crucial for keeping your batteries in optimal condition.

Materials and Tools:

- Solar battery charger - 1 unit

- Cables - As needed

- Multimeter - 1 unit

Step-by-Step Guide:

1. **Choosing the Right Solar Battery Charger**:

   a. **Compatibility**: Ensure the solar charger is compatible with your battery type (lead-acid, lithium-ion, etc.) and system voltage. Some chargers are universal, while others are designed specifically for certain battery chemistries.

    b. **Charging Efficiency**: Look for chargers with high charging efficiency and features like MPPT to maximize the power harvested from your solar panels. A good charger will also have built-in protections against overcharging, short circuits, and reverse polarity.

2. **Connecting the Charger**:

    a. **Wiring the Charger**: Connect the solar charger to your battery bank using appropriately sized cables. Ensure the connections are secure and that the charger is set to the correct voltage for your battery bank.

    b. **Monitoring the Charge**: Use a multimeter to monitor the charging process and ensure that the battery is charging at the correct rate. The charger should display the charging current and battery voltage.

3. **Placement and Setup**:

    a. **Charger Placement**: Place the charger in a well-ventilated area, away from direct sunlight and moisture. If the charger has a display or indicator lights, ensure they are easily visible for monitoring.

    b. **Testing the Charger**: After setup, test the charger by fully charging a battery and monitoring its performance. Ensure the charger shuts off or enters a maintenance mode once the battery is fully charged.

Maintenance:

- **Regular Cleaning**: Keep the charger and its connections clean and free of dust and debris. This ensures efficient operation and reduces the risk of overheating.

- **Performance Monitoring**: Periodically check the charger's output to ensure it is working correctly and not overcharging or undercharging the batteries.

Complexity:

Easy to Moderate. Requires basic understanding of battery charging and safe electrical connections.

Estimated Time:

- 1-2 hours for installation and testing.

3.2.6 HOW TO CHOOSE A SOLAR CHARGER

Selecting the right solar charger for your off-grid system is crucial for ensuring that your batteries remain charged and in good condition. This subchapter provides a comprehensive guide on what to look for when choosing a solar charger, including key features, compatibility, and efficiency.

Materials and Tools:

- Solar charger comparison chart - 1 unit

- Calculator - 1 unit

- Multimeter - 1 unit

Step-by-Step Guide:

1. **Determine Your Battery Type and Voltage**:

    a. **Battery Chemistry**: Identify the type of batteries you are using (lead-acid, lithium-ion, etc.) as this will determine the type of solar charger you need. Some chargers are designed specifically for certain battery types, while others are more versatile.

    b. **System Voltage**: Know the voltage of your battery bank (12V, 24V, 48V, etc.). The solar charger must be compatible with this voltage to work effectively.

2. **Consider Charging Efficiency**:

   a. **MPPT vs. PWM**: MPPT (Maximum Power Point Tracking) chargers are more efficient than PWM (Pulse Width Modulation) chargers, especially in systems with higher voltages or varying sunlight conditions. MPPT chargers can increase charging efficiency by up to 30%.

   b. **Efficiency Rating**: Check the efficiency rating of the charger. Higher efficiency means more of the solar energy is converted into usable electricity for charging your batteries.

3. **Look for Essential Features**:

   a. **Overcharge Protection**: Ensure the charger has built-in overcharge protection to prevent damage to your batteries.

   b. **Temperature Compensation**: This feature adjusts the charging voltage based on the battery temperature, which helps maintain battery health in varying climates.

   c. **Display and Monitoring**: A charger with a clear display or the ability to connect to a monitoring app allows you to keep track of charging status, voltage, and current.

4. **Consider Durability and Build Quality**:

   a. **Weatherproofing**: If your charger will be exposed to the elements, make sure it is weatherproof or can be installed in a protected enclosure.

   b. **Quality of Components**: Choose a charger with high-quality components and a solid build to ensure longevity and reliability in off-grid conditions.

Maintenance:

- **Monitor Charger Performance**: Regularly check the charger's performance to ensure it is operating within specifications and providing the correct charge to your batteries.

- **Update Firmware (if applicable)**: If your charger supports firmware updates, keep it updated to benefit from any performance improvements or new features.

Complexity:

Moderate. Requires understanding battery technology and charger features.

Estimated Time:

- 1-2 hours for selection and setup.

3.3 STEP-BY-STEP GUIDE FOR SOLAR SETUP

Setting up an off-grid solar power system involves several key steps, from calculating your home's electrical load to installing the solar panels and connecting all the components. This comprehensive guide walks you through the entire process, ensuring that your system is properly sized, installed, and ready to provide reliable power.

3.3.1 STEP 1: HOW TO CALCULATE HOME ELECTRICAL LOAD

Determining your home's electrical load is a crucial step in designing a solar power system that meets your needs. By calculating the total wattage of all the appliances and devices you plan to use, you can ensure your solar system is properly sized to handle both everyday usage and peak power demands.

Step-by-Step Guide:

1. **Inventory of Essential Appliances**:

   a. **Identify Critical Devices**: Begin by listing all the essential appliances you want to power with your solar setup, especially during emergencies like power outages. For example, you might prioritize keeping your refrigerator running to preserve food, maintaining lighting for safety, cooling a room with an air conditioner, using a toaster, and keeping your laptop charged for communication.

2. **Determine Running and Starting Watts**:

   a. **Running Watts Calculation**: Each appliance has a rated or running wattage, which indicates how much power it consumes during regular operation. Sum these values to find your total running wattage. Here's an example with common household items, taken from https://generatorist.com/power-consumption-of-household-appliances:

Selected Appliances	Rated (Running) Watts	Additional Starting Watts
Toaster	850 W	0 W
Refrigerator / Freezer	700 W	2,200 W
Laptop	50 W	0 W
Lamp (2 Lightbulbs)	150 W	0 W
Window AC (10,000 BTU)	1,200 W	3,600 W
TOTAL	**2,950 W**	**6,550 W**

   b. In this scenario, the combined running wattage of all the appliances is 2,950 watts (850 + 700 + 50 + 150 + 1,200 = 2,950 W). This means your solar power system needs to support at least 2,950 watts of continuous power.

   c. **Starting Watts Calculation**: Some appliances, especially those with motors, require additional surge or starting watts when they first power on. This surge is usually short-lived but can be several times higher than the running wattage. To ensure your solar setup can handle these surges, you need to account for the highest starting wattage among your devices. In this example, the highest starting surge comes from the window AC unit, adding 3,600 watts to the system's requirements. Therefore, your system should be capable of providing at least 6,550 watts (2,950 W + 3,600 W = 6,550 W) during startup, as long as the other devices requiring additional surge do not power on at the same time.

3. **Estimating Watts for Unlabeled Appliances**:

   a. **Using Voltage and Current**: If an appliance doesn't list its wattage, you can calculate it using the voltage (V) and current (A) specifications usually found on the device's label. The formula is straightforward:

   Watts (W) = Volts (V) × Amps (A)

   For example, if an appliance operates at 120 volts and draws 5 amps, the power consumption would be:

   Watts = 120V × 5A = 600W

   This formula, a practical application of Ohm's Law from basic physics, helps estimate the power requirements of any electrical device.

Maintenance:

- **Review and Adjust**: Periodically review your list of essential appliances and adjust your calculations if you add or remove devices, ensuring your solar system continues to meet your needs efficiently.

Complexity:

Moderate. Requires careful inventory of appliances and understanding of electrical concepts to ensure accurate calculations.

Estimated Time:

- 1-2 hours to list appliances, calculate wattages, and determine overall power needs.

3.3.2 STEP 2: SOLAR PANELS AND PEAK SUN HOURS

Understanding how to size your solar panel array based on your location's peak sun hours is crucial for ensuring that your system can generate enough power to meet your needs.

Materials and Tools:

- Solar irradiance map or app - 1 unit
- Calculator - 1 unit

Step-by-Step Guide:

1. **Determine Peak Sun Hours**:
   a. **Use a Solar Map**: Find your location on a solar irradiance map or use an app to determine your average daily peak sun hours. Peak sun hours represent the time when sunlight intensity is strong enough to generate the maximum possible power from your solar panels.
   b. **Check the U.S. Annual Solar GHI**: Available from National Renewable Energy Laboratory (NREL). This map provides annual average daily total solar resource using 1998-2016 data (PSM v3) covering 0.038-degree latitude by 0.038-degree longitude (nominally 4 km x 4 km):

   https://www.nrel.gov/gis/assets/images/solar-annual-ghi-2018-usa-scale-01.jpg

2. **Calculate Required Solar Panel Capacity**:
   a. **Divide by Peak Sun Hours**: Divide your total daily electrical load (in watt-hours) by the number of peak sun hours to calculate the required solar panel capacity in watts. This will give you the total wattage needed from your solar panels to meet your energy needs.

3. **Select Solar Panels**:
   a. **Panel Sizing**: Choose solar panels that match or exceed the calculated capacity. Consider the efficiency and space requirements of different panel types (monocrystalline, polycrystalline, thin-film) when making your selection.

Maintenance:

- **Panel Cleaning**: Keep the panels clean to ensure they operate at maximum efficiency.
- **Check for Obstructions**: Regularly check for new obstructions, such as growing trees, that could reduce sunlight reaching your panels.

Complexity:

Moderate. Requires basic math and understanding of solar energy.

Estimated Time:

- 1-2 hours for calculation and selection.

3.3.3 STEP 3: BATTERY DECISIONS

Choosing the right batteries and properly sizing your battery bank is critical for storing the energy generated by your solar panels.

Materials and Tools:

- Battery comparison chart - 1 unit
- Calculator - 1 unit

Step-by-Step Guide:

1. **Choose Battery Type**:

   a. **Lead-Acid vs. Lithium-Ion**: Consider the pros and cons of different battery types. Lead-acid batteries are cheaper but require maintenance and have a shorter lifespan. Lithium-ion batteries are more expensive but offer better performance and longevity.

2. **Calculate Battery Capacity**:

   a. **Energy Storage Needs**: Multiply your daily electrical load by the number of days you want your system to run without sunlight (usually 2-3 days). Divide this by the battery's voltage to determine the total amp-hours required.

3. **Battery Bank Configuration**:

   a. **Series vs. Parallel**: Decide whether to connect your batteries in series or parallel, depending on whether you need to increase voltage or capacity.

Maintenance:

- **Regular Checks**: Monitor battery health and charge levels regularly to ensure optimal performance.

Complexity:

Moderate. Requires understanding battery technology and proper installation.

Estimated Time:

- 1-2 hours for calculation and selection.

3.3.4 STEP 4: INVERTERS

Inverters are essential for converting the DC power stored in your batteries into AC power, which is used by most household appliances.

Materials and Tools:

- Inverter (pure sine wave or modified sine wave) - 1 unit
- Wiring - As needed
- Multimeter - 1 unit

Step-by-Step Guide:

1. **Choose the Right Inverter**:

   a. **Pure Sine Wave vs. Modified Sine Wave**: Pure sine wave inverters are recommended for sensitive electronics, while modified sine wave inverters are cheaper but may not work with all appliances.

2. **Sizing the Inverter**:

   a. **Calculate Peak Power**: Add up the wattage of all devices you plan to run simultaneously and choose an inverter that can handle this load with a 20-30% safety margin.

3. **Installation**:

    a. **Connect to Battery Bank**: Wire the inverter to your battery bank using appropriately sized cables. Ensure all connections are secure and protected from short circuits.

Maintenance:

- **Regular Inspection**: Check the inverter for any signs of malfunction and ensure it is operating within its specifications.

Complexity:

Moderate. Requires electrical knowledge and proper installation.

Estimated Time:

- 1-2 hours for sizing and installation.

3.3.5 STEP 5: CHARGE CONTROLLER

The charge controller is crucial for regulating the flow of electricity from your solar panels to your batteries, preventing overcharging and ensuring battery longevity.

Materials and Tools:

- Charge controller (PWM or MPPT) - 1 unit
- Wiring - As needed
- Multimeter - 1 unit

Step-by-Step Guide:

1. **Choose the Right Controller**:

   a. **PWM vs. MPPT**: MPPT controllers are more efficient, especially for larger systems. Choose a controller that matches your system's voltage and current output.

2. **Install the Controller**:

   a. **Wiring Connections**: Connect the solar panels to the controller, then connect the controller to the battery bank. Use the appropriate wire gauge to handle the current.

Maintenance:

- **Monitor Performance**: Regularly check the controller's performance and ensure it is protecting the batteries as expected.

Complexity:

Moderate. Requires understanding of electrical systems and proper installation.

Estimated Time:

- 1-2 hours for sizing and installation.

3.3.6 STEP 6: CABLES AND MISCELLANEOUS

Proper cabling is essential for ensuring that your off-grid solar power system operates safely and efficiently. This step covers the selection and installation of cables, fuses, and other miscellaneous components.

Materials and Tools:

- Electrical cables (various gauges) - As needed
- Fuses and circuit breakers - As needed
- Cable ties - As needed

- Multimeter - 1 unit

Step-by-Step Guide:

1. **Choose the Right Cable Gauge**:

    a. **Calculate Current Load**: Use your system's current load to determine the correct wire gauge. Thicker wires are required for higher currents to prevent overheating and power loss.

2. **Install Fuses and Circuit Breakers**:

    a. **Safety First**: Install fuses or circuit breakers between major components, such as between the panels and charge controller, and between the charge controller and battery bank, to protect against short circuits and overloads.

3. **Secure Cables**:

    a. **Cable Management**: Use cable ties and conduit to organize and protect cables. Ensure all connections are secure and properly insulated to prevent short circuits.

Maintenance:

- **Regular Inspections**: Check all cables and connections for signs of wear, corrosion, or damage. Replace any components as needed to maintain system safety and efficiency.

Complexity:

Moderate. Requires basic electrical knowledge and attention to detail.

Estimated Time:

- 1-2 hours for installation.

3.3.7 STEP 7: SOLAR SETUP INSTRUCTIONS

This final step brings together all the components of your off-grid solar power system, from solar panels to batteries, charge controllers, and inverters, into a cohesive and functional system.

Materials and Tools:

- Solar panels, batteries, charge controller, inverter, and cables - As needed
- Multimeter - 1 unit
- Screwdriver set - 1 unit
- Drill - 1 unit
- Ladder (if installing rooftop panels) - 1 unit

Step-by-Step Guide:

1. **Install Solar Panels**:

    a. **Positioning**: Mount the solar panels on your roof or on a ground-based frame, ensuring they are angled to capture the maximum amount of sunlight. Ideally, panels should face true south (in the Northern Hemisphere) or true north (in the Southern Hemisphere) at an angle equal to your latitude.

    b. **Wiring**: Connect the solar panels in series or parallel, depending on your system's voltage requirements. Use appropriately sized wiring to connect the panels to the charge controller. Ensure the wiring is secure, weatherproof, and protected from the elements.

2. **Install the Battery Bank**:

    a. **Location**: Place the batteries in a cool, dry location with good ventilation. Ensure they are easily accessible for maintenance but protected from extreme temperatures and moisture.

b. **Battery Connections**: Connect the batteries in series or parallel, depending on your system voltage. Use heavy-duty cables to connect the batteries to the charge controller and inverter, ensuring all connections are tight and secure.

3. **Connect the Charge Controller**:

   a. **Wiring Setup**: Connect the solar panels to the charge controller, then connect the controller to the battery bank. Follow the manufacturer's instructions for proper wiring and setup. Use a multimeter to verify that the system voltage and current are within the expected range.

   b. **Mounting and Placement**: Install the charge controller in a location that is easily accessible for monitoring and maintenance. Ensure it is well-ventilated to prevent overheating.

4. **Install the Inverter**:

   a. **Connection to Batteries**: Connect the inverter to the battery bank using heavy-duty cables. Ensure the inverter is located in a well-ventilated area to prevent overheating. If the inverter supports multiple output voltages (e.g., 120V and 240V), ensure it is configured correctly for your household appliances.

   b. **AC Output Connections**: Connect the inverter's AC output to your home's electrical panel or directly to specific appliances. Ensure that all connections are properly insulated and protected from short circuits.

5. **Test the System**:

   a. **Initial Testing**: Turn on the system and monitor the output from the solar panels, the charge level of the batteries, and the power output from the inverter. Use a multimeter to verify that all components are operating within their expected ranges.

   b. **Adjustments**: Make any necessary adjustments to the panel angle, wiring connections, or component settings to optimize system performance.

Maintenance:

- **Ongoing Monitoring**: Regularly monitor the system's performance and make adjustments as needed to ensure long-term reliability and efficiency. Use system monitoring tools or apps to track performance metrics like voltage, current, and battery state of charge.

- **Annual Inspections**: Conduct an annual inspection of all components, including solar panels, batteries, wiring, and inverters. Check for signs of wear, corrosion, or damage, and replace any faulty components promptly.

Complexity:

Hard. This final step requires integrating all the components into a fully functional system and ensuring everything operates correctly.

Estimated Time:

- 2-4 days for installation and testing.

3.4 OFF-GRID WIND POWER

Off-grid wind power generates electricity from wind, providing a sustainable solution for those seeking self-sufficiency. This project enables the creation of a personal energy source, reducing dependence on traditional grids and fossil fuels. By utilizing wind energy, utility costs decrease, and the carbon footprint is minimized, contributing to environmental preservation.

The significance of off-grid wind power goes beyond energy generation. As climate change threatens ecosystems and communities, adopting renewable energy is essential. Wind power offers a clean alternative that lowers greenhouse gas emissions, aligning with sustainability goals for a healthier planet for future generations.

A key advantage of off-grid wind power is independence. For those in remote areas, traditional power sources may be limited. Installing a wind turbine ensures a reliable energy supply for essential needs, enhancing quality of life without reliance on external providers.

Wind power also complements other renewable systems like solar. A hybrid approach maximizes energy generation, as wind turbines can produce consistent energy even when solar panels underperform in winter, ensuring steady power supply year-round.

Additionally, having an off-grid wind power system builds resilience. In natural disasters or grid failures, a personal energy source keeps essential appliances running, supporting preparedness and sustainability.

The project involves selecting the right wind turbine, determining the best installation site, and setting up battery storage. Understanding local wind patterns is crucial for effective turbine placement and energy generation.

Knowledge of turbine specifications is also necessary, as models vary in power output, height, and installation needs. Assessing energy requirements, budget, and space will help choose the appropriate turbine.

Safety is vital when working with wind power systems. Proper installation and secure electrical connections are essential for longevity and effectiveness. Following safety guidelines minimizes risks and maximizes investment.

In summary, starting an off-grid wind power project is a significant step toward energy independence and environmental stewardship. With careful planning and execution, wind energy can support a sustainable lifestyle for individuals and the planet.

3.4.1 TYPES OF SMALL WIND TURBINES

Wind turbines harness the power of the wind to generate electricity, making them an essential component of off-grid energy systems. These devices convert the kinetic energy from moving air into electrical energy, offering a renewable and sustainable source of power. For those pursuing self-sufficiency, small wind turbines provide numerous benefits. They reduce reliance on fossil fuels, lower electricity costs, and minimize environmental impact. Whether you're powering a cabin, a tiny home, or a full-fledged homestead, incorporating wind power can significantly enhance your energy independence.

This guide explores the different types of small wind turbines, detailing their characteristics, advantages, and disadvantages. Understanding these distinctions will help you choose the right turbine for your specific needs, wind conditions, and energy goals.

Overview of Wind Turbines:

Wind turbines generally fall into two main categories: horizontal axis wind turbines (HAWT) and vertical axis wind turbines (VAWT). Each type has unique design features and operational characteristics suited for various environments and energy requirements.

Horizontal Axis Wind Turbines (HAWT)

HAWTs are the most common type of wind turbine, characterized by their blades that rotate around a horizontal axis. Typically resembling traditional windmills, these turbines feature a tall tower and a rotor mounted at the top. The rotor spins when the wind blows, generating electricity through a generator connected to the turbine.

Pros:

- **Efficiency**: HAWTs are generally more efficient than VAWTs. They can capture wind energy at higher speeds, producing more electricity, particularly in areas with consistent, strong winds.

- **Height Advantage**: The tall towers elevate the rotor to catch faster winds that occur at higher altitudes.

- **Scalability**: HAWTs are available in various sizes, from small units suitable for homes to larger models for commercial use.

Cons:

- **Noise**: The rotor blades can produce noise, which may be a concern in residential areas.

- **Space Requirements**: HAWTs require more space for installation, as they need to be positioned away from obstacles that could disrupt airflow.

- **Complex Installation**: Setting up a HAWT can be more complicated, often requiring professional installation due to the height and structural considerations.

Vertical Axis Wind Turbines (VAWT)

VAWTs have blades that rotate around a vertical axis. They can take various forms, including the Darrieus and Savonius designs. These turbines are typically shorter and more compact, making them suitable for residential use and areas with limited space.

Pros:

- **Omnidirectional**: VAWTs can capture wind from any direction, eliminating the need for a yaw mechanism that adjusts the turbine's position in relation to the wind.

- **Lower Height**: They are easier to install and maintain, often requiring less specialized equipment or expertise.

- **Safety**: VAWTs are generally safer, as their lower height reduces the risk of accidents during installation or maintenance.

Cons:

- **Lower Efficiency**: VAWTs are typically less efficient than HAWTs, particularly in high-wind conditions. They may produce less electricity in areas with consistent strong winds.

- **Less Common**: Fewer manufacturers produce VAWTs, leading to limited options for consumers.

- **Durability Issues**: Some VAWT designs can experience more wear and tear due to the stress of wind pushing against the blades.

How to Choose the Right Wind Turbine

Selecting the appropriate wind turbine for your off-grid setup requires careful consideration of various factors, including location, energy needs, and personal preferences. Here are key points to help guide your decision:

- **Assess Wind Conditions**: Conduct a wind resource assessment for your site. Use an anemometer to measure wind speed and direction over a period of time. Ideally, look for locations with average wind speeds of at least 10 mph (4.5 m/s). The more data you collect, the better informed your decision will be.

- **Determine Energy Needs**: Calculate your household's energy consumption. Identify the appliances, lighting, and systems you intend to power with wind energy. This calculation helps determine the size of the turbine needed to meet your energy demands. Smaller turbines typically produce between 400 to 10,000 watts, while larger models can generate significantly more.

- **Consider Space and Zoning Regulations**: Evaluate the available space for turbine installation. HAWTs need more room for optimal airflow, while VAWTs can be installed in tighter spaces. Additionally, check local zoning regulations regarding turbine installation, as some areas have restrictions on height and placement.

- **Evaluate Cost and Budget**: Analyze the costs associated with purchasing, installing, and maintaining a wind turbine. HAWTs often require a higher initial investment due to their size and complexity. Consider whether you can manage the installation yourself or if you will need professional help, which can add to the overall cost.

- **Factor in Aesthetics and Noise**: Consider how the turbine's appearance and noise level may affect your living environment. If you live in a residential area, a quieter VAWT might be more suitable. A HAWT, while efficient, may produce noise that could disturb neighbors.

- **Research Manufacturer Options**: Investigate different manufacturers and models. Look for warranties, customer reviews, and after-sales support. Ensure the chosen turbine meets quality and performance standards, as well as your energy production goals.

- **Long-Term Sustainability**: Assess how the wind turbine fits into your overall off-grid strategy. Ensure it aligns with your goals for sustainability, cost savings, and energy independence.

- **Conclusion:** Understanding the different types of wind turbines empowers you to make informed decisions about integrating wind power into your off-grid lifestyle. HAWTs and VAWTs each offer unique advantages and challenges, allowing you to tailor your energy system to fit your specific needs and conditions. By carefully considering your location, energy demands, and preferences, you can select a wind turbine that enhances your self-sufficiency and contributes to a sustainable future.

3.4.2 DIY Your Own Wind Turbine

Building a wind turbine using PVC for the blades offers a cost-effective and practical approach to generating renewable energy at home. This project empowers individuals to harness wind energy, a clean and sustainable power source, crucial for off-grid living or DIY energy solutions. By constructing a wind turbine, you not only reduce reliance on conventional energy but also gain a deeper understanding of renewable technologies. The benefits of this project extend beyond energy savings; it fosters self-sufficiency, encourages innovation, and provides an opportunity to engage with nature. This guide will take you through the steps necessary to create your own wind turbine, focusing on building the rotor blades, assembling the rotor and hub, constructing the tail and yaw mechanism, erecting the tower, wiring and electrical connections, and finally, testing and fine-tuning the turbine for optimal performance.

Materials and Tools:

- PVC pipe (schedule 40, 2-inch diameter) - 2 pieces, 4 feet long

- PVC pipe (schedule 40, 3-inch diameter) - 1 piece, 2 feet long

- PVC end caps (2-inch) - 2 units

- PVC end cap (3-inch) - 1 unit

- Wooden dowel (3/4 inch diameter) - 1 unit, 5 feet long

- 2x4 lumber - 2 pieces, 4 feet long (for the tower)

- Heavy-duty hinge - 1 unit

- Angle brackets - 4 units

- Electrical wire (14-gauge) - 50 feet

- Charge controller - 1 unit

- Deep cycle battery - 1 unit

- DC motor (12V) - 1 unit

- Diode - 1 unit

- Anemometer - 1 unit (for wind speed measurement)

- Drill with 1/4 inch drill bit - 1 unit

- Screwdriver - 1 unit

- Saw (for cutting wood and PVC) - 1 unit

- Measuring tape - 1 unit

- Safety goggles - 1 unit
- Work gloves - 1 unit

Step-by-Step Guide:

1. **Building the Rotor Blades**:

   a. **Cut PVC Pipe**: Cut two pieces of 2-inch PVC pipe into 3 equal lengths, each 2 feet long, to serve as rotor blades.

   b. **Shape the Blades**: Use a saw to create a slight curve along one side of each PVC blade to enhance aerodynamics. Aim for a gentle arc.

   c. **Drill Holes**: Drill a 1/4 inch hole at one end of each blade, 1 inch from the edge. Ensure holes are aligned to facilitate attachment to the hub.

2. **Assembling the Rotor and Hub**:

   a. **Prepare the Hub**: Take the 3-inch PVC end cap and drill a 1/4 inch hole in the center. This hole will fit onto the wooden dowel for mounting.

   b. **Attach Blades to Hub**: Align the blades with the drilled holes on the hub. Use screws to secure each blade to the hub, ensuring they are evenly spaced around the circumference.

   c. **Mount the Hub**: Slide the hub onto the wooden dowel. Secure it with a washer and nut, tightening it until the hub is stable but can still rotate freely.

3. **Constructing the Tail and Yaw Mechanism**:

   a. **Create the Tail**: Cut a piece of 2x4 lumber to 3 feet long. This will serve as the tail fin.

   b. **Attach the Tail**: Use angle brackets to secure one end of the tail to the bottom of the wooden dowel, allowing it to pivot.

   c. **Install the Yaw Mechanism**: Attach a heavy-duty hinge at the point where the tail connects to the dowel. This allows the tail to pivot, keeping the rotor aligned with the wind direction.

4. **Constructing the Tower**:

   a. **Prepare Tower Base**: Cut two pieces of 2x4 lumber to 4 feet long. These will serve as the vertical supports for the tower.

   b. **Construct the Frame**: Create a rectangular frame using the two 4-foot pieces and two additional 2-foot pieces. Secure corners with screws and angle brackets.

   c. **Attach the Rotor**: Drill a hole through the top of the tower frame to insert the wooden dowel. Position the rotor assembly at the top, ensuring it is securely mounted and can rotate freely.

5. **Wiring and Electrical Connections**:

   a. **Connect the DC Motor**: Attach the wires from the DC motor to the charge controller, ensuring proper polarity. The motor will generate electricity when the rotor spins.

   b. **Wire to Battery**: Connect the charge controller to the deep cycle battery using 14-gauge electrical wire. Follow the manufacturer's wiring diagram to ensure correct connections.

   c. **Install Diode**: Connect a diode between the charge controller and the battery to prevent backflow of electricity, protecting the system from potential damage.

6. **Testing and Fine-Tuning**:

   a. **Check Connections**: Before testing, double-check all electrical connections for tightness and correctness.

b. **Measure Wind Speed**: Use the anemometer to measure wind speed at your location. This helps in understanding the efficiency of the turbine.

c. **Test the Turbine**: Place the turbine in an open area with unobstructed wind flow. Observe the rotor; it should begin to spin in response to wind.

d. **Fine-Tune Positioning**: Adjust the tail fin's angle if necessary to ensure the rotor aligns with prevailing wind directions for maximum efficiency.

Maintenance:

- **Monthly**: Inspect all connections and fasteners for wear or looseness. Tighten as necessary. Clean the rotor blades and ensure no debris obstructs their movement.

- **Annually**: Check the structural integrity of the tower and base. Replace any rotting wood or damaged parts. Inspect the electrical components, including the battery and charge controller, for any signs of corrosion or wear.

Complexity:

This project is moderate in complexity, requiring basic carpentry skills, familiarity with electrical components, and some mechanical understanding. Challenges may arise in ensuring proper alignment and securing the rotor assembly. However, with patience and attention to detail, most individuals can successfully complete the project.

Estimated Time:

- **Setup**: 4-6 hours to gather materials, cut and assemble the turbine components.

- **Ongoing maintenance**: 30 minutes monthly for inspections and cleaning.

- **Testing**: 1-2 hours to set up the turbine and fine-tune its positioning.

3.4.3 HOW TO INSTALL A SMALL WIND TURBINE

Installing a small wind turbine provides a sustainable energy solution for off-grid living, reducing reliance on fossil fuels and contributing to a self-sufficient lifestyle. This project harnesses the power of wind to generate electricity, which can be used for various applications, including lighting, appliances, and charging batteries. By creating your own wind energy system, you not only cut energy costs but also contribute to environmental preservation by minimizing your carbon footprint. The installation process involves careful site selection, tower preparation, turbine assembly, and electrical setup. This guide aims to equip you with the knowledge and skills needed to successfully install a small wind turbine, ensuring efficient energy production and long-term reliability.

Materials and Tools:

- Small wind turbine kit (includes rotor, generator, and mounting hardware) - 1 unit

- Galvanized steel pipe (for tower) - 1 unit, 10-20 feet

- Concrete mix - 1 bag, 60 pounds

- Rebar (for tower stability) - 3 pieces, 3 feet each

- 12-volt battery bank - 1 unit

- Charge controller - 1 unit

- Inverter (if AC power is needed) - 1 unit

- Weather-resistant electrical wire - 100 feet

- Drill with ¼ inch drill bit - 1 unit

- Wrench set - 1 unit

- Screwdriver set - 1 unit
- Level - 1 unit
- Safety goggles - 1 unit
- Gloves - 1 pair

Step-by-Step Guide:

1. **Site Selection and Assessment**:

   a. **Choose a Location**: Select an open area away from trees, buildings, or other structures that may obstruct wind flow. Aim for a location with consistent wind speeds of at least 10 mph.

   b. **Conduct a Wind Assessment**: Use a handheld anemometer to measure wind speeds at different times throughout the day. Document average wind speeds over a week to determine the site's viability.

   c. **Check Local Regulations**: Review local zoning laws and regulations regarding wind turbine installations. Obtain any necessary permits before proceeding.

2. **Tower Selection and Preparation**:

   a. **Select Tower Type**: Choose a suitable tower type (e.g., freestanding, guyed) based on your wind turbine's height and expected wind conditions. A galvanized steel pipe tower is often preferred for durability.

   b. **Prepare the Ground**: Clear the installation area of debris, rocks, and vegetation. Ensure the ground is level to provide a stable base for the tower.

3. **Assembling the Wind Turbine**:

   a. **Unpack the Turbine Kit**: Lay out all components from the wind turbine kit, including the rotor, generator, and mounting hardware. Refer to the manufacturer's instructions for specific assembly details.

   b. **Attach the Rotor Blades**: Securely attach the rotor blades to the generator, ensuring that each blade is evenly spaced and tightened. Use the provided bolts and a wrench for this step.

   c. **Mount the Generator**: Attach the generator to the mounting bracket, following the manufacturer's specifications. Ensure all connections are secure.

   d. **Install the Hub**: If your turbine has a hub, connect it to the generator according to the provided instructions. This component helps transfer mechanical energy to electrical energy.

4. **Raising the Tower**:

   a. **Prepare the Concrete Base**: Dig a hole approximately 3 feet deep and 2 feet wide. Mix the concrete according to package instructions and pour it into the hole.

   b. **Insert Rebar**: Place three pieces of rebar into the concrete while it is still wet, ensuring they are evenly spaced for added stability. Leave about 1 foot of rebar above ground.

   c. **Position the Tower**: Once the concrete has set (allow 24-48 hours), carefully position the tower over the rebar, ensuring it is vertical. Use a level to confirm that the tower is straight.

   d. **Secure the Tower**: Fill the base with additional concrete around the tower base, ensuring it is well-supported. Allow the concrete to cure for the recommended time.

5. **Electrical Wiring and Grounding**:

   a. **Run Electrical Wire**: Use weather-resistant electrical wire to connect the generator to the charge controller. Ensure the wire is rated for outdoor use and has adequate insulation.

    b. **Ground the System**: Connect a grounding wire from the tower to a grounding rod driven into the ground. This protects the system from electrical surges and lightning strikes.

    c. **Connect to Battery Bank**: Connect the charge controller to your battery bank, following the manufacturer's wiring diagram. Ensure all connections are secure and insulated.

    d. **Connect Inverter**: If using an inverter for AC power, connect it to the battery bank, following the provided instructions. This allows you to use standard household appliances.

6. **Testing and Initial Operation**:

    a. **Power Up the System**: Turn on the charge controller and check for any error messages or warnings. Ensure the system is functioning correctly before proceeding.

    b. **Test Voltage Output**: Use a multimeter to measure the voltage output from the generator. Confirm that it matches the expected output according to the manufacturer's specifications.

    c. **Monitor Wind Conditions**: Allow the turbine to operate for a few hours, monitoring its performance. Check for unusual noises, vibrations, or any signs of malfunction.

    d. **Initial Adjustments**: If necessary, make adjustments to the turbine's position or angle to optimize performance based on wind conditions. Ensure that all bolts and connections remain tight.

Maintenance:

- **Monthly**: Inspect the turbine and tower for signs of wear or damage. Tighten any loose bolts and check the integrity of electrical connections.

- **Every 6 Months**: Lubricate any moving parts as recommended by the manufacturer. Check the grounding system to ensure it remains intact.

- **Annually**: Conduct a thorough inspection of the entire system, including the turbine, tower, and electrical components. Replace any worn or damaged parts as necessary.

Complexity:

The project is rated as moderate in complexity. While basic mechanical skills are necessary for assembly, a solid understanding of electrical systems is crucial for proper wiring and grounding. Challenges may arise in ensuring proper tower installation and achieving optimal turbine performance based on local wind conditions.

Estimated Time:

- **Site Selection and Assessment**: 1-2 days for research and wind measurements.

- **Tower Selection and Preparation**: 1 day for site preparation and tower selection.

- **Assembling the Wind Turbine**: 3-4 hours for assembly and installation.

- **Raising the Tower**: 1 day for concrete work and tower positioning.

- **Electrical Wiring and Grounding**: 2-3 hours for wiring and connections.

- **Testing and Initial Operation**: 1-2 hours for testing and adjustments.

3.5 DIY ENERGY PROJECTS

DIY energy projects empower individuals to take control of their energy needs, offering practical solutions for sustainable living. These projects range from creating simple backup power systems to harnessing renewable energy sources. As the world increasingly faces energy challenges, DIY energy projects present a way for people to reduce their reliance on conventional power grids and embrace self-sufficiency.

The motivation behind these projects is multifaceted. Individuals may seek to cut energy costs, prepare for emergencies, or simply enjoy the satisfaction of building their own energy systems. With growing concerns about environmental impact, DIY energy solutions also allow for a more sustainable lifestyle by utilizing renewable resources and minimizing waste.

There are numerous DIY energy projects suitable for various skill levels. One such project is creating protection against electromagnetic pulses (EMPs), which can disrupt electrical systems. By building an EMP shield, individuals can safeguard sensitive electronics, ensuring they remain operational during unforeseen events. This project often involves using conductive materials and understanding basic principles of electromagnetic fields.

Another accessible project is the pedal-powered generator. This system converts human energy into electrical power, allowing users to generate electricity through pedaling. It combines fitness with functionality, making it an engaging way to produce energy while promoting physical activity. The complexity varies, but basic mechanical skills suffice for assembly.

The hand crank charger project is similarly straightforward. It enables users to charge small electronic devices by cranking a handle, transforming manual effort into electrical energy. This project requires minimal materials and can be completed quickly, making it ideal for beginners.

DIY candle making is an excellent way to create alternative lighting solutions while adding a personal touch to home decor. Crafting candles involves melting wax, pouring it into molds, and adding fragrances or colours, which appeals to those looking to combine creativity with practicality.

Finally, building a DIY solar oven allows individuals to harness the sun's energy for cooking or heating. This project demonstrates the principles of solar energy while providing a functional tool for outdoor cooking. The complexity ranges from simple cardboard designs to more advanced models with better insulation and reflectors.

Each of these projects presents unique challenges and learning opportunities. While some may require basic tools and materials, others might demand more advanced skills in electronics or mechanics. Regardless of the complexity, DIY energy projects encourage innovation, creativity, and a proactive approach to energy independence.

3.5.1 ELECTROMAGNETIC PULSES (EMPS) AND PROTECTION

Electromagnetic pulses (EMPs) are bursts of electromagnetic energy that can disrupt or damage electronic equipment. These pulses can occur naturally, such as from solar flares, or can be man-made, often as a result of nuclear detonations. For those living off-grid or pursuing self-sufficiency, understanding EMPs and how to protect electronic devices becomes crucial. A successful EMP protection system shields vital electronics from damage, ensuring that communication, power generation, and essential appliances remain operational. By implementing a robust EMP protection project, individuals not only safeguard their investments but also enhance their resilience against unforeseen disruptions. This guide provides detailed steps to create an effective EMP shield, utilizing readily available materials and straightforward techniques.

Materials and Tools:

- Metal container (e.g., ammo can or Faraday bag) - 1 unit
- Conductive material (e.g., aluminum foil) - 1 roll
- Non-conductive padding (e.g., cardboard or bubble wrap) - 1 unit
- Grounding wire (copper or aluminum) - 10 feet
- Soldering iron - 1 unit
- Solder - 1 spool
- Electrical tape - 1 roll
- Multimeter - 1 unit
- Wire cutters/strippers - 1 unit

- Safety goggles - 1 unit

Step-by-Step Guide:

1. **Select a Container**: Choose a metal container, such as an ammo can, that can completely enclose your electronics. Ensure it has a tight-fitting lid.

2. **Prepare Conductive Material**: Unroll aluminum foil and cut enough to line the inside of the metal container. The foil should cover all sides, including the bottom and lid, without gaps.

3. **Line the Container**: Place the aluminum foil inside the metal container, pressing it against the sides and bottom. Ensure there are no wrinkles or holes that could allow electromagnetic waves to penetrate.

4. **Add Non-Conductive Padding**: Cut a piece of cardboard or bubble wrap to fit inside the container. This padding will protect your electronics from physical damage and should be placed over the aluminum lining.

5. **Test Grounding**: Cut a 10-foot length of grounding wire. Strip both ends of the wire to expose the metal. Use a multimeter to test for continuity, ensuring that your grounding setup is functional.

6. **Connect Grounding Wire**: Solder one end of the grounding wire to the aluminum foil inside the container. Ensure the solder is secure and covers a sufficient area for good conductivity. Wrap electrical tape around the connection to reinforce it.

7. **Attach Grounding Point**: Find a suitable grounding point outside your home, such as a grounding rod or metal water pipe. Attach the other end of the grounding wire securely to this point using clamps or electrical tape.

8. **Store Electronics**: Place your essential electronics inside the container, ensuring they are wrapped in additional non-conductive padding for protection. This includes items like radios, solar chargers, and batteries.

9. **Seal the Container**: Close the lid of the metal container tightly. Ensure there are no gaps that could allow electromagnetic interference to enter.

10. **Conduct a Test**: To verify your setup, use a multimeter to check the grounding connection. Place one probe on the grounding point and the other on the container. A successful connection will show continuity on the multimeter.

Maintenance:

- **Monthly**: Inspect the grounding wire and connections for corrosion or wear. Clean any exposed metal with a wire brush to ensure a solid connection.

- **Yearly**: Test the integrity of the aluminum lining and container. Check for any signs of wear or damage that could compromise the shielding effectiveness. Replace any damaged materials immediately.

Complexity: The project is moderate in complexity, requiring basic skills in soldering and electrical safety. Challenges may arise when ensuring a proper ground connection or verifying the effectiveness of the shield. However, with careful attention to detail, these challenges can be effectively managed.

Estimated Time:

- **Setup**: 2-3 hours to gather materials, prepare the container, and complete all assembly steps.

- **Ongoing maintenance**: 10-15 minutes monthly for inspections and testing.

- **Annual check-up**: 1 hour to evaluate and reinforce the system's integrity.

3.5.2 PEDAL POWERED GENERATOR

A pedal-powered generator is a unique solution that converts human energy into electrical energy through pedaling. This project is essential for off-grid living, providing a sustainable energy source that relies solely on physical activity. By creating your own pedal-powered generator, you harness renewable energy, reduce reliance on fossil fuels, and cultivate a self-sufficient lifestyle. This system can power small appliances, charge batteries, or provide lighting, making it invaluable for those living off the grid or seeking to enhance their DIY capabilities. Engaging in this project not only contributes to personal energy independence but also fosters a deeper connection with sustainable practices.

Materials and Tools:

- Bicycle (old or used) - 1 unit
- Alternator or DC motor (12V) - 1 unit
- Wooden platform (1" x 4" x 48") - 1 unit
- Plywood (3/4" x 24" x 24") - 1 unit
- Pulley system (pulley wheels and belt) - 1 set
- Battery (12V deep cycle) - 1 unit
- Battery charger (12V) - 1 unit
- Voltage regulator - 1 unit
- Wire (14 gauge, stranded) - 50 feet
- Connectors (ring terminals, butt connectors) - 1 pack
- Tools (drill, screwdriver, wrenches) - As needed
- Safety goggles - 1 unit
- Gloves - 1 pair

Step-by-Step Guide:

1. **Prepare the Bicycle**: Remove the front wheel of the bicycle, leaving the rear wheel intact for pedaling.
2. **Construct the Platform**: Cut the wooden platform to size (1" x 4" x 48") and attach it securely to the plywood base using screws, ensuring it is sturdy enough to hold the bicycle.
3. **Position the Bicycle**: Securely mount the bicycle to the platform, aligning the rear wheel with the edge of the plywood. Use clamps or brackets to hold the bike in place.
4. **Install the Alternator**: Attach the alternator or DC motor to the platform, ensuring the pulley system aligns with the rear wheel. Use bolts and brackets to secure it firmly.
5. **Attach the Pulley System**: Connect a pulley wheel to the rear wheel of the bicycle. Thread the belt through the pulley system, ensuring it is tight enough to transfer power without slipping.
6. **Connect Wiring**: Use 14-gauge wire to connect the alternator or DC motor output to the battery. Strip the wire ends and attach them using ring terminals for a secure connection.
7. **Install Voltage Regulator**: Integrate a voltage regulator into the wiring system between the alternator and the battery to maintain stable voltage output and protect the battery.
8. **Secure the Battery**: Position the battery on the platform, ensuring it is stable and protected from movement during operation. Use straps or brackets to secure it.
9. **Add Battery Charger**: Connect the battery charger to the battery for recharging when not pedaling. Follow the manufacturer's instructions for installation.

10. **Test the System**: Begin pedaling the bicycle to generate power. Monitor the battery charging indicator to ensure the system is functioning correctly. Adjust pulley tension if necessary.

11. **Safety Check**: Ensure all components are securely fastened and that wiring is protected from wear. Wear safety goggles and gloves while testing to prevent injuries.

Maintenance:

- **Weekly**: Inspect the wiring connections for signs of wear or corrosion. Replace any damaged wires immediately. Check the tension on the pulley belt, adjusting as necessary to ensure efficient power transfer.

- **Monthly**: Clean the bicycle and generator components to prevent dust buildup that could affect performance. Test the battery voltage to ensure it holds a charge effectively. Replace the battery if performance declines significantly.

- **Yearly**: Perform a thorough inspection of the entire system, checking for loose connections, damaged parts, or signs of wear. Replace any components as needed. Update any worn-out belts in the pulley system to maintain efficiency.

Complexity:

The project is moderate in complexity, suitable for individuals with basic mechanical skills. Challenges may arise in aligning the pulley system or securing components effectively. Familiarity with electrical systems is beneficial for wiring connections and understanding battery management.

Estimated Time:

- **Setup**: 4-6 hours for gathering materials, constructing the platform, and assembling the generator.

- **Ongoing maintenance**: 30 minutes weekly for inspections and minor adjustments.

- **Annual maintenance**: 1-2 hours for a comprehensive system check and parts replacement as needed.

3.5.3 HAND CRANK CHARGER

The hand crank charger project creates a simple, effective way to generate electricity manually. This project holds particular significance for those pursuing off-grid living or DIY sustainability. In emergencies or remote situations where traditional power sources are unavailable, a hand crank charger allows you to power small devices such as lights, radios, or mobile phones. This generator empowers you with self-sufficiency, enabling you to harness your physical energy to produce electricity. Building a hand crank charger is not only practical but also educational, providing insight into basic electrical principles and renewable energy. The project showcases how human effort can translate into useful power, emphasizing resilience in the face of energy scarcity.

Materials and Tools:

- DC motor (5-12V) - 1 unit

- Hand crank (can be salvaged from an old device) - 1 unit

- Rectifier diode - 1 unit

- Battery (rechargeable, 6V or 12V) - 1 unit

- Wire (22 AWG) - 10 feet

- Wooden board (for base) - 1 unit, 1 inch thick, 12 x 12 inches

- Screws (wood screws) - 4 units

- Drill - 1 unit

- Screwdriver - 1 unit

- Soldering iron - 1 unit
- Solder - 1 unit
- Heat shrink tubing - 2 units
- Electrical tape - 1 roll

Step-by-Step Guide:

1. **Prepare the Base**: Cut the wooden board to a 12 x 12 inch square to serve as the base for the charger.

2. **Mount the Motor**: Secure the DC motor to the center of the wooden base using screws. Ensure that the shaft of the motor is positioned upright.

3. **Attach the Hand Crank**: Connect the hand crank to the shaft of the DC motor. If necessary, use a small piece of rubber tubing to create a snug fit between the crank and the motor shaft.

4. **Install the Diode**: Solder the rectifier diode to the positive terminal of the DC motor. This prevents backflow of electricity, protecting the motor and connected devices.

5. **Connect Wires**: Cut a 2-foot length of 22 AWG wire. Strip the ends and connect one end to the negative terminal of the DC motor. Connect the other end to the negative terminal of the battery.

6. **Connect to Battery**: Use another length of 22 AWG wire to connect the other end of the diode to the positive terminal of the battery. Ensure the connections are secure and insulated with heat shrink tubing or electrical tape.

7. **Secure Everything**: Ensure all components are firmly attached to the wooden base and that there are no loose wires. Double-check all connections.

8. **Test the Charger**: Start cranking the handle at a steady pace. Use a multimeter to measure the voltage output from the battery. If the connections are correct, the battery should begin to charge.

9. **Maintain Proper Usage**: Use the charger regularly to ensure all components remain in good working order. Avoid over-cranking the motor to prevent damage.

Maintenance:

- **Monthly**: Check all electrical connections for wear or corrosion. Tighten any loose connections and replace damaged wires as needed.

- **Every 6 Months**: Inspect the motor and hand crank for signs of wear. Lubricate the motor shaft if necessary to ensure smooth operation.

- **Annually**: Test the output voltage of the battery to confirm it holds a charge effectively. Replace the battery if it shows significant degradation.

Complexity:

This project is rated as moderate in complexity. It requires basic mechanical skills for assembly and a fundamental understanding of electrical connections. Challenges may arise in soldering and ensuring proper insulation of connections. Attention to detail is essential to avoid shorts or failures.

Estimated Time:

- **Setup**: 2-3 hours to gather materials, cut the wooden base, and assemble components.

- **Testing**: 30 minutes to test the connections and verify the charger works correctly.

- **Ongoing Maintenance**: 10-15 minutes monthly for checks and adjustments.

3.5.4 DIY CANDLE MAKING

Making candles at home provides a sustainable and practical solution for lighting needs, especially in off-grid living situations. This project allows you to create custom candles that not only illuminate your space but also add ambiance and a personal touch. Homemade candles can utilize natural ingredients, such as beeswax or soy wax, which are environmentally friendly compared to commercial paraffin candles. By mastering the art of candle making, you gain control over the materials and scents used, creating a healthier indoor environment. Additionally, this skill offers a way to repurpose leftover wax and other materials, reducing waste. Candle making serves not just as a functional craft but also as a rewarding hobby that can enhance self-sufficiency and creativity.

Materials and Tools:

- Wax (beeswax or soy wax) - 2 pounds
- Candle wicks (cotton or wood) - 10 units
- Wick holder or adhesive - 1 unit
- Double boiler or heat-safe container - 1 unit
- Thermometer (candy or cooking) - 1 unit
- Pouring pitcher or ladle - 1 unit
- Molds or containers (glass jars, metal tins) - 5 units
- Essential oils or fragrance oils (optional) - 1 ounce
- Dye (optional) - As needed
- Stirring utensil (wooden or metal) - 1 unit

Step-by-Step Guide:

1. **Prepare Workspace**: Clear a flat, stable surface to work on, and lay down newspaper or a drop cloth to catch any spills.

2. **Measure Wax**: Weigh 2 pounds of wax and cut it into smaller pieces for easier melting.

3. **Set Up Double Boiler**: Fill the bottom pot of a double boiler with water and place it on the stove over medium heat. If you don't have a double boiler, use a heat-safe container placed in a pot of simmering water.

4. **Melt the Wax**: Add the wax to the top pot or heat-safe container. Monitor the temperature with a thermometer, aiming for around 170-180°F (77-82°C).

5. **Prepare Wicks**: While the wax melts, trim the candle wicks to about 1 inch longer than the height of your mold or container. Secure the wick to the bottom of the mold with adhesive or a wick holder.

6. **Add Fragrance and Dye**: Once the wax reaches the desired temperature, remove it from heat. If using fragrance or dye, add it now, following the manufacturer's recommended amounts. Stir gently to combine.

7. **Pour the Wax**: Carefully pour the melted wax into the prepared molds or containers, leaving a small amount of wax in the pouring pitcher for topping off later.

8. **Stabilize the Wick**: Ensure the wick remains centered and straight as the wax cools. Use a wick holder if necessary.

9. **Cool the Candles**: Allow the candles to cool completely at room temperature, which may take several hours. Avoid moving them during this time to prevent imperfections.

10. **Top Off if Necessary**: If the surface of the candle sinks or creates a depression, reheat the remaining wax and pour it over the top to create a smooth finish.

11. **Trim Wicks**: Once the candles are fully cooled and set, trim the wicks to about ¼ inch above the surface of the wax.

12. **Label and Store**: Label the candles with their scent and date made, then store them in a cool, dark place until ready for use.

Maintenance:

- **Weekly**: Inspect candles for any cracks or imperfections. Store them upright and avoid exposing them to heat or direct sunlight.

- **Monthly**: If you have made multiple batches, rotate their storage to ensure even usage. Check wicks for proper length, trimming as necessary before lighting.

- **Yearly**: Consider making new candles as needed, using up any leftover wax or materials from previous projects to maintain a sustainable practice.

Complexity:

The project is straightforward, suitable for beginners. Key skills include measuring, melting, and pouring wax. Challenges may arise in achieving the right temperature and managing the wick's position, but with practice, these become manageable.

Estimated Time:

- **Setup**: 30 minutes for preparing the workspace and gathering materials.

- **Melting and pouring**: 1-2 hours for melting wax, adding scents and dyes, and pouring into molds.

- **Cooling**: 4-6 hours, or overnight, for candles to fully set.

- **Trimming and labeling**: 30 minutes after cooling is complete.

- **Total estimated time**: Approximately 6-8 hours, including cooling time.

3.5.5 DIY SOLAR OVEN

Building a solar oven offers an innovative solution for cooking food using renewable energy. This project not only aligns with sustainable living principles but also serves as a practical tool for off-grid enthusiasts. A solar oven harnesses sunlight, converting it into heat for cooking, baking, or dehydrating food. This process significantly reduces reliance on conventional energy sources, lowering both costs and environmental impact. By using a solar oven, you can prepare meals without electricity, making it an invaluable resource for camping, emergency situations, or daily cooking. The ability to create a functioning solar oven empowers you to utilize natural resources, highlighting the importance of self-sufficiency and eco-friendliness in an off-grid lifestyle.

Materials and Tools:

- Cardboard box - 1 unit - 20 inches x 20 inches x 12 inches

- Aluminum foil - 1 roll

- Clear plastic wrap - 1 roll - 24 inches wide

- Black construction paper - 1 sheet - 22 inches x 22 inches

- Duct tape - 1 roll

- Scissors - 1 unit

- Ruler - 1 unit

- Craft knife - 1 unit

- Optional: Small cooking pot or baking dish - 1 unit

Step-by-Step Guide:

1. **Prepare the Box**: Cut a flap on the top of the cardboard box, leaving about 1 inch of border around three sides. This flap should create a hinge, allowing it to open and close.

2. **Line the Interior**: Cover the inner surfaces of the box with aluminum foil. Ensure that the shiny side faces inward for optimal reflection. Use duct tape to secure the foil in place, making sure it lies flat and smooth.

3. **Create a Cooking Surface**: Place a sheet of black construction paper at the bottom of the box. The black color absorbs heat, increasing cooking efficiency.

4. **Seal the Oven**: Lay clear plastic wrap over the opening created by the flap. Stretch it tightly to prevent heat from escaping. Secure the edges with duct tape, ensuring a tight seal.

5. **Position the Flap**: Angle the flap to reflect sunlight into the box. Adjust the flap's position throughout the day to capture the most sunlight.

6. **Add the Cooking Pot**: Place your small cooking pot or baking dish on top of the black construction paper. Cover it with a lid if available to trap heat.

7. **Monitor Temperature**: Use a thermometer to check the internal temperature of the solar oven. Ideal cooking temperatures range from 200°F to 250°F, depending on what you're preparing.

8. **Cook Your Meal**: Depending on the sunlight intensity, cooking times will vary. Expect longer cooking times than traditional methods. For example, baking bread may take 1-2 hours, while reheating food can take 30 minutes to 1 hour.

9. **Adjust and Reflect**: Throughout the cooking process, adjust the flap's angle to maximize sunlight reflection into the oven. Reassess the cooking pot's position as needed to ensure it captures the heat efficiently.

Maintenance:

- **Monthly**: Inspect the solar oven for wear and tear. Repair any damaged sections of the cardboard with duct tape. Clean the aluminum foil and plastic wrap to maintain reflectivity.

- **Yearly**: If using the solar oven regularly, consider replacing the cardboard box every 1-2 years, as prolonged exposure to sunlight and weather can deteriorate its structural integrity.

Complexity:

This project is straightforward and suitable for beginners. The primary challenges include ensuring proper insulation and positioning the flap correctly for optimal sunlight capture. Basic skills in cutting, measuring, and assembling materials are all that is required.

Estimated Time:

- **Setup**: 1-2 hours to gather materials, cut the box, and assemble the oven.

- **Cooking**: Varies based on the recipe; typically 30 minutes to several hours depending on sunlight and food type.

- **Maintenance**: 15-30 minutes monthly for inspections and cleaning.

4. FOOD PRODUCTION AND PRESERVATION

4.1 INTRODUCTION

Permaculture principles and design for small-scale gardens introduce a sustainable approach to food production that aligns with the ethos of no-grid living. Permaculture, a portmanteau of "permanent agriculture," is the development of agricultural ecosystems intended to be sustainable and self-sufficient. It's about working with nature, rather than against it, to create productive environments that mimic the diversity, stability, and resilience of natural ecosystems. For beginners, it starts with observing your immediate environment and understanding the resources at your disposal—sunlight, water, soil, and local flora and fauna. Designing a garden based on permaculture involves integrating food plants with trees, shrubs, perennials, and animals to create a symbiotic ecosystem. This method reduces waste, conserves water, and improves soil health, making it ideal for those striving for self-sufficiency.

Building a no-grid greenhouse or cold frame is a practical step towards extending the growing season of your garden. A greenhouse allows for the cultivation of plants year-round, protecting them from harsh weather conditions, while a cold frame, which is a simpler and smaller version of a greenhouse, can be used to harden off seedlings before transplanting them outside or to grow cold-tolerant plants during winter. Both structures can be constructed using salvaged materials such as old windows, doors, and frames, making this a cost-effective project. The key is to ensure adequate ventilation and sunlight, factors crucial for plant growth. These structures not only enhance food production but also provide a rewarding DIY project that bolsters your self-reliance.

DIY container gardening, vertical gardening, and hydroponics present innovative solutions for growing food in limited spaces. Container gardening involves growing plants in pots or containers, an ideal method for those with small yards or living in urban settings. Vertical gardening takes this concept a step further by utilizing vertical space, such as walls or fences, to grow food, effectively increasing your growing area without requiring more ground space. Hydroponics, on the other hand, is the method of growing plants in a water-based, nutrient-rich solution, without soil. It's a highly efficient system that can significantly increase yield and growth rates, though it requires a bit more technical knowledge to set up and maintain. Each of these methods demonstrates how limitations in space can be creatively overcome, ensuring that even the smallest of spaces can contribute to your food supply.

Food preservation techniques such as canning, dehydrating, and fermenting are essential for extending the shelf life of your harvest and ensuring a year-round supply of food. Canning involves processing food in sealed containers at high temperatures to kill microorganisms and enzymes that cause food spoilage. Dehydrating, another preservation method, removes moisture from food, inhibiting the growth of microorganisms and enzymes. Fermentation, a process that uses microorganisms to convert sugars into alcohol or organic acids, not only preserves food but also enhances its nutritional value and flavor. These preservation methods are invaluable for no-grid living, allowing you to store surplus produce and diversify your diet. They require minimal equipment and can be done at home, making them accessible to beginners eager to maximize their self-sufficiency.

Foraging for wild edibles and using them in cooking introduces an element of adventure into no-grid living, connecting you directly with your natural surroundings. Foraging involves the gathering of wild food from their natural habitat, offering a sustainable way to supplement your diet with nutritious, locally sourced food. It's important, however, to approach foraging with respect for the environment and knowledge of safe and sustainable harvesting practices. Identifying edible plants, understanding their habitats, and knowing the right time to harvest are crucial skills for any forager. Incorporating wild edibles into your cooking not only diversifies your diet but also deepens your connection to the land, reinforcing the principles of self-sufficiency and sustainability that underpin the no-grid lifestyle.

Raising small animals for meat and eggs, such as chickens, rabbits, and fish, provides a reliable source of protein and can be an integral part of living off the grid. Chickens offer the dual benefits of egg production and meat, while rabbits are known for their rapid reproduction and lean meat. Fish, particularly in aquaponic systems, can be raised in symbiosis with plants, creating a closed-loop system that produces both vegetables and protein. These practices require some initial setup and ongoing care, but they significantly contribute to food security and self-sufficiency. Understanding the needs of each type of animal, including their housing, diet, and health management, is crucial for success. Moreover, integrating these animals into your permaculture system can enhance soil fertility and pest management, creating a more resilient and productive garden.

DIY food storage systems such as root cellars, pantries, and shelves are essential for organizing and maintaining the quality of your preserved foods. A well-designed storage system not only extends the shelf life of your food but also helps in inventory management, ensuring that nothing goes to waste. Root cellars, which can be as simple as a buried container or as complex as an underground room, provide a cool, dark, and humid environment ideal for storing root vegetables, canned goods, and other perishables. Pantries and shelves should be organized to keep frequently used items accessible while storing bulk or seldom-used items securely. Using clear labeling and maintaining a rotation system ensures that older items are used first, reducing waste and keeping your food supply fresh.

Incorporating these practices into your no-grid lifestyle not only enhances your self-reliance but also connects you with the cycles of nature, providing a deep sense of fulfillment and resilience. The journey towards self-sufficiency is a continuous learning process, filled with challenges and rewards. As you become more adept at growing, preserving, and storing your food, you'll discover a profound appreciation for the resources nature provides. This journey is not just about survival; it's about thriving in harmony with the environment, building a sustainable future for yourself and your community.

Remember, the transition to a no-grid lifestyle is a step-by-step process. Start small, perhaps with a container garden or a few chickens, and gradually expand your projects as you gain confidence and experience. Each step you take brings you closer to a life of independence and sustainability. The skills you develop, from gardening and animal husbandry to food preservation and storage, are not only practical but also incredibly rewarding. They empower you to take control of your food supply, reduce your dependence on commercial systems, and contribute to a healthier planet.

By embracing these practices, you're not just preparing for a crisis or disaster; you're adopting a lifestyle that values self-sufficiency, sustainability, and resilience. The knowledge and skills you acquire through these projects are invaluable, providing you with the means to thrive in any situation. So, take the first step today, and begin your journey towards a more self-reliant and sustainable future.

4.2 PERMACULTURE FOR SMALL GARDENS

4.2.1 PERMACULTURE GARDEN DESIGN

Permaculture principles and design for small-scale gardens offer a roadmap to creating sustainable and productive outdoor spaces, even with limited resources. At its core, permaculture is about mimicking the patterns and relationships found in nature to develop ecosystems that are more resilient and self-sustaining. For those new to this concept, it begins with three foundational ethics: care for the earth, care for the people, and sharing the surplus. These ethics guide the design and development of permaculture gardens, ensuring that they not only provide for human needs but also enhance the environment.

The first step in applying permaculture principles to a small-scale garden is observation. Spend time understanding the natural flows of sunlight, wind, and water in your space. Notice areas that are particularly sunny, shaded, or prone to becoming waterlogged. This information is crucial in deciding where to place different elements of your garden to maximize their productivity and health.

One of the key principles of permaculture is "Each element performs many functions." In practice, this means choosing plants and features that serve multiple purposes. For example, a tree can provide shade, fruit, support for climbing plants, and habitat for beneficial insects all at once. Similarly, a pond can offer water storage, habitat for aquatic plants and animals, and a cool microclimate for nearby plants.

Another principle is "Use edges and value the marginal." The edges of your garden, where different ecosystems meet, are often the most productive areas. Utilizing these spaces for planting can yield surprising results. Similarly, areas that might initially seem less useful, like rocky patches or slopes, can be transformed with a bit of creativity, perhaps into a rock garden or terraced planting beds.

"Stacking functions" is a concept where you design your garden in layers to mimic a natural ecosystem. Start with a canopy layer of tall trees, followed by smaller fruit trees, shrubs, herbaceous plants, ground cover, and finally, root crops below the soil. This approach not only maximizes the use of space but also creates a diverse habitat that supports a variety of wildlife and beneficial insects.

Water conservation is a critical aspect of permaculture. Techniques such as rainwater harvesting, using swales to capture runoff, and drip irrigation can help maintain your garden with minimal external water input. Composting and mulching are essential practices that recycle organic waste into valuable nutrients for your soil, reducing the need for chemical fertilizers.

Integrating animals into your garden can also be part of permaculture design. Chickens, for example, can provide pest control, manure for fertilizer, and eggs. The key is to create a system where the waste product of one element becomes the resource for another, creating a closed-loop system that minimizes waste and maximizes efficiency.

For those starting their journey into permaculture, it's important to begin small and gradually expand as you gain experience and confidence. Start with a few raised beds or containers, experimenting with companion planting and observing what works best in your unique environment. Remember, permaculture is not a one-size-fits-all approach but rather a set of principles and ethics that guide you in creating sustainable, productive, and resilient gardens tailored to your specific circumstances.

By adopting permaculture principles in your small-scale garden, you're not just growing food or flowers; you're cultivating an ecosystem that supports and sustains itself and its inhabitants. It's a step towards living more harmoniously with nature, reducing your ecological footprint, and contributing to a healthier planet for future generations. As you apply these principles, you'll discover the joy and satisfaction that comes from nurturing a garden that thrives in balance with the natural world.

Materials and Tools:

- Site assessment tools (compass, measuring tape) - 1 set
- Garden plan sketch paper - 1 pad
- Soil test kit - 1 unit
- Organic mulch (straw, wood chips) - 2 cubic yards
- Native plants and seeds (vegetables, herbs, flowers) - As needed
- Compost (homemade or store-bought) - 1 cubic yard
- Rainwater collection system (barrel, gutters) - 1 unit
- Raised bed materials (wood, bricks, or stones) - As needed
- Hand tools (shovel, rake, trowel, hoe) - 1 set
- Watering can or hose - 1 unit
- Organic fertilizer (bone meal, blood meal) - As needed
- Protective gear (gloves, goggles) - 1 set

Step-by-Step Guide:

1. **Conduct a Site Assessment**: Use a compass and measuring tape to identify sunlight exposure, wind patterns, and existing vegetation on your property.
2. **Sketch a Garden Plan**: On garden plan sketch paper, draw your proposed layout, marking zones for planting, paths, and structures based on your site assessment.
3. **Test the Soil**: Utilize a soil test kit to evaluate pH and nutrient levels, determining what amendments may be necessary for optimal plant growth.
4. **Prepare the Garden Area**: Clear the designated garden space of debris and weeds, ensuring a clean slate for your permaculture design.
5. **Build Raised Beds**: Construct raised beds using wood, bricks, or stones, aiming for dimensions of 4 feet wide and 4-6 inches deep. This structure improves drainage and soil quality.
6. **Add Compost**: Fill the raised beds with a mixture of compost and native soil, creating a nutrient-rich environment for planting.

7. **Incorporate Mulch**: Spread organic mulch, such as straw or wood chips, around the garden beds to suppress weeds, retain moisture, and improve soil health.

8. **Select Plants Wisely**: Choose a variety of native plants, vegetables, herbs, and flowers that complement each other and thrive in your local climate. Aim for diversity to attract beneficial insects.

9. **Plant Seeds and Transplants**: Follow planting guidelines for each species, spacing seeds or transplants according to their mature size, and ensure proper planting depth.

10. **Install a Rainwater Collection System**: Set up a rain barrel or gutter system to capture runoff from roofs, providing a sustainable water source for your garden.

11. **Monitor Watering Needs**: Regularly check soil moisture levels, watering plants as necessary, and utilizing the collected rainwater when possible.

12. **Maintain Plant Health**: Use organic fertilizers and compost to nourish plants, and monitor for pests or diseases, employing natural remedies as needed.

13. **Observe and Adjust**: Regularly assess the garden's performance, adjusting planting arrangements or strategies based on what works best in your unique environment.

Maintenance:

- **Weekly**: Check soil moisture levels, watering as needed, especially during dry spells. Inspect plants for pests and diseases, treating them with organic solutions if necessary.

- **Monthly**: Refresh mulch layers to maintain moisture retention and weed suppression. Evaluate plant growth and spacing, making adjustments to optimize light and airflow.

- **Annually**: Conduct a soil test to assess nutrient levels and amend soil as necessary. Rotate crops to prevent soil depletion and pest buildup, ensuring diverse planting each season.

Complexity:

The complexity of permaculture garden design is moderate, requiring a mix of planning, manual labor, and ongoing observation. Challenges may include understanding plant compatibility and managing soil health, but these can be navigated with careful research and attention. Basic gardening skills are beneficial, though beginners can learn through hands-on experience.

Estimated Time:

- **Setup**: 8-10 hours to conduct site assessment, sketch plans, prepare the area, build raised beds, and plant.

- **Ongoing maintenance**: 1-2 hours weekly for watering, monitoring plant health, and adjusting care as needed.

- **Annual review**: 2-3 hours to test soil, refresh mulch, and rotate crops, ensuring continued productivity and health of the garden.

4.2.2 BUILDING A NO-GRID GREENHOUSE OR COLD FRAME

Building a no-grid greenhouse or cold frame enables you to extend the growing season, providing a controlled environment for your plants regardless of the external weather conditions. This approach is particularly beneficial for starting seedlings early in the season, growing plants that require a warmer climate, and protecting your harvest from frost. The beauty of constructing these structures lies in their simplicity and the opportunity to utilize recycled or locally sourced materials, making this project accessible to everyone, regardless of their building experience or budget.

For a no-grid greenhouse, focus on materials that maximize sunlight exposure and retain heat. Frames can be built from PVC pipes, wood, or even repurposed materials like old window frames. The covering should be a clear, durable material such as polyethylene film, polycarbonate panels, or even old windows for those looking to recycle. The foundation can be as simple as treated wood or concrete blocks. Ensure that your greenhouse has a south-facing orientation to capture the maximum amount of sunlight throughout the day. Ventilation is crucial to prevent overheating and to ensure a steady supply of fresh air; this can be achieved through manual or automatic vent openings on the roof and sides.

Cold frames, on the other hand, are smaller, simpler structures that serve as miniature greenhouses, trapping heat from the sun to create a microclimate. A basic cold frame can be constructed using a wooden box without a bottom and a transparent lid, often made from an old window or a clear polycarbonate sheet. The box should be placed in a sunny, sheltered location, ideally facing south. The lid should be hinged for easy access and to regulate temperature and humidity. Cold frames are perfect for hardening off seedlings, extending the growing season for leafy greens and herbs, or protecting tender plants from frost.

Both greenhouses and cold frames can be enhanced with thermal mass, such as water barrels or stone, which absorbs heat during the day and releases it at night, maintaining a more consistent temperature. Additionally, incorporating a rainwater collection system can provide a sustainable water source for your plants. For those looking to further optimize their no-grid greenhouse, consider using solar panels to power fans or small heaters, though this is not necessary for the success of most greenhouse or cold frame projects.

The key to a successful no-grid greenhouse or cold frame is monitoring and adjusting the internal environment to meet the needs of your plants. This might include opening vents on hot days, insulating with bubble wrap during colder nights, or introducing shade cloth to prevent scorching in the peak of summer. Regularly check on your plants, looking out for signs of distress, and be prepared to adjust your approach as needed.

By building a no-grid greenhouse or cold frame, you're taking a significant step towards self-sufficiency and resilience. These structures not only extend your growing capabilities but also deepen your connection to the cycles of nature, allowing you to grow a wider variety of plants and secure your food supply. With some basic materials, a bit of creativity, and a willingness to learn and adapt, you can enhance your no-grid living experience and enjoy the bounty of your garden year-round.

Materials and Tools:

- PVC pipes (1-inch diameter) - 10 units - 10 feet each

- Polyethylene greenhouse film - 1 roll - 6 mil thickness, 10 feet x 25 feet

- Wooden stakes (for anchoring) - 8 units - 4 feet each

- Hinged window (for cold frame) - 1 unit - 3 feet x 2 feet

- Wooden boards (for frame construction) - 6 units - 1 inch x 6 inches x 8 feet

- Screws (for assembly) - 1 box - 1.5 inches

- Drill with ¼ inch drill bit - 1 unit

- Saw (hand saw or power saw) - 1 unit

- Measuring tape - 1 unit

- Level - 1 unit

- Shovel (for site preparation) - 1 unit

- Hammer - 1 unit

- Clear plastic containers (for thermal mass) - 5 units - 1-gallon size

- Water (for filling containers) - As needed

Step-by-Step Guide:

1. **Select a Site**: Choose a location that receives full sun, preferably with southern exposure, ensuring at least six hours of direct sunlight daily.

2. **Prepare the Ground**: Clear the selected area of debris, rocks, and weeds. Level the ground using a shovel to create a stable base for the greenhouse or cold frame.

3. **Build the Frame**: For the greenhouse, cut wooden boards into six 8-foot lengths and six 4-foot lengths. Assemble the frame in a rectangle using screws to secure the corners, creating a sturdy base.

4. **Add Vertical Supports**: Insert the PVC pipes into the corners of the frame as vertical supports. Cut the pipes to a height of 6 feet for the greenhouse, or 3 feet for the cold frame.

5. **Attach the Roof**: For the greenhouse, create an arched roof by bending the PVC pipes over the frame and securing them with screws. For the cold frame, attach the hinged window directly to the top of the wooden frame.

6. **Install the Covering**: Unroll the polyethylene film over the greenhouse frame, stretching it tightly. Secure it with clips or staples along the edges. For the cold frame, place the hinged window over the top, ensuring it fits snugly.

7. **Anchor the Structure**: Drive wooden stakes into the ground around the perimeter of the greenhouse to anchor it securely. Ensure they are at least 1 foot deep to withstand wind.

8. **Add Thermal Mass**: Fill the clear plastic containers with water and place them inside the greenhouse or cold frame. This thermal mass helps regulate temperature by absorbing heat during the day and releasing it at night.

9. **Ventilation**: For the greenhouse, install a manual vent at the top or sides to allow for airflow. For the cold frame, ensure the hinged window opens easily to regulate internal temperature.

10. **Monitor and Adjust**: After construction, monitor the internal temperature and humidity levels. Open vents or the cold frame lid as needed to maintain a suitable environment for your plants.

Maintenance:

- **Weekly**: Check for any damage to the film or structure, repairing as necessary. Open vents or the cold frame lid to regulate temperature, especially on sunny days.

- **Monthly**: Clean the interior of the greenhouse or cold frame to prevent mold or pests. Inspect thermal mass containers, refilling with water if needed.

- **Annually**: Reassess the structure for any wear and tear, replacing materials as necessary. Clean the exterior covering to maximize sunlight exposure.

Complexity:

This project ranks as moderate in complexity, requiring basic carpentry skills and familiarity with tools. Challenges may include ensuring proper ventilation and managing temperature fluctuations. However, with careful planning and attention, these hurdles can be effectively managed.

Estimated Time:

- **Setup**: 4-6 hours to gather materials, prepare the site, and construct the greenhouse or cold frame.

- **Ongoing maintenance**: 10-15 minutes weekly for checking structural integrity and regulating conditions.

- **Annual review**: 1-2 hours to inspect and maintain the structure as needed.

4.3 INNOVATIVE HOME GARDENING TECHNIQUES

Container gardening offers a flexible and accessible way to grow your own food, even in the smallest of spaces. By using pots, buckets, and other containers, you can cultivate a variety of vegetables, herbs, and even small fruit trees right on your patio, balcony, or windowsill. The key to successful container gardening lies in choosing the right containers—anything from traditional clay pots to recycled plastic buckets will do, as long as they provide adequate drainage. Fill them with a high-quality potting mix, which is specifically designed to hold moisture and provide the nutrients your plants need to thrive. Regular watering is crucial, as container plants can dry out more quickly than those in the ground. However, be mindful not to overwater, as soggy soil can lead to root rot and other diseases. With a bit of care, container gardening can yield a bounty of fresh produce, even in the most limited spaces.

Vertical gardening takes the concept of space-efficient gardening a step further by using vertical structures to grow plants. Trellises, wall planters, and hanging baskets are all excellent options for maximizing your growing area vertically. This method is particularly effective for climbing plants like tomatoes, cucumbers, and beans, as well as for creating lush, living walls of herbs and greens. Vertical gardening not only saves space but can also reduce pest problems and make harvesting easier. To get started, choose a sunny wall or fence and select plants that are suited to vertical growth. Ensure your vertical structures are sturdy and provide adequate support for the plants as they grow. With creativity and strategic planning, vertical gardening can transform even the narrowest of spaces into a productive and beautiful green oasis.

Hydroponics introduces a soil-free method of gardening that can significantly increase growth rates and yields. This technique uses a nutrient-rich water solution to feed plants, allowing for more precise control over the growing conditions. Hydroponic systems can range from simple, passive setups using wicking or deep water culture to more complex, active systems with nutrient film technique or aeroponics. Starting with hydroponics might seem daunting, but even beginners can achieve success with a bit of research and a simple setup. Lettuce, herbs, and strawberries are among the many plants that thrive in hydroponic systems. The initial investment in equipment and nutrients can be offset by the high efficiency and productivity of hydroponic gardening. Plus, it allows for year-round growing, free from the constraints of soil quality and weather conditions.

Each of these gardening methods—container, vertical, and hydroponics—offers a unique set of advantages for maximizing food production in limited spaces. By understanding and applying these techniques, you can enjoy fresh, home-grown produce regardless of your living situation. These methods not only provide a practical solution to food production challenges but also offer the satisfaction of nurturing plants and harvesting your own food. As you experiment and learn, you'll find that these gardening practices can be adapted and combined to fit your specific needs and preferences, further enhancing your journey toward self-sufficiency and resilience.

4.3.1 CONTAINER GARDENING

Container gardening allows individuals to cultivate fresh vegetables in limited spaces, making it an ideal solution for off-grid living or DIY sustainability. This project transforms ordinary pots, buckets, or any suitable containers into productive growing spaces, providing easy access to home-grown food. It not only promotes self-sufficiency but also reduces reliance on store-bought produce, which can be costly and environmentally taxing. Container gardening offers flexibility; you can rearrange your plants as needed, whether on a balcony, patio, or even indoors. Additionally, growing vegetables in containers helps mitigate pest issues and improves soil management, as you control the growing medium and conditions. This guide focuses on five vegetables that thrive in containers: tomatoes, peppers, lettuce, radishes, and herbs. Each offers unique flavors and nutritional benefits, making them perfect choices for your container garden.

Materials and Tools:

- Plastic or clay pots (at least 12 inches in diameter) - 5 units
- Potting mix (high-quality, well-draining) - 2 bags (1.5 cubic feet each)
- Fertilizer (balanced, slow-release) - 1 bag (5 pounds)
- Watering can or hose with spray nozzle - 1 unit
- Trowel - 1 unit
- Garden gloves - 1 pair
- Labels or markers - 5 units

- Mulch (straw or wood chips) - 1 bag (2 cubic feet)

- Seeds or seedlings:

- Tomato (variety of choice) - 1 pack

- Bell pepper (variety of choice) - 1 pack

- Lettuce (leaf or head variety) - 1 pack

- Radish (any variety) - 1 pack

- Herb seeds (basil, parsley, or cilantro) - 1 pack

Step-by-Step Guide:

1. **Choose Containers**: Select five containers that are at least 12 inches in diameter. Ensure they have drainage holes to prevent waterlogging.

2. **Prepare Potting Mix**: Fill each container with a high-quality potting mix, leaving about 2 inches of space at the top. This allows room for watering and mulching.

3. **Add Fertilizer**: Mix a balanced, slow-release fertilizer into the potting mix according to package instructions. This provides essential nutrients for your plants.

4. **Plant Seeds or Seedlings**:

    a. For tomatoes, plant 1 seedling per container at a depth of 2 inches.

    b. For peppers, plant 1 seedling per container at a depth of 1 inch.

    c. For lettuce, scatter seeds on the surface, then cover lightly with soil.

    d. For radishes, plant 10 seeds per container, spaced evenly, at a depth of 1 inch.

    e. For herbs, plant 3-5 seeds per container, spaced evenly, at a depth of ¼ inch.

5. **Water Thoroughly**: After planting, water each container thoroughly until water drains from the bottom. Ensure the soil is evenly moist but not soggy.

6. **Label Containers**: Use labels or markers to identify each type of plant. This helps track growth and care for different vegetables.

7. **Mulch the Soil**: Apply a layer of mulch (straw or wood chips) on top of the soil in each container to retain moisture and suppress weeds.

8. **Monitor and Water**: Check the moisture level daily, especially in hot weather. Water when the top inch of soil feels dry, ensuring water reaches the roots.

9. **Prune and Support Plants**: As tomatoes and peppers grow, provide support with stakes or cages. Prune excess leaves to promote airflow and reduce disease risk.

10. **Harvest Vegetables**:

    a. Harvest tomatoes when they are fully ripe and have a deep color.

    b. Pick peppers when they reach desired size and color.

    c. Cut lettuce leaves as needed, allowing the plant to continue growing.

    d. Harvest radishes when they are firm and reach the desired size.

    e. Snip herbs as needed, ensuring not to remove more than one-third of the plant at a time.

Maintenance:

- **Weekly**: Check for pests and diseases. Remove any affected leaves immediately. Water containers as needed, ensuring consistent moisture levels.

- **Monthly**: Reapply slow-release fertilizer as per package instructions to maintain nutrient levels. Refresh mulch if it decomposes or washes away.

- **Seasonally**: Rotate crops by planting different vegetables in the containers to prevent soil depletion and pest buildup. Clean containers thoroughly at the end of the growing season to prepare for new plants.

Complexity:

The complexity of container gardening is low, making it accessible for beginners. Basic gardening skills are required, such as planting seeds and monitoring moisture. Challenges may include managing watering schedules and addressing pest issues, but these can be easily handled with regular observation and care.

Estimated Time:

- **Setup**: 1-2 hours to gather materials, prepare soil, and plant seeds or seedlings.

- **Ongoing maintenance**: 15-30 minutes weekly for watering, monitoring, and pruning.

- **Harvesting**: 1 hour as vegetables reach maturity, depending on the quantity harvested.

4.3.2 VERTICAL GARDENING

Vertical gardening is an innovative approach that allows you to maximize space by growing plants upward rather than outward. This method is particularly beneficial for those with limited gardening space, such as urban dwellers or individuals living off-grid. By utilizing vertical structures like trellises, walls, or even hanging planters, you create an efficient growing environment that enhances air circulation and light exposure for your plants. This project not only reduces the footprint of your garden but also adds an aesthetic element to your living space. Additionally, vertical gardening can lead to higher yields in smaller areas, making it an ideal choice for self-sufficiency. You cultivate fresh produce right at home, contributing to your overall sustainability goals while enjoying the satisfaction of growing your own food.

Materials and Tools:

- Wooden pallets or trellis - 1 unit
- Potting soil - 1 bag - 1 cubic foot
- Planters or small pots - 5 units
- Drill with ¼ inch drill bit - 1 unit
- Screws (1.5 inches) - 1 box - 50 units
- Nails (1 inch) - 1 box - 100 units
- Watering can - 1 unit
- Measuring tape - 1 unit
- Garden gloves - 1 pair
- Organic fertilizer - 1 bag - 5 pounds

Step-by-Step Guide:

1. **Select a Location**: Choose a sunny area that receives at least 6-8 hours of sunlight daily for your vertical garden.

2. **Prepare the Pallet or Trellis**: If using a wooden pallet, sand any rough edges to prevent splinters. If using a trellis, ensure it is sturdy and can support the weight of your plants.

3. **Mount the Structure**: Secure the pallet or trellis vertically against a wall or fence using screws and a drill. Ensure it is stable and won't tip over.

4. **Add Planters**: Attach small planters or pots to the pallet or trellis using nails. Space them evenly, allowing enough room for plants to grow without overcrowding.

5. **Fill with Potting Soil**: Fill each planter with potting soil, leaving about an inch of space at the top for watering.

6. **Choose Your Vegetables**: Select five vegetables ideal for vertical gardening:

    a. **Tomatoes**: Opt for determinate varieties, which grow to a certain height and produce fruit in a shorter time.

    b. **Cucumbers**: Choose bush varieties for compact growth and attach them to the trellis for support.

    c. **Pole Beans**: These climbing plants naturally grow upward and can reach impressive heights, perfect for vertical gardening.

    d. **Peas**: Sugar snap or snow peas thrive in cooler temperatures and will climb easily with support.

    e. **Lettuce**: Opt for loose-leaf varieties that do not require as much vertical space and can thrive in smaller planters.

7. **Plant the Seeds or Seedlings**: Follow the planting instructions for each vegetable. Generally, plant seeds or seedlings at the depth specified on the seed packet, ensuring they are adequately spaced for healthy growth.

8. **Water Regularly**: Water the vertical garden thoroughly after planting. Maintain consistent moisture, especially in warmer weather, as vertical gardens can dry out faster than traditional gardens.

9. **Fertilize**: Apply organic fertilizer according to package instructions every 4-6 weeks to ensure your plants receive necessary nutrients.

10. **Monitor Growth**: Check your plants regularly for signs of pests or diseases. Support growing plants with additional ties if necessary to keep them secure.

Maintenance:

- **Weekly**: Water the vertical garden, ensuring the soil remains moist but not soggy. Inspect for pests or diseases.

- **Monthly**: Fertilize with organic fertilizer. Trim any dead or yellowing leaves to promote healthy growth.

- **Annually**: At the end of the growing season, remove all plant debris from the vertical garden and clean the planters to prevent diseases in the following year.

Complexity:

This project is moderately complex. It requires basic woodworking skills to secure the structure and some understanding of plant care. The challenges may include ensuring adequate sunlight, managing moisture levels, and monitoring plant health. However, with attention and care, you can successfully cultivate a vibrant vertical garden.

Estimated Time:

- **Setup**: 2-3 hours to gather materials, prepare the structure, and plant the vegetables.

- **Ongoing maintenance**: 15-20 minutes weekly for watering, inspecting, and fertilizing.

- **Seasonal clean-up**: 1-2 hours at the end of the growing season to clear out plant debris and prepare for the next year.

4.3.3 HYDROPONICS

Hydroponics is a method of growing plants without soil, using nutrient-rich water instead. This technique is crucial for off-grid living, as it allows you to cultivate fresh vegetables in a controlled environment, regardless of soil quality or climate. The PVC pipe hydroponic system offers an affordable, accessible solution for home gardeners. It maximizes space and minimizes water usage, making it an ideal choice for small backyards, balconies, or indoor setups. This project empowers you to grow your own food efficiently while conserving resources, aligning perfectly with the principles of self-sufficiency and sustainability.

Materials and Tools:

- PVC pipe (4 inches diameter, 10 feet long) - 1 unit
- PVC end caps (4 inches) - 2 units
- PVC elbows (90 degrees, 4 inches) - 2 units
- Net pots (3 inches diameter) - 10 units
- Hydroponic nutrient solution - 1 gallon
- Water pump (submersible, 200 GPH) - 1 unit
- Air pump with air stone - 1 unit
- Tubing (1/2 inch) - 10 feet
- Drill with hole saw attachment (3 inches) - 1 unit
- Water reservoir (plastic container, 5 gallons) - 1 unit
- Measuring cup - 1 unit
- Timer (for pump operation) - 1 unit
- Clean water - As needed

Step-by-Step Guide:

1. **Cut the PVC Pipe**: Cut the PVC pipe into two 5-foot lengths using a saw.
2. **Drill Holes**: Use a drill with a 3-inch hole saw attachment to create holes in the top of each PVC pipe section. Space the holes 6-8 inches apart for optimal plant growth.
3. **Attach End Caps**: Securely attach the PVC end caps to one end of each pipe section to create a closed system.
4. **Connect Elbows**: Attach the 90-degree PVC elbows to the open ends of the pipes, creating a U-shape with both pipe sections.
5. **Prepare the Water Reservoir**: Fill the 5-gallon plastic container with clean water and mix in the hydroponic nutrient solution according to package instructions.
6. **Install the Water Pump**: Place the submersible water pump in the reservoir. Connect the tubing to the pump outlet and run it to one of the pipe sections.
7. **Set Up Air Pump**: Position the air pump outside the reservoir. Connect it to the air stone and place the stone inside the water. This aerates the water, promoting healthy root development.
8. **Insert Net Pots**: Place net pots into the drilled holes, ensuring they fit snugly. These will hold the plants.
9. **Fill Net Pots**: Fill the net pots with a growing medium, such as clay pellets or rock wool, to support the seedlings.
10. **Add Plants**: Transplant seedlings into the net pots, ensuring the roots make contact with the growing medium.
11. **Water the System**: Turn on the water pump and check for leaks. Ensure water flows evenly through each pipe section.

12. **Set Timer**: Program the timer to operate the water pump for 15-30 minutes every hour, ensuring consistent moisture without overwatering.

13. **Vegetables Perfect for Hydroponics**:

   a. **Lettuce**: Grows quickly in a hydroponic system and thrives in nutrient-rich water.

   b. **Spinach**: Prefers cooler temperatures and offers a quick harvest.

   c. **Kale**: Nutrient-dense and adaptable, kale flourishes in various conditions.

   d. **Basil**: This aromatic herb grows well in hydroponics, enhancing both flavor and aroma in dishes.

   e. **Tomatoes**: Although slightly more demanding, tomatoes can yield bountiful harvests with proper care.

Maintenance:

- **Weekly**: Check the water level in the reservoir, topping off with clean water as needed. Inspect plants for pests or diseases, removing any affected foliage. Clean the net pots and growing medium to prevent algae buildup.

- **Monthly**: Replace the nutrient solution in the reservoir to ensure optimal nutrient levels. Test the pH of the water, adjusting as necessary to keep it between 5.5 and 6.5.

Complexity:

This project is moderately complex. It requires basic DIY skills, including cutting and assembling PVC components. You may encounter challenges in maintaining the right balance of nutrients and ensuring proper water flow, but these can be addressed with attention and regular monitoring.

Estimated Time:

- **Setup**: 2-3 hours for gathering materials, cutting pipes, drilling holes, and assembling the system.

- **Ongoing maintenance**: 30 minutes weekly for checking plants, water levels, and nutrient solutions.

- **Nutrient solution replacement**: 1 hour monthly for draining, cleaning the reservoir, and refilling with fresh solution.

4.4 FOOD PRESERVATION METHODS

Canning, dehydrating, and fermenting stand as pillars in the realm of food preservation, each method offering a unique way to extend the shelf life of your harvest while locking in nutritional value and flavor. Canning involves the process of packing fruits, vegetables, meats, and seafood into jars and heating them to a temperature that destroys microorganisms and enzymes that could cause spoilage. This method requires some basic equipment: a canner, canning jars with lids and rings, a jar lifter, and a funnel. There are two main types of canning: water bath canning, suitable for acidic foods like fruits, tomatoes, pickles, and jams; and pressure canning, necessary for low-acid foods like vegetables, meats, and fish. The key to successful canning is following tested recipes and processing times to ensure safety and quality.

Dehydrating is another effective preservation technique, especially useful for fruits, vegetables, and herbs. By removing moisture, dehydrating inhibits the growth of bacteria, yeasts, and molds. Dehydrators, ovens, or even the sun can be used for this purpose. The process is relatively simple and requires minimal equipment, making it accessible for beginners. Sliced or chopped food is spread on trays in a single layer and heated at a low temperature for several hours until dry but still pliable. Properly dehydrated foods can last for months or even years when stored in airtight containers in a cool, dark place. This method not only preserves your food but also concentrates flavors, making for delicious snacks and ingredients.

Fermenting is perhaps the most intriguing of the three methods, relying on the natural process of lacto-fermentation to preserve food. This process involves submerging vegetables or fruits in a brine or using their natural juices to create an environment where beneficial bacteria thrive and harmful bacteria are inhibited.

Common fermented foods include sauerkraut, kimchi, pickles, and yogurt. Fermentation not only extends the shelf life of foods but also enhances their nutritional value, introducing probiotics that support digestive health. Getting started with fermentation requires minimal equipment: a jar, a weight to keep the food submerged in brine, and a cloth to cover the jar, allowing gases to escape while keeping contaminants out.

Each of these methods—canning, dehydrating, and fermenting—offers a way to preserve the bounty of your garden, forage, or hunt, ensuring a diverse and nutritious diet year-round. They allow you to take full control of your food supply, reduce waste, and enjoy the fruits of your labor even in the off-season. Moreover, these techniques can transform your approach to cooking and eating, encouraging a deeper connection with the food you consume and a greater appreciation for the cycles of nature. As you embark on these preservation projects, remember to start small, experiment with different foods and flavors, and most importantly, enjoy the process. With practice, you'll find that these age-old methods of food preservation are not only practical but also deeply rewarding, offering a tangible link to the past and a sustainable path forward.

4.4.1 CANNING

Canning serves as a vital method for preserving food, particularly for those embracing off-grid living or DIY sustainability. This process involves sealing food in jars and heating them to destroy harmful bacteria, yeasts, and enzymes that contribute to spoilage. By canning, you ensure a stable supply of nutritious, homemade meals throughout the year, reducing reliance on store-bought goods. The benefits of canning extend beyond food preservation; it empowers you to control ingredients, avoid additives, and minimize food waste. Canning allows you to savor the flavors of your harvest long after the growing season ends, providing a practical solution for food security. This project covers the essential steps and considerations for canning vegetables and meats, focusing on five ideal candidates for this method: green beans, carrots, corn, chicken, and beef.

Materials and Tools:

- Water bath canner or pressure canner - 1 unit
- Canning jars with lids and rings (pint or quart size) - 12 units
- Jar lifter - 1 unit
- Canning funnel - 1 unit
- Ladle - 1 unit
- Measuring spoons - 1 set
- Large pot for blanching - 1 unit
- Tongs - 1 unit
- Clean dishcloths - 2 units
- Kitchen timer - 1 unit
- Labels and marker - 1 set
- Fresh green beans - 2 pounds (for canning)
- Fresh carrots - 2 pounds (for canning)
- Fresh corn - 6 ears (for canning)
- Fresh chicken - 2 pounds (for canning)
- Fresh beef - 2 pounds (for canning)
- Salt (non-iodized) - As needed
- Water - As needed

Step-by-Step Guide:

1. **Prepare Canner**: Fill the canner with water and place it on the stove to heat, ensuring it's ready for processing jars.

2. **Sanitize Jars**: Wash jars and lids in hot, soapy water. Rinse thoroughly and keep them warm until ready to use.

3. **Blanch Vegetables**: For green beans and carrots, blanch in boiling water for 3-5 minutes. Remove and transfer them to an ice bath to stop cooking.

4. **Prepare Corn**: Husk the corn and remove the kernels using a sharp knife. Set aside.

5. **Prepare Chicken and Beef**: Cut chicken and beef into bite-sized pieces, trimming excess fat.

6. **Fill Jars**: Use the canning funnel to pack blanched green beans into jars, leaving 1-inch headspace. Add ½ teaspoon of non-iodized salt per pint.

7. **Repeat for Carrots**: Pack blanched carrot pieces into another jar, leaving 1-inch headspace, and add ½ teaspoon of salt.

8. **Fill Corn Jars**: Fill jars with corn kernels, leaving 1-inch headspace, and add ½ teaspoon of salt.

9. **Fill Meat Jars**: Pack raw chicken pieces into jars, leaving 1-inch headspace, and do not add salt. For beef, follow the same method.

10. **Seal Jars**: Wipe the rims of the jars with a clean cloth to remove any residue. Place lids on jars and screw on rings until fingertip-tight.

11. **Process Jars**: For green beans and corn, process in a pressure canner at 10 pounds of pressure for 20 minutes. For carrots, process at 10 pounds for 25 minutes. For chicken and beef, process at 10 pounds for 75 minutes.

12. **Cool Jars**: After processing, turn off the heat and let the canner cool down naturally. Remove jars using the jar lifter and place them on a clean towel to cool completely.

13. **Label Jars**: Once jars are cool, label them with the contents and date, storing them in a cool, dark place.

Maintenance:

- **Monthly**: Inspect stored jars for any signs of spoilage, such as leaks or bulging lids. Replace any compromised jars.

- **Annually**: Rotate canned goods to use older jars first, ensuring you consume food before the recommended shelf life.

Complexity:

The project has a moderate complexity level. Canning requires precise measurements and timing to ensure safety. Familiarity with pressure canners is essential, especially for low-acid foods like meats. Beginners may face challenges with processing times and understanding pressure adjustments, but these can be mitigated with practice and adherence to tested recipes.

Estimated Time:

- **Setup**: 30 minutes to gather materials, sanitize jars, and prepare ingredients.

- **Canning Process**: 2-3 hours for blanching, filling jars, and processing them in the canner.

- **Cooling and labeling**: 1 hour for cooling jars and completing labels.

4.4.2 DEHYDRATING

Building a DIY off-grid solar dehydrator offers a practical solution for preserving fruits, vegetables, and herbs using the sun's natural energy. This project is crucial for off-grid living or anyone seeking to reduce food waste and maintain a self-sufficient lifestyle. Dehydrating food extends its shelf life, concentrating flavors and nutrients, while reducing the need for refrigeration. With a solar dehydrator, you harness renewable energy, making it a cost-effective method to prepare for emergencies or simply enjoy seasonal produce year-round. The dehydrator uses a small solar-powered fan to facilitate ventilation, ensuring even drying and preventing moisture buildup. By completing this project, you empower yourself with the ability to preserve food sustainably and healthily.

Materials and Tools:

- Wooden pallets - 2 units (for the frame)
- Plywood sheet (1/2 inch thick) - 1 unit (for the base)
- Clear plastic sheet (UV-resistant) - 1 unit (for the cover)
- Small solar-powered fan - 1 unit (for ventilation)
- Hinges - 2 units (for the door)
- Screws (1.5 inches) - 1 box (for assembly)
- Wood glue - 1 bottle (for additional support)
- Wire mesh (1/4 inch) - 1 roll (for the drying trays)
- L-brackets - 4 units (for added stability)
- Paint or sealant (non-toxic) - 1 can (for weatherproofing)
- Measuring tape - 1 unit (for accurate measurements)
- Saw (hand or power) - 1 unit (for cutting wood)
- Drill - 1 unit (for making holes and driving screws)

Step-by-Step Guide:

1. **Build the Frame**: Use the wooden pallets to construct a rectangular frame measuring 3 feet wide by 4 feet tall. Secure the corners with screws and wood glue.

2. **Attach the Base**: Cut the plywood sheet to 3 feet by 4 feet. Attach it to the bottom of the frame using screws to create a sturdy base for the dehydrator.

3. **Create the Cover**: Cut the clear plastic sheet to fit over the top of the frame. Secure it with screws, ensuring it is airtight to trap heat inside.

4. **Install the Fan**: Cut an opening in one side of the frame for the solar-powered fan. Attach the fan using screws, ensuring it blows air into the dehydrator to enhance ventilation.

5. **Make Drying Trays**: Cut wire mesh into four rectangles measuring 2 feet by 3 feet. Create a frame for each tray using leftover wood, securing the mesh to the frame with screws.

6. **Position Trays**: Stack the drying trays inside the dehydrator, allowing space for air to circulate around each tray. Ensure they fit snugly but can be easily removed.

7. **Attach the Door**: Cut another piece of plywood for the front door. Use hinges to attach it to one side of the frame, allowing for easy access to the trays.

8. **Seal the Dehydrator**: Apply a non-toxic paint or sealant to the exterior of the dehydrator to protect it from moisture and UV damage. Allow it to dry completely.

9. **Test the Dehydrator**: Place a thermometer inside the dehydrator to monitor the internal temperature. Aim for a temperature of at least 130°F to effectively dehydrate food.

10. **Prepare Vegetables**: Wash and slice vegetables evenly to ensure uniform drying. Ideal candidates for dehydrating include:

   a. Zucchini: Slice into 1/4-inch rounds.

   b. Bell Peppers: Chop into strips or small pieces.

   c. Carrots: Cut into thin rounds or julienne.

   d. Tomatoes: Halve or quarter, removing excess moisture.

   e. Green Beans: Trim ends and cut into 1-inch pieces.

11. **Start Dehydrating**: Arrange the prepared vegetables on the drying trays in a single layer. Close the door and allow the sun to heat the dehydrator throughout the day.

Maintenance:

- **Weekly**: Inspect the dehydrator for any signs of wear or damage. Ensure the fan operates properly and check the seals for air leaks.

- **Monthly**: Clean the trays with warm, soapy water to remove any residue. Rinse thoroughly and allow them to dry completely before storage.

- **Annually**: Reapply paint or sealant as needed to maintain weather resistance. Check the structural integrity of the frame and make any necessary repairs.

Complexity:

This project is moderate in complexity, requiring basic woodworking skills and tools. The primary challenges include ensuring proper insulation and ventilation. Familiarity with working with wood and basic electrical knowledge for the solar fan installation is beneficial but not mandatory.

Estimated Time:

- **Setup**: 2-3 hours to gather materials, cut wood, and assemble the dehydrator.

- **Drying Time**: 6-12 hours depending on the vegetable type and thickness.

- **Ongoing maintenance**: 10-15 minutes weekly for inspections and cleaning.

4.4.3 FERMENTING

Fermenting vegetables transforms ordinary produce into tangy, flavorful foods packed with probiotics and nutrients. This process, rooted in ancient preservation methods, enhances the shelf life of vegetables while promoting gut health. For those engaged in off-grid living or DIY sustainability, fermenting offers an accessible way to store surplus harvests, reduce food waste, and diversify diets with minimal equipment. The fermentation process involves using beneficial bacteria to convert sugars into acids, creating an environment that preserves food and develops complex flavors. In this guide, you will learn how to ferment five vegetables that excel in this preservation method: cabbage, carrots, radishes, cucumbers, and beets. Each vegetable brings its unique flavor and health benefits, making them ideal candidates for fermentation.

Materials and Tools:

- Fermentation jar (with airlock lid) - 1 unit - 1 gallon

- Sharp knife - 1 unit

- Cutting board - 1 unit

- Measuring cup - 1 unit

- Sea salt (non-iodized) - 1 cup

- Filtered water - As needed

- Fresh cabbage - 2 pounds

- Fresh carrots - 2 pounds

- Fresh radishes - 2 pounds

- Fresh cucumbers - 2 pounds

- Fresh beets - 2 pounds

- Grater or food processor - 1 unit (optional)

- Weights (to submerge vegetables) - As needed

Step-by-Step Guide:

1. **Prepare Vegetables**: Wash all vegetables thoroughly under cold running water to remove dirt and pesticides.

2. **Chop Cabbage**: Remove the outer leaves from the cabbage and slice it into thin strips, approximately ¼ inch wide.

3. **Shred Carrots**: Peel the carrots and either grate them using a box grater or chop them into thin matchsticks.

4. **Slice Radishes**: Trim the ends of the radishes and slice them into thin rounds, about ⅛ inch thick.

5. **Cut Cucumbers**: Wash cucumbers and slice them into spears or rounds, depending on your preference.

6. **Peel and Dice Beets**: Wearing gloves to avoid staining, peel the beets and dice them into small cubes, roughly ½ inch in size.

7. **Mix Saltwater Brine**: In a measuring cup, dissolve 1 cup of sea salt in 1 quart of filtered water to create a brine.

8. **Combine Vegetables**: In a large mixing bowl, combine the chopped cabbage, shredded carrots, sliced radishes, cucumber pieces, and diced beets.

9. **Pack Vegetables into Jar**: Layer the mixed vegetables into the fermentation jar, pressing down firmly with each layer to release air and pack them tightly.

10. **Add Weights**: Place fermentation weights on top of the packed vegetables to keep them submerged below the brine. This prevents exposure to air and potential spoilage.

11. **Pour Brine**: Pour the saltwater brine over the packed vegetables until they are fully submerged. Leave about an inch of headspace at the top of the jar.

12. **Seal the Jar**: Secure the airlock lid onto the fermentation jar. This allows gases to escape while preventing air from entering.

13. **Ferment**: Place the jar in a cool, dark area (ideally 60-70°F or 15-21°C) and let it ferment for 1-4 weeks, depending on your taste preference. Check weekly for flavor and adjust fermentation time as desired.

14. **Store Finished Ferments**: Once fermented to your liking, transfer the jar to the refrigerator to slow down the fermentation process. The fermented vegetables can be stored for several months.

Maintenance:

- **Weekly**: Check the jar for any signs of mold on the surface. If present, carefully skim it off with a clean spoon. Ensure that the vegetables remain submerged in the brine; add more brine if necessary.

- **Monthly**: Taste the fermented vegetables to assess flavor development. Adjust storage conditions if they seem too warm or too cold.

Complexity:

This project ranks as moderate in complexity. Basic skills include chopping and mixing ingredients. Challenges may arise in monitoring fermentation and managing the brine level, but these can be overcome with attention to detail.

Estimated Time:

- **Preparation**: 1-2 hours for washing, chopping, and packing vegetables.

- **Fermentation**: 1-4 weeks, depending on desired flavor.

- **Storage**: 30 minutes to transfer to the refrigerator once fermentation is complete.

4.5 COOKING WITH WILD EDIBLES

Foraging for wild edibles opens up a world of nutritional and culinary opportunities, enabling you to supplement your diet with a variety of fresh, organic, and free ingredients right from your backyard or local wilderness. Embarking on the journey of foraging not only connects you with nature but also empowers you with the knowledge to identify and utilize the abundance of edible plants, berries, nuts, and mushrooms that grow in the wild. Before you begin, it's crucial to arm yourself with reliable resources such as field guides and, if possible, the wisdom of experienced foragers to accurately identify safe-to-eat plants and avoid those that are toxic.

Safety is paramount when foraging for wild edibles. Always be 100% certain of a plant's identity before consuming it, as some edible plants have dangerous look-alikes. Start with easily recognizable species and gradually expand your knowledge. Learning about the habitats where these plants thrive can also lead you to more fruitful foraging grounds. Remember, the goal is not only to forage safely but to do so sustainably, ensuring that you leave enough for others and for the plants to reproduce.

Incorporating wild edibles into your cooking can transform ordinary meals into extraordinary ones, adding unique flavors and nutritional benefits. Many wild greens, for instance, pack a more potent nutritional punch than their cultivated counterparts. Dandelion greens, wild garlic, and nettles can be used in salads, soups, and pestos, offering a burst of flavor and vitamins. Wild berries and fruits can be made into jams, jellies, or simply enjoyed fresh, adding a natural sweetness to your diet. Nuts and seeds gathered from the wild, such as acorns and pine nuts, can be used in baking or as crunchy additions to salads.

Mushrooms, while a delicious foraging find, require extra caution due to the difficulty in distinguishing between edible and poisonous varieties. Only forage mushrooms if you are thoroughly educated on the species in your area or are accompanied by an expert. Edible mushrooms like morels, chanterelles, and oyster mushrooms can elevate any dish, from simple sautés to gourmet sauces.

Preservation techniques such as drying, pickling, and fermenting can extend the shelf life of your foraged bounty, allowing you to enjoy the flavors of the season long after they've passed. Dried herbs and mushrooms can add depth to dishes year-round, while pickled wild vegetables can provide a tangy crunch.

Foraging not only enriches your diet but also encourages a deeper appreciation for the land and its cycles. It's a practice that fosters a sense of independence and self-sufficiency, aligning perfectly with the ethos of no-grid living. As you become more proficient in identifying and preparing wild edibles, you'll find that nature offers a generous pantry just waiting to be explored. The act of foraging itself is a rewarding experience, connecting you with the natural world in a profound and personal way. With each foray into the wild, you'll gather not just food, but knowledge, skills, and memories that nourish both body and soul. So, step outside, and let the earth's bounty inspire your next culinary adventure.

4.5.1 DANDELION SALAD WITH HONEY MUSTARD DRESSING

Dandelion Salad with Honey Mustard Dressing offers a refreshing way to incorporate wild edibles into your diet. This vibrant salad features tender dandelion greens, known for their peppery flavor and rich nutritional profile, including vitamins A, C, and K, along with minerals like iron and calcium. For those pursuing off-grid living or

DIY sustainability, this recipe serves as a perfect example of utilizing foraged ingredients that promote self-sufficiency and a connection to the land. Harvesting dandelion greens requires minimal effort, making it an accessible project for anyone interested in exploring the bounty of nature. Additionally, the honey mustard dressing adds a sweet and tangy contrast, enhancing the natural flavors of the greens. This dish not only satisfies your taste buds but also embodies the spirit of resourcefulness and health-conscious eating.

Materials and Tools:

- Dandelion greens (freshly foraged) - 4 cups
- Cherry tomatoes - 1 cup
- Cucumber - 1 medium
- Red onion - ½ medium
- Olive oil - ¼ cup
- Honey - 2 tablespoons
- Dijon mustard - 1 tablespoon
- Apple cider vinegar - 2 tablespoons
- Salt - to taste
- Black pepper - to taste
- Mixing bowl - 1 unit
- Salad serving bowl - 1 unit
- Whisk or fork - 1 unit
- Knife - 1 unit
- Cutting board - 1 unit

Step-by-Step Guide:

1. **Forage Dandelion Greens**: Identify and harvest dandelion greens from a clean area, avoiding locations near roadsides or areas treated with pesticides. Collect about 4 cups of young, tender leaves.

2. **Wash Greens**: Rinse the dandelion greens thoroughly under cold water to remove any dirt or insects. Shake off excess water or use a salad spinner to dry them.

3. **Prepare Vegetables**: Slice the cucumber into thin rounds, chop the cherry tomatoes in half, and finely slice the red onion.

4. **Combine Salad Ingredients**: In a mixing bowl, add the washed dandelion greens, cucumber slices, halved cherry tomatoes, and red onion. Toss gently to combine.

5. **Make Dressing**: In a separate bowl, whisk together ¼ cup of olive oil, 2 tablespoons of honey, 1 tablespoon of Dijon mustard, and 2 tablespoons of apple cider vinegar until well blended.

6. **Season Dressing**: Add salt and black pepper to the dressing according to taste. Whisk again to ensure even seasoning.

7. **Dress Salad**: Drizzle the honey mustard dressing over the salad mixture in the mixing bowl. Toss the salad gently to coat all ingredients evenly with the dressing.

8. **Serve**: Transfer the dressed salad into a salad serving bowl. Optionally, garnish with additional cherry tomatoes or a sprinkle of seeds for added texture.

9. **Enjoy**: Serve immediately for the freshest taste, or allow the salad to sit for a few minutes to let the flavors meld.

Maintenance:

- **Weekly**: Check for any remaining dandelion greens that may not have been used and ensure they are stored in a cool, dry place if not consumed immediately.

- **Monthly**: Replenish your dandelion supply by foraging fresh greens during the growing season to maintain a consistent supply for salads.

Complexity:

The project is low in complexity, making it suitable for beginners. Basic skills required include foraging, washing, and preparing fresh ingredients. The main challenge may lie in accurately identifying edible dandelion greens, but this can be overcome with proper guidance and practice.

Estimated Time:

- **Foraging**: 30 minutes to 1 hour, depending on the availability of dandelions in your area.

- **Preparation**: 15-20 minutes for washing, chopping, and mixing ingredients.

- Total Time: Approximately 45 minutes to 1 hour to gather, prepare, and serve the salad.

4.5.2 WILD GARLIC PESTO

Wild Garlic Pesto showcases the vibrant, aromatic flavors of foraged wild garlic, also known as ramsons or bear's garlic. This recipe captures the essence of wild edibles, transforming simple ingredients into a deliciously versatile condiment. Wild garlic grows abundantly in damp woodlands during spring, making it an ideal candidate for those engaged in off-grid living or DIY sustainability. Harvesting wild garlic not only provides a free and nutritious ingredient but also connects you to the local ecosystem. The pesto serves as a delightful spread for bread, a sauce for pasta, or a topping for grilled meats and vegetables. By learning to create wild garlic pesto, you enhance your culinary repertoire while embracing a lifestyle of self-sufficiency and resourcefulness.

Materials and Tools:

- Wild garlic leaves - 2 cups

- Pine nuts (or walnuts) - ¼ cup

- Grated Parmesan cheese - ½ cup

- Olive oil - ½ cup

- Lemon juice - 2 tablespoons

- Salt - to taste

- Black pepper - to taste

- Food processor - 1 unit

- Spatula - 1 unit

- Measuring cups - 1 set

- Measuring spoons - 1 set

- Airtight container for storage - 1 unit

Step-by-Step Guide:

1. **Forage Wild Garlic**: Identify and gather 2 cups of young wild garlic leaves from a clean area, ensuring you recognize the distinctive broad leaves and garlic scent.

2. **Wash Leaves**: Rinse the wild garlic leaves thoroughly under cold water to remove any dirt or insects. Shake off excess water or use a salad spinner.

3. **Toast Pine Nuts**: In a dry skillet over medium heat, toast ¼ cup of pine nuts until golden brown, stirring frequently to prevent burning. This enhances their flavor.

4. **Prepare Food Processor**: Add the washed wild garlic leaves, toasted pine nuts, and ½ cup of grated Parmesan cheese to the food processor.

5. **Blend Ingredients**: Pulse the mixture until finely chopped, scraping down the sides with a spatula as needed to ensure even blending.

6. **Add Olive Oil**: With the food processor running, slowly drizzle in ½ cup of olive oil until the mixture reaches a smooth consistency.

7. **Incorporate Lemon Juice**: Add 2 tablespoons of lemon juice to the mixture and pulse briefly to combine. This adds brightness and helps preserve the vibrant colour.

8. **Season to Taste**: Add salt and black pepper to taste, then pulse again to mix thoroughly. Adjust seasoning as desired.

9. **Transfer to Container**: Use a spatula to transfer the wild garlic pesto into an airtight container. Smooth the top to remove air pockets.

10. **Store Pesto**: Cover the pesto with a thin layer of olive oil to prevent oxidation, then seal the container and store it in the refrigerator.

11. **Enjoy**: Use the wild garlic pesto within 1-2 weeks, adding it to pasta, spreading it on bread, or using it as a flavorful topping for various dishes.

Maintenance:

- **Weekly**: Check the pesto for freshness. If you notice any discoloration or off smells, discard it.
- **Monthly**: Consider making a new batch as wild garlic is seasonal, ensuring you have a steady supply of this vibrant condiment throughout the spring.

Complexity:

The project is low to moderate in complexity, making it accessible for beginners. Key skills involve foraging, food processing, and seasoning. The main challenges may include accurately identifying wild garlic and achieving the desired consistency in the pesto. With practice, these challenges become manageable.

Estimated Time:

- **Foraging**: 30 minutes to 1 hour, depending on the availability of wild garlic in your area.
- **Preparation**: 15-20 minutes for washing, toasting, and blending ingredients.
- **Total Time**: Approximately 45 minutes to 1 hour to gather, prepare, and store the wild garlic pesto.

4.5.3 NETTLE SOUP

Nettle soup is a nourishing and flavorful dish that harnesses the unique taste and nutritional benefits of stinging nettles, a wild edible often found in abundance during spring. For those living off-grid or pursuing DIY sustainability, this recipe exemplifies resourcefulness by transforming foraged ingredients into a wholesome meal. Nettles are rich in vitamins A, C, and K, along with essential minerals like iron and calcium. Incorporating nettles into your diet not only reduces reliance on store-bought produce but also fosters a deeper connection with nature and the seasonal rhythms of the environment. This project not only serves as a delicious meal option but also promotes self-sufficiency by utilizing readily available wild edibles. Preparing nettle soup empowers you to embrace the flavors of your surroundings while minimizing waste and environmental impact.

Materials and Tools:

- Fresh stinging nettles - 4 cups (packed)

- Onion - 1 medium (chopped)
- Potato - 1 large (peeled and diced)
- Vegetable broth - 4 cups
- Olive oil - 2 tablespoons
- Garlic - 2 cloves (minced)
- Salt - to taste
- Black pepper - to taste
- Lemon juice - 1 tablespoon
- Blender or immersion blender - 1 unit
- Large pot - 1 unit (4-6 quarts)
- Wooden spoon - 1 unit
- Knife - 1 unit
- Cutting board - 1 unit
- Ladle - 1 unit

Step-by-Step Guide:

1. **Forage Nettles**: Wear gloves and harvest 4 cups of fresh stinging nettles from a clean, pesticide-free area. Choose young, tender leaves for the best flavor.
2. **Wash Nettles**: Rinse the nettles thoroughly under cold water to remove dirt and insects. Shake off excess water.
3. **Prepare Ingredients**: Chop 1 medium onion, peel and dice 1 large potato, and mince 2 cloves of garlic.
4. **Heat Oil**: In a large pot, heat 2 tablespoons of olive oil over medium heat until shimmering.
5. **Sauté Onion and Garlic**: Add the chopped onion and minced garlic to the pot. Sauté for 5-7 minutes until the onion becomes translucent.
6. **Add Potato**: Stir in the diced potato and cook for an additional 5 minutes, allowing the potato to absorb the flavors.
7. **Pour Broth**: Add 4 cups of vegetable broth to the pot, bringing the mixture to a gentle boil.
8. **Incorporate Nettles**: Carefully add the washed nettles to the boiling broth. Stir well and reduce heat to a simmer.
9. **Cook Soup**: Simmer the soup for 15-20 minutes, or until the potatoes are tender and the nettles have wilted.
10. **Blend Soup**: Remove the pot from heat. Using a blender or immersion blender, puree the soup until smooth, taking care to avoid splattering.
11. **Season**: Return the blended soup to low heat. Season with salt and black pepper to taste, and stir in 1 tablespoon of lemon juice for brightness.
12. **Serve**: Ladle the nettle soup into bowls and enjoy immediately, garnished with a drizzle of olive oil if desired.

Maintenance:

- **Weekly**: If any leftovers remain, store the nettle soup in an airtight container in the refrigerator. Consume within 3-4 days for optimal freshness.

- **Monthly**: Review your foraging techniques and locations to identify any new areas where nettles may grow. This helps maintain a sustainable source for future recipes.

Complexity:

The complexity of making nettle soup is low. The project requires basic cooking skills, including chopping, sautéing, and blending. Challenges may arise from foraging, as accurately identifying stinging nettles is essential. However, with proper identification techniques and a willingness to learn, anyone can successfully prepare this nourishing soup.

Estimated Time:

- **Foraging**: 30 minutes to 1 hour, depending on the availability of nettles in your area.

- **Preparation**: 15 minutes for washing, chopping, and gathering ingredients.

- **Cooking**: 30 minutes to bring the soup to a boil, simmer, and blend.

- **Total Time**: Approximately 1-1.5 hours to forage, prepare, and serve the nettle soup.

4.5.4 FORAGED MUSHROOM RISOTTO

Foraged mushroom risotto combines the earthy flavors of wild mushrooms with the creamy texture of Arborio rice. This dish is a celebration of nature's bounty, particularly appealing to those pursuing off-grid living or DIY culinary adventures. Sourcing mushrooms from local woods not only enhances self-sufficiency but also deepens one's connection to the land. Risotto serves as a versatile canvas for showcasing seasonal ingredients, making it a practical meal that can adapt to whatever mushrooms are available. Beyond taste, this recipe provides a rich source of nutrients, particularly when prepared with foraged varieties, promoting a sustainable lifestyle. By mastering this dish, you gain the ability to transform simple, foraged ingredients into a gourmet meal, ensuring minimal reliance on store-bought goods.

Materials and Tools:

- Arborio rice - 1 cup

- Fresh foraged mushrooms (e.g., chanterelles, morels, or porcini) - 2 cups, chopped

- Vegetable broth - 4 cups

- White wine (optional) - ½ cup

- Onion - 1 medium, finely chopped

- Garlic - 2 cloves, minced

- Olive oil - 2 tablespoons

- Butter - 2 tablespoons

- Fresh parsley - ¼ cup, chopped

- Parmesan cheese - ½ cup, grated (optional)

- Salt - to taste

- Pepper - to taste

- Large skillet - 1 unit

- Wooden spoon - 1 unit

- Ladle - 1 unit

- Cutting board - 1 unit

- Knife - 1 unit

Step-by-Step Guide:

1. **Prepare Broth**: Heat 4 cups of vegetable broth in a pot on low heat, keeping it warm but not boiling.

2. **Sauté Aromatics**: In a large skillet, heat 2 tablespoons of olive oil and 2 tablespoons of butter over medium heat. Add 1 medium finely chopped onion and sauté until translucent, about 5 minutes.

3. **Add Garlic**: Stir in 2 minced garlic cloves and sauté for an additional minute, allowing the garlic to become fragrant.

4. **Cook Mushrooms**: Add 2 cups of chopped foraged mushrooms to the skillet. Sauté for 5-7 minutes until the mushrooms release their moisture and begin to brown.

5. **Incorporate Rice**: Stir in 1 cup of Arborio rice, coating the grains in the oil and butter mixture. Cook for 2-3 minutes until the rice becomes slightly translucent.

6. **Deglaze with Wine**: If using, pour in ½ cup of white wine. Stir continuously until the wine has mostly evaporated, leaving behind a rich flavor.

7. **Add Broth Gradually**: Begin adding the warm vegetable broth to the rice mixture, one ladle at a time. Stir continuously, allowing the rice to absorb the broth before adding more. Repeat this process until all the broth is used, about 20-25 minutes.

8. **Check for Doneness**: Taste the risotto for doneness. The rice should be creamy and al dente. If necessary, add a little more broth or water to achieve the desired consistency.

9. **Season and Finish**: Once the risotto reaches the right texture, stir in ¼ cup of chopped fresh parsley, and season with salt and pepper to taste. For an extra touch, mix in ½ cup of grated Parmesan cheese if desired.

10. **Serve Immediately**: Spoon the risotto onto plates or into bowls. Garnish with additional parsley or cheese as preferred.

Maintenance:

- **Weekly**: Check for any leftover risotto. Store in an airtight container in the refrigerator and consume within 3-4 days.

- **Monthly**: If foraging for mushrooms, review your mushroom identification skills and ensure you're confident in distinguishing edible varieties from toxic ones. Attend a local foraging workshop if necessary.

Complexity:

This recipe is of moderate complexity. It requires basic culinary skills such as chopping, sautéing, and monitoring cooking times. Foraging adds an additional layer of challenge, as identifying edible mushrooms can be daunting for beginners. Those new to cooking may find the process of stirring and adding broth a bit demanding, but with practice, it becomes easier.

Estimated Time:

- **Preparation**: 15 minutes to gather and chop ingredients.

- **Cooking**: 30-35 minutes to sauté, simmer, and stir the risotto until creamy.

- **Total time**: Approximately 45-50 minutes to complete the dish from start to finish.

4.5.5 ACORN PANCAKES

Acorn pancakes offer a unique culinary experience rooted in foraging and self-sufficiency. These pancakes transform acorns, often considered mere wildlife food, into a hearty and nutritious dish. Acorns are rich in carbohydrates, healthy fats, and fiber, making them a valuable addition to your diet, especially in off-grid living situations where resources may be limited. By incorporating acorns into your meals, you not only utilize local and abundant resources but also embrace a sustainable lifestyle that values natural ingredients. This recipe guides you through the process of harvesting, processing, and cooking acorns, resulting in delicious pancakes that connect you to the land and its offerings.

Materials and Tools:

- Acorns (preferably white or red oak) - 2 cups
- Water - 4 cups
- Baking powder - 1 tablespoon
- Salt - ½ teaspoon
- Honey or maple syrup - 2 tablespoons
- Eggs - 2 large
- Milk (or plant-based alternative) - 1 cup
- All-purpose flour (or whole wheat flour) - 1 cup
- Mixing bowl - 1 unit
- Whisk - 1 unit
- Skillet or griddle - 1 unit
- Spatula - 1 unit
- Strainer or cheesecloth - 1 unit

Step-by-Step Guide:

1. **Harvest Acorns**: Collect acorns from oak trees, choosing those that are firm and unblemished. Gather at least 2 cups of acorns.

2. **Remove Shells**: Crack open the acorns using a nutcracker or hammer. Discard the outer shells and inner skins, keeping only the nutmeat.

3. **Leach Tannins**: Place the acorn meat in a pot, cover with 4 cups of water, and bring to a boil. Boil for 10 minutes, then strain the water using a strainer or cheesecloth. Repeat this process 3-4 times until the water runs clear, indicating that the tannins have been removed.

4. **Blend Acorns**: Once leached, place the acorn meat in a mixing bowl. Mash or blend it until it reaches a smooth consistency, similar to a thick paste.

5. **Mix Dry Ingredients**: In a separate mixing bowl, whisk together 1 cup of flour, 1 tablespoon of baking powder, and ½ teaspoon of salt until evenly combined.

6. **Combine Ingredients**: In the bowl with the acorn paste, add 2 eggs, 1 cup of milk, and 2 tablespoons of honey or maple syrup. Mix until the ingredients are fully integrated.

7. **Incorporate Dry Mixture**: Gradually add the dry ingredient mixture to the wet mixture, stirring gently until just combined. Avoid over-mixing to maintain a light texture.

8. **Preheat Skillet**: Heat a skillet or griddle over medium heat. Add a small amount of oil or butter to prevent sticking.

9. **Cook Pancakes**: Pour ¼ cup of batter onto the preheated skillet for each pancake. Cook until bubbles form on the surface, approximately 3-4 minutes. Flip the pancakes and cook for another 2-3 minutes until golden brown.

10. **Serve**: Stack the pancakes on a plate and serve warm, topped with additional honey, maple syrup, or fresh fruit as desired.

Maintenance:

- **Weekly**: Ensure you have an adequate supply of leached acorn flour for pancake preparation. Check the pantry for other ingredients like flour and baking powder.

- **Monthly**: Replenish your stock of acorns by foraging in the fall when they are plentiful. Store processed acorns in a cool, dry place to prevent spoilage.

- **Annually**: Review your foraging techniques and consider expanding your wild edible knowledge to incorporate other ingredients into your diet.

Complexity:

The project ranks as moderate in complexity. It requires basic cooking skills and some knowledge of foraging and food processing. The most challenging aspect is leaching the tannins from acorns, which can be time-consuming but is essential for palatable pancakes.

Estimated Time:

- **Foraging and harvesting acorns**: 1-2 hours, depending on location and availability.

- **Processing acorns (leaching)**: 1-2 hours, including boiling and straining multiple times.

- **Pancake preparation and cooking**: 30-45 minutes.

- **Total time**: Approximately 2.5 to 5 hours, considering the entire process from foraging to serving.

4.5.6 CLOVER TEA

Clover tea, made from the flowers and leaves of the clover plant, offers a soothing beverage rich in vitamins and minerals. It serves as a herbal remedy known for its potential health benefits, including anti-inflammatory properties and support for respiratory health. For those embracing off-grid living, clover tea embodies a sustainable approach to foraging and utilizing local flora. It allows you to tap into nature's bounty, transforming simple ingredients into a nourishing drink. This recipe highlights the ease of preparing clover tea, making it a valuable skill for anyone looking to enhance their self-sufficiency while enjoying a natural, healthful beverage.

Materials and Tools:

- Clover flowers (fresh or dried) - 1 cup

- Water - 4 cups

- Saucepan - 1 unit

- Strainer - 1 unit

- Teapot or heatproof container - 1 unit

- Honey or sweetener (optional) - As needed

Step-by-Step Guide:

1. **Harvest Clover**: Identify and harvest clover flowers from a clean area, avoiding spots near roadways or contaminated soil. Gather 1 cup of fresh or dried flowers.

2. **Prepare Water**: Measure 4 cups of water and pour it into a saucepan.

3. **Heat Water**: Place the saucepan on the stove over medium heat. Bring the water to a gentle boil.

4. **Add Clover**: Once the water reaches a boil, add the clover flowers directly to the saucepan.

5. **Steep**: Reduce heat to low and cover the saucepan. Allow the mixture to steep for 10-15 minutes, releasing the clover's beneficial properties.

6. **Strain Tea**: After steeping, remove the saucepan from heat. Use a strainer to separate the clover flowers from the liquid, pouring the tea into a teapot or heatproof container.

7. **Sweeten (Optional)**: If desired, add honey or your preferred sweetener to taste. Stir until dissolved.

8. **Serve**: Pour the clover tea into cups and enjoy warm. Alternatively, chill the tea for a refreshing cold beverage.

Maintenance:

- **Weekly**: If harvesting clover regularly, ensure you only take flowers from abundant areas to promote sustainable foraging. Refrain from over-harvesting.

- **Monthly**: If storing dried clover flowers, check the storage container for moisture. Keep in a cool, dry place to prevent mold growth.

- **Annually**: Reassess your foraging areas and ensure they remain free from pollutants. Rotate locations to allow clover populations to thrive.

Complexity:

The complexity of preparing clover tea is low. It requires basic skills such as foraging, boiling water, and straining tea. Challenges may include correctly identifying clover and ensuring it's free from contaminants. With proper knowledge, these challenges are easily overcome.

Estimated Time:

- **Harvesting**: 15-30 minutes, depending on availability and abundance of clover.

- **Preparation**: 20 minutes for boiling water and steeping.

- **Total time**: Approximately 35-50 minutes for the entire process, including harvesting and preparation.

4.5.7 WILD BERRY JAM

Wild berry jam is a delightful and versatile preserve made from foraged or homegrown berries, perfect for enhancing meals and snacks. This recipe emphasizes the importance of utilizing natural resources, particularly for those living off-grid or practicing DIY sustainability. Making wild berry jam allows you to reduce food waste by transforming excess berries into a long-lasting product. This jam not only preserves the vibrant flavors of summer but also provides a rich source of vitamins and antioxidants, contributing to a healthier diet. By creating your own wild berry jam, you gain control over ingredients, avoiding preservatives and added sugars often found in store-bought versions. This project empowers you to embrace self-sufficiency while enjoying the fruits of your labor, making it a valuable addition to any off-grid lifestyle.

Materials and Tools:

- Fresh wild berries (strawberries, blueberries, raspberries, or blackberries) - 4 cups

- Granulated sugar - 2 cups

- Lemon juice - ¼ cup

- Pectin (powdered or liquid) - 1 box (1.75 oz for powdered or 1 cup for liquid)

- Canning jars with lids - 4 jars (8 oz each)

- Large pot - 1 unit (at least 8 quarts)

- Wooden spoon - 1 unit

- Ladle - 1 unit

- Jar lifter - 1 unit

- Canning funnel - 1 unit

- Food thermometer - 1 unit (optional)

- Clean cloths - 2 units

Step-by-Step Guide:

1. **Gather Berries**: Forage or purchase 4 cups of fresh wild berries, ensuring they are ripe and free of mold or damage.

2. **Prepare Jars**: Wash 4 canning jars and lids in hot, soapy water. Rinse thoroughly and place them in a large pot of boiling water for 10 minutes to sterilize.

3. **Mash Berries**: In a large pot, add the berries and mash them lightly with a wooden spoon to release juices. Aim for a chunky consistency, leaving some whole berries for texture.

4. **Add Ingredients**: Stir in 2 cups of granulated sugar and ¼ cup of lemon juice. Mix well until the sugar dissolves.

5. **Incorporate Pectin**: Follow the instructions on your pectin package. If using powdered pectin, stir it into the berry mixture and allow it to sit for 10 minutes. For liquid pectin, add it after the mixture reaches a rolling boil.

6. **Cook Mixture**: Place the pot on medium heat and bring the mixture to a rolling boil. Stir constantly to prevent sticking, allowing it to boil for 1-2 minutes until it thickens.

7. **Test Consistency**: If using a food thermometer, check that the mixture reaches 220°F (104°C) for proper jelling. If not, use the spoon test: dip a spoon into the jam; if it coats the back and drips slowly, it's ready.

8. **Fill Jars**: Remove sterilized jars from boiling water. Use a canning funnel to ladle the hot jam into the jars, leaving ¼ inch of headspace at the top.

9. **Seal Jars**: Wipe the rims of the jars with a clean cloth to remove any residue. Place the sterilized lids on top and screw on the metal bands until fingertip-tight.

10. **Process Jars**: Place the filled jars back into the pot of boiling water. Ensure the water covers the jars by at least an inch. Boil for 10-15 minutes to seal.

11. **Cool Jars**: Remove jars from boiling water using a jar lifter and place them on a clean towel or cooling rack. Allow them to cool completely for 12-24 hours.

12. **Check Seals**: After cooling, check that the jars are sealed by pressing down on the center of each lid. If it pops back, the jar is not sealed and should be refrigerated and consumed within a week.

Maintenance:

- **Monthly**: Inspect stored jars for signs of spoilage or leakage. If any jars are compromised, discard them immediately.

- **Yearly**: Reassess the storage conditions, ensuring jars are kept in a cool, dark place. Consume jams within one year for optimal flavor and quality.

Complexity:

This project rates as moderate in complexity. Basic cooking skills and attention to detail are necessary for successful preservation. Challenges may include ensuring proper sealing of jars and achieving the correct consistency in the jam.

Estimated Time:

- **Preparation**: 30 minutes for gathering and preparing ingredients.

- **Cooking**: 20-30 minutes for cooking and thickening the jam.

- **Canning**: 30 minutes for filling, sealing, and processing the jars.

- **Total time**: Approximately 1.5 to 2 hours for the entire process.

4.6 SMALL-SCALE LIVESTOCK FARMING: CHICKENS, RABBITS, FISH

Raising small animals for meat and eggs is a fundamental step towards achieving self-sufficiency and resilience in a no-grid lifestyle. Chickens, rabbits, and fish are among the most manageable and rewarding livestock to keep, providing a sustainable source of protein and nutrients. Each of these animals requires different care and facilities, but with a basic understanding and commitment, even beginners can succeed in nurturing these valuable resources.

Chickens are often the first choice for homesteaders due to their dual-purpose nature, offering both eggs and meat. Starting with a small flock requires minimal investment in housing and feed. A secure coop protects chickens from predators and the elements, while allowing them space to roam reduces feed costs and improves their health through natural foraging. Learning to manage a flock includes routine tasks such as feeding, watering, collecting eggs, and monitoring for health issues. Chickens also contribute to a homestead's ecosystem by providing manure for compost and controlling pests.

Rabbits are another excellent option for meat production, known for their rapid reproduction rate and efficient feed conversion. Housing can be as simple as well-ventilated hutches that protect them from weather and predators. Rabbits are quiet, clean, and require less space than most livestock, making them suitable for smaller properties. Their diet consists of hay, commercial pellets, and vegetable scraps. Breeding rabbits is a straightforward process that can significantly increase your self-reliance for meat production.

Fish farming, or aquaculture, introduces an aquatic component to your homestead, offering a continuous protein source. Systems can range from simple backyard ponds to more complex aquaponics setups that integrate fish farming with plant cultivation. Tilapia and catfish are popular choices due to their hardiness and growth rate. Fish farming requires knowledge of water quality management, feeding, and disease control. The benefits extend beyond food production, as fish waste provides an excellent fertilizer for garden plants in integrated systems.

Starting with any of these livestock options brings you closer to a sustainable lifestyle, reducing your reliance on commercial food sources. Success hinges on research, preparation, and a willingness to learn from experience. Local agricultural extensions, experienced homesteaders, and reputable online forums are invaluable resources for troubleshooting and advice. As you gain confidence and skills, you may find these small-scale farming activities not only contribute to your household's nutrition but also bring a profound sense of satisfaction and connection to the cycles of life and nature. Engaging with these practices encourages a deeper understanding of the responsibilities and joys of no-grid living, reinforcing the importance of stewardship, patience, and hard work.

4.6.1 SMALL-SCALE LIVESTOCK FARMING: CHICKENS

Small-scale livestock farming, particularly raising chickens, plays a crucial role in off-grid living and DIY sustainability. Chickens provide a reliable source of protein through both meat and eggs, making them an invaluable addition to any homestead. This project enables individuals to take control of their food supply, reducing dependence on commercial agriculture while enhancing self-sufficiency. Beyond nutrition, chickens contribute to soil health by producing manure that enriches compost, promoting a sustainable cycle of nutrient recycling. The joy of raising chickens extends to their engaging behaviors and the benefits they bring to garden pest management. With minimal space requirements and a relatively low startup cost, anyone can embark on this rewarding venture.

Materials and Tools:

- Chicken coop or portable chicken tractor - 1 unit (size varies based on flock size)

- Chicken feed (starter, grower, or layer) - 50 pounds

- Waterer (5-gallon capacity) - 1 unit

- Feeder (adjustable height) - 1 unit

- Nesting boxes (1 box per 3-4 hens) - Quantity as needed
- Bedding material (straw, wood shavings, or shredded paper) - 2 bales or bags
- Wire mesh (hardware cloth, 1/2 inch) - 25 feet
- Lumber for coop construction (2x4s, plywood) - Quantity varies
- Hinges and latches for doors - Quantity as needed
- Drill with drill bits - 1 unit
- Saw (hand saw or power saw) - 1 unit
- Hammer - 1 unit
- Measuring tape - 1 unit
- Safety gloves - 1 pair

Step-by-Step Guide:

1. **Choose a Location**: Select a well-drained, sunny spot in the yard for the chicken coop, away from strong winds and predators.

2. **Design the Coop**: Plan the coop's dimensions based on the number of chickens. Allow 4 square feet per bird for adequate space inside the coop.

3. **Gather Materials**: Acquire all materials listed above, ensuring quality for durability and safety.

4. **Build the Frame**: Cut lumber into pieces according to the coop design, using 2x4s for the frame. Assemble the base and walls using screws for strength.

5. **Attach the Roof**: Secure plywood to the top of the coop to create a weatherproof roof. Ensure it overhangs to prevent rain from entering.

6. **Install Nesting Boxes**: Build or purchase nesting boxes and mount them inside the coop, ideally 18 inches off the ground for easy access.

7. **Create Ventilation**: Cut ventilation holes in the upper sides of the coop, covering them with wire mesh to allow airflow while keeping predators out.

8. **Install the Door**: Cut a door opening and attach it with hinges. Secure it with a latch to ensure it closes tightly.

9. **Add Bedding**: Layer 2-3 inches of bedding material on the floor of the coop to absorb moisture and provide comfort for the chickens.

10. **Set Up Feeders and Waterers**: Place the feeder and waterer inside the coop, ensuring they are easily accessible but elevated to prevent contamination.

11. **Introduce Chickens**: Once the coop is ready, introduce the chickens to their new home. Allow them time to explore and acclimate.

12. **Monitor Health**: Observe the chickens daily for signs of distress or illness. Provide fresh water and food daily.

13. **Collect Eggs**: Check nesting boxes daily for eggs, collecting them gently to prevent breakage.

14. **Rotate Pasture**: If using a portable chicken tractor, move it to fresh grass every few days to provide new foraging opportunities.

15. **Maintain Cleanliness**: Clean the coop weekly, removing soiled bedding and replacing it with fresh material to prevent odors and disease.

16. **Monitor Feed Levels**: Keep an eye on feed levels and replenish as necessary, ensuring chickens receive a balanced diet.

Maintenance:

- **Weekly**: Clean the coop by removing old bedding and replacing it with fresh material. Check the waterer and feeder for cleanliness and refill as needed.

- **Monthly**: Inspect the coop for wear and tear, tightening screws or replacing damaged parts. Check for pests and apply appropriate treatments if necessary.

- **Annually**: Deep clean the coop and conduct a thorough inspection to prepare for the next laying season. Repaint or treat the exterior if wood shows signs of wear.

Complexity:

The complexity of raising chickens is moderate, suitable for individuals with basic DIY skills. Key challenges include constructing a predator-proof coop and managing the flock's health and wellbeing. Regular monitoring and maintenance ensure success, as do proper feeding and care practices.

Estimated Time:

- **Setup**: 4-6 hours for constructing the coop and setting up the necessary equipment.

- **Ongoing maintenance**: 15-30 minutes daily for feeding, watering, and collecting eggs.

- **Deep cleaning and annual maintenance**: 1-2 hours once a year to ensure the coop remains in good condition.

4.6.2 SMALL-SCALE LIVESTOCK FARMING: RABBITS

Small-scale livestock farming with rabbits provides a sustainable and efficient means of food production, particularly valuable for those pursuing off-grid living or DIY self-sufficiency. Raising rabbits offers multiple benefits, including a steady supply of lean meat, rich manure for gardening, and a low-cost source of fur. Their compact size makes them suitable for small spaces, whether in a backyard or on a larger homestead. Moreover, rabbits reproduce quickly, allowing for rapid population growth, which translates to increased meat production in a short period. This project emphasizes the importance of self-reliance, ecological balance, and resourcefulness. By engaging in rabbit farming, individuals contribute to their food security while practicing responsible animal husbandry.

Materials and Tools:

- Rabbit hutch (two compartments) - 1 unit (size: 4 feet long x 2 feet wide x 2 feet high)

- Wire mesh (1-inch squares) - 25 feet

- Plywood sheets (for flooring and walls) - 2 sheets (4 feet x 8 feet)

- Wooden pallets (for base support) - 2 units

- Rabbit feed (commercial pellets) - 50 pounds

- Waterer (automatic or gravity-fed) - 1 unit

- Feeder (hanging or ground) - 1 unit

- Bedding material (straw or wood shavings) - 2 bags (10 pounds each)

- Nesting boxes (for females) - 2 units

- Basic hand tools (screwdriver, hammer, saw, drill) - 1 set

- Measuring tape - 1 unit

- Safety gloves - 1 pair

Step-by-Step Guide:

1. **Select a Location**: Choose a shaded area in the yard that is well-drained and protected from strong winds and direct sunlight.

2. **Design the Hutch**: Sketch a design for the hutch with two compartments: one for the male and one for the female. Each compartment should be at least 2 feet by 2 feet.

3. **Gather Materials**: Collect all materials listed above, ensuring they are of high quality and suitable for outdoor use.

4. **Build the Base**: Use wooden pallets to create a sturdy base for the hutch. Position them to provide enough elevation for drainage and ventilation.

5. **Construct the Hutch Walls**: Cut plywood sheets to fit the sides and back of the hutch. Attach them to the base using screws for stability.

6. **Add Wire Mesh**: Cut the wire mesh to cover the front of the hutch and any ventilation holes. Secure it with staples or screws, ensuring there are no sharp edges.

7. **Install the Roof**: Use a plywood sheet to create a roof, sloping it slightly for rain runoff. Attach it securely to the hutch walls.

8. **Create Compartments**: Divide the hutch into two sections using additional plywood, allowing each rabbit to have its own space.

9. **Install Nesting Boxes**: Place nesting boxes inside the female's compartment, ideally 12 inches off the ground for easy access.

10. **Set Up Feeders and Waterers**: Position the feeder and waterer in each compartment, ensuring they are accessible but elevated to avoid contamination.

11. **Add Bedding**: Layer 2-3 inches of bedding material in each compartment for comfort and to absorb waste.

12. **Introduce Rabbits**: After completing the hutch, introduce the rabbits to their new home. Allow them time to adjust and explore.

13. **Monitor Health**: Observe the rabbits daily for signs of distress or illness. Ensure they have fresh water and food available at all times.

14. **Breeding Considerations**: If breeding, introduce the male and female during the appropriate season. Monitor the female for signs of pregnancy.

15. **Maintain Cleanliness**: Clean the hutch weekly, removing soiled bedding and replacing it with fresh material to maintain a healthy environment.

Maintenance:

- **Weekly**: Clean the hutch by removing old bedding and replacing it with fresh bedding. Check water levels in the waterer and refill as necessary.

- **Monthly**: Inspect the hutch for wear and tear, tightening screws or replacing damaged parts. Assess the rabbits' health, adjusting their diet if necessary.

- **Annually**: Conduct a deep clean of the hutch, disinfecting surfaces to prevent disease. Check for any signs of pests and apply treatments as needed.

Complexity:

The complexity of raising rabbits is low to moderate, suitable for individuals with basic construction skills. Challenges may include ensuring proper ventilation in the hutch and managing the rabbits' health. With regular monitoring and care, these challenges are manageable.

Estimated Time:

- **Setup**: 4-5 hours for constructing the hutch and setting up the necessary equipment.

- **Ongoing maintenance**: 15-30 minutes daily for feeding, watering, and checking on the rabbits.

- **Deep cleaning and annual maintenance**: 1-2 hours once a year to ensure the hutch remains in good condition.

4.6.3 SMALL-SCALE LIVESTOCK FARMING: FISH

Small-scale fish farming, or aquaculture, offers a sustainable and efficient way to produce protein, especially for those living off the grid or pursuing self-sufficiency. Integrating fish farming with gardening systems, such as hydroponics, creates a symbiotic environment where fish waste nourishes plants, and plants help purify the water for fish. This project guide focuses on establishing a small-scale fish farming system that can be managed independently, providing a steady food source while minimizing reliance on external resources. Fish farming is particularly advantageous due to its space efficiency, making it suitable for various scales of operation, from backyard ponds to larger homestead setups. The guide emphasizes resourcefulness, ecological balance, and the importance of self-reliance.

Materials and Tools:

- Fish tank or pond liner (minimum 300 gallons) - 1 unit

- Water pump (appropriate for tank size) - 1 unit

- Aerator or air pump (sized for tank capacity) - 1 unit

- Filtration system (mechanical and biological filter) - 1 unit

- Fish feed (commercial pellets or flakes) - 50 pounds

- Fish species (e.g., tilapia, catfish, or trout) - 50-100 fingerlings

- PVC pipes (1-inch diameter) - 20 feet

- Netting or cover (to prevent fish jumping and debris) - 1 unit

- Water testing kit (pH, ammonia, nitrites, nitrates) - 1 unit

- Thermometer (submersible) - 1 unit

- Measuring tape - 1 unit

- Basic hand tools (screwdriver, pliers, saw) - 1 set

- Safety gloves - 1 pair

Step-by-Step Guide:

1. **Select a Location**: Choose a well-drained, shaded area for your fish tank or pond that is protected from direct sunlight and extreme weather conditions.

2. **Prepare the Tank or Pond**: If using a tank, place it on a level surface. For a pond, dig a hole and line it with the pond liner, ensuring there are no wrinkles. Install the filtration system according to the manufacturer's instructions.

3. **Install the Aeration System**: Place the aerator or air pump in the tank or pond to ensure proper oxygenation. This is crucial for the health of the fish.

4. **Set Up the Filtration System**: Connect the water pump to the filtration system using PVC pipes. Ensure the filter is correctly installed to handle both mechanical debris and biological waste.

5. **Fill the Tank or Pond**: Fill the tank or pond with water, ensuring it is free from chlorine and other harmful chemicals. If using tap water, let it sit for 24-48 hours or use a dechlorinator.

6. **Test Water Quality**: Use the water testing kit to check pH levels, ammonia, nitrite, and nitrate levels. Adjust as necessary to create a safe environment for the fish.

7. **Introduce Fish**: Acclimate the fish to the water temperature by floating the bag of fish in the tank or pond for 15-30 minutes. Gradually release the fish into their new environment.

8. **Set Up Feeding Routine**: Feed the fish twice daily with commercial fish feed, adjusting the amount according to the number of fish and their size. Avoid overfeeding to prevent water quality issues.

9. **Monitor Fish Health**: Regularly observe the fish for signs of illness or distress. Check water temperature and quality daily to ensure optimal conditions.

10. **Maintain the System**: Clean the filtration system weekly and replace any worn or damaged parts. Check the aerator and water pump for functionality.

11. **Harvesting Fish**: Once the fish reach maturity, begin harvesting as needed. Use a net to catch the fish, and ensure the remaining population has enough space and resources to continue growing.

Maintenance:

- **Daily**: Check water quality, temperature, and fish health. Feed the fish and remove any uneaten food to prevent water contamination.

- **Weekly**: Clean the filtration system, check the aerator and pump, and ensure all equipment is functioning correctly.

- **Monthly**: Test water quality more comprehensively, checking for any changes in pH, ammonia, nitrites, and nitrates. Adjust the system as needed.

Complexity:

The complexity of fish farming is moderate to high, depending on the scale of the operation and the species of fish being farmed. Challenges include maintaining water quality, ensuring adequate oxygenation, and managing the health of the fish population. With regular monitoring and proper system maintenance, these challenges can be effectively managed.

Estimated Time:

- **Setup**: 6-8 hours for constructing the tank or pond, setting up the filtration and aeration systems, and preparing the water for the fish.

- **Ongoing maintenance**: 30-60 minutes daily for feeding, water quality checks, and system maintenance.

- **Harvesting and annual maintenance**: 2-3 hours for harvesting fish, deep cleaning the system, and making any necessary repairs or upgrades.

4.7 DIY FOOD STORAGE SOLUTIONS

Creating effective DIY food storage systems such as root cellars, pantries, and shelves is a cornerstone of maintaining a sustainable, no-grid lifestyle. These systems enable you to store the bounty of your garden, foraged goods, and bulk purchases, ensuring a steady supply of food throughout the year, especially during lean months.

Root cellars are an age-old solution for storing fruits and vegetables in a cool, dark, humid environment where they remain fresh for much longer than at room temperature. Constructing a root cellar can be as simple as burying a new, clean trash can in a shaded area of your yard or as complex as excavating a portion of your property to create a large underground storage space. The key is maintaining the right conditions: a temperature just above freezing and humidity levels between 80-95%. This can be achieved by ensuring proper insulation and ventilation to regulate temperature and moisture.

Pantries provide a different kind of food storage solution, one that's more accessible on a day-to-day basis. A well-organized pantry can store not only canned goods and dried foods but also grains, spices, and other non-perishables. When setting up a pantry, consider the space's temperature and light exposure. Keep it cool, dry, and dark to prolong the shelf life of your stored foods. Use shelving units to maximize space, and organize items so that older stock is used first. Clear, airtight containers can help keep pests out and make it easy to see what you have on hand.

Shelves, whether in a pantry, kitchen, or cellar, are critical for maximizing storage space and keeping things organized. They can be custom-built to fit specific areas or repurposed from other furniture pieces. When designing shelves, consider the weight of the items you'll be storing and ensure that the materials and supports you use are sturdy enough to hold them safely. Adjustable shelving can be particularly useful, allowing you to change the spacing between shelves as your storage needs evolve.

Incorporating these DIY food storage systems into your home doesn't require expert carpentry skills or a large budget. With some basic tools, materials, and a willingness to learn, you can create efficient, durable solutions that support your self-sufficient lifestyle. Remember, the goal is to create a system that works for your specific needs, taking into account the types of foods you're storing, the climate you live in, and the space you have available. By investing the time and effort into building these systems, you'll ensure that your hard-earned harvests, foraged finds, and bulk purchases provide nourishment and enjoyment for months to come, reinforcing your independence and resilience.

4.7.1 BUILDING A ROOT CELLAR OR UNDERGROUND STORAGE

Building a root cellar, or underground storage, serves as an essential project for anyone seeking to enhance self-sufficiency, particularly in off-grid living scenarios. This underground space allows individuals to store vegetables, fruits, and other perishables in a controlled environment, significantly extending their shelf life. Root cellars utilize the earth's natural insulation, maintaining cooler temperatures and higher humidity levels than above-ground storage. This natural method of preservation is crucial for reducing food waste and ensuring a reliable food supply throughout the year. By investing in a root cellar, individuals can harvest their crops in bulk and store them, promoting a sustainable lifestyle and minimizing reliance on external sources. The project's scope includes constructing a structure that is durable, insulated, and properly ventilated to foster ideal storage conditions. This guide details every aspect of building a root cellar, empowering readers to create their own effective underground storage solution.

Materials and Tools:

- Shovels - 2 units

- Pickaxe - 1 unit

- Level - 1 unit

- Tape measure - 1 unit

- Wood (2x4 inches) - 10 units, 8 feet long

- Plywood (3/4 inch thick) - 2 sheets, 4x8 feet

- Concrete blocks - 30 units

- Gravel - 1 cubic yard

- Insulation board (polystyrene) - 2 sheets, 4x8 feet

- Hinges - 2 units

- Latch - 1 unit

- Door handle - 1 unit

- Waterproof sealant - 1 quart

- Roofing material (metal or shingles) - As needed

- Ventilation pipe (4 inches diameter) - 2 units, 5 feet long

- Tarps - 2 units, 10x12 feet

- Safety goggles - 1 pair

- Work gloves - 1 pair

- Dust mask - 1 unit

Step-by-Step Guide:

1. **Select Location**: Choose a shaded area on your property with well-drained soil and minimal tree roots, ideally near your garden.

2. **Mark Dimensions**: Use a tape measure to mark a rectangular area measuring 8 feet by 10 feet for the root cellar's footprint.

3. **Excavate Site**: Use shovels and a pickaxe to dig down 4-5 feet deep within the marked area. Ensure the sides are as vertical as possible to prevent cave-ins.

4. **Level the Base**: Use a level to ensure the bottom of the excavation is flat. This creates a stable foundation for the walls.

5. **Lay Concrete Blocks**: Begin stacking concrete blocks along the perimeter of the excavated area, creating a wall that is 2 blocks high. Ensure each block is level before placing the next.

6. **Install Insulation**: Cut the insulation board to fit snugly between the concrete blocks, placing it on the inner walls to maintain temperature control.

7. **Construct the Roof Frame**: Build a frame using 2x4 wood, creating a rectangular shape that matches the dimensions of the root cellar. The frame should be sturdy enough to support the weight of the roof material.

8. **Attach Plywood**: Secure plywood sheets to the top of the frame using screws, creating a solid roof. This will help keep moisture out and provide structural integrity.

9. **Add Ventilation Pipes**: Cut holes in the roof and sides of the cellar to insert ventilation pipes. Ensure that one pipe leads outside and another remains inside to promote airflow.

10. **Seal Gaps**: Apply waterproof sealant around the edges of the plywood roof and between the concrete blocks to prevent moisture infiltration.

11. **Construct the Door**: Create a door frame using 2x4 wood, then attach plywood to the frame. Secure hinges to one side and a latch on the opposite side for easy access.

12. **Cover with Soil**: Once the structure is complete, carefully cover the roof with a layer of soil, creating a mound to encourage drainage away from the cellar.

13. **Install Drainage**: Dig a small trench around the cellar to direct water away from the structure. Fill this trench with gravel to promote drainage.

14. **Add Final Touches**: Place tarps over the soil mound for added insulation during colder months. Ensure that the ventilation pipes are unobstructed.

Maintenance:

- **Monthly**: Check the door seal for any signs of wear and ensure the latch functions correctly. Inspect the ventilation pipes for blockages.

- **Seasonally**: Monitor the internal conditions of the root cellar, ensuring it remains cool and dry. Remove any spoiled produce promptly to prevent rot.

- **Annually**: Evaluate the structural integrity of the root cellar, checking for any cracks in the walls or roof. Repair any issues with waterproof sealant as necessary.

Complexity:

The complexity of building a root cellar is moderate. It requires basic construction skills, including measuring, cutting, and leveling. Challenges may arise during excavation or if encountering rocky soil. Ensuring proper ventilation is critical to prevent mold growth, which requires attention to detail.

Estimated Time:

- **Preparation and Planning**: 2 hours for site selection and material gathering.
- **Excavation**: 4-6 hours, depending on soil conditions.
- **Construction**: 8-10 hours to build walls, roof, and door.
- **Finishing Touches**: 2 hours for sealing and covering.
- **Total Estimated Time**: 16-20 hours spread over a weekend or two days, depending on individual pacing and experience level.

4.7.2 PANTRY ORGANIZATION SYSTEM

Creating a pantry organization system transforms chaos into order, ensuring easy access to essential food supplies. This project is crucial for individuals living off-grid or pursuing a DIY lifestyle, where self-sufficiency and efficient food storage are paramount. An organized pantry not only maximizes space but also enhances food preservation, reduces waste, and streamlines meal preparation. By categorizing items and implementing storage solutions, individuals can easily locate ingredients, manage inventory, and minimize the risk of spoilage. This guide provides a comprehensive approach to designing and building a functional pantry organization system that meets the unique needs of off-grid living.

Materials and Tools:

- Wooden shelving units - 2 units, 4 feet high, 3 feet wide
- Clear plastic bins - 8 units, 12 quarts
- Labels - 1 pack, waterproof
- Marker - 1 unit, permanent
- Storage jars (glass or plastic) - 10 units, various sizes
- Measuring tape - 1 unit
- Level - 1 unit
- Screwdriver - 1 unit
- Wall anchors - 10 units (if mounting shelves)
- Bungee cords - 2 units (for securing loose items)
- Hooks - 6 units (for hanging utensils or tools)

Step-by-Step Guide:

1. **Assess Pantry Space**: Measure the dimensions of the pantry area using a measuring tape, noting the height, width, and depth.
2. **Select Shelving Units**: Choose two wooden shelving units that fit comfortably within the pantry space, allowing room for additional items on the floor if necessary.
3. **Install Shelves**: If mounting the shelving units to the wall, use a level to ensure they are straight, and secure with wall anchors for stability.

4. **Sort Food Items**: Categorize pantry items into groups such as grains, canned goods, snacks, and spices. This streamlines the organization process.

5. **Choose Bins**: Select eight clear plastic bins to store grouped items. This aids in visibility and access, allowing quick identification of contents.

6. **Label Bins**: Using waterproof labels and a permanent marker, label each bin according to its contents, such as "Pasta," "Canned Vegetables," and "Snacks."

7. **Store Jars**: Fill ten storage jars with bulk items like rice, beans, and flour. Ensure the jars are clean and dry before adding food to prevent moisture buildup.

8. **Arrange Items on Shelves**: Place the labeled bins and jars on the shelving units, arranging them by category for easy access. Keep frequently used items at eye level.

9. **Utilize Hooks**: Install six hooks on the pantry door or side walls to hang utensils, measuring cups, or small tools, maximizing vertical space.

10. **Secure Loose Items**: Use bungee cords to secure any loose items on the shelves, preventing them from tipping over during pantry access.

11. **Conduct a Final Check**: Review the entire setup to ensure everything is accessible, well-organized, and stable. Make adjustments as needed for optimal flow.

Maintenance:

- **Monthly**: Inspect the pantry for expired items and remove them promptly. Reorganize as necessary to maintain efficiency.

- **Seasonally**: Evaluate the overall organization system. Consider any changes in food inventory and adjust bin categories or shelf placements accordingly.

- **Annually**: Conduct a thorough cleanout of the pantry, checking for pest issues, and sanitizing surfaces. Replace any damaged bins or jars to maintain integrity.

Complexity:

The complexity of creating a pantry organization system is low to moderate. Basic skills in measuring, sorting, and labeling are sufficient. Challenges may arise in maximizing space, especially in smaller pantries, but these can be managed with creative solutions and adaptability.

Estimated Time:

- **Assessment and Planning**: 1 hour for measuring and categorizing items.

- **Installation of Shelves**: 2 hours, including wall mounting if necessary.

- **Sorting and Organizing**: 2 hours for sorting food items and labeling bins.

- **Final Setup**: 1 hour for arranging items and conducting a final check.

- **Total Estimated Time**: 6 hours, which can be spread over a day or two, depending on individual pacing and pantry size.

4.7.3 DIY SHELVING UNITS

Building DIY shelving units is a fundamental project that enhances storage capacity and organization in any space, particularly in off-grid living environments. These units provide practical solutions for maximizing vertical space, accommodating a variety of items from pantry supplies to tools. The significance of this project lies in its ability to create customized storage solutions tailored to specific needs, promoting efficient use of resources and space. With limited access to commercial products, constructing shelving units becomes an essential skill for those seeking self-sufficiency. This project aims to guide individuals through the process of designing and building sturdy shelving units that will not only improve organization but also withstand the rigors of an off-grid lifestyle.

Materials and Tools:

- Plywood sheets (¾ inch thick) - 2 units, 4 feet x 8 feet
- 2x4 lumber - 6 units, 8 feet long
- Wood screws (3 inches) - 1 box, 100 count
- Wood glue - 1 bottle, 8 ounces
- Sandpaper (medium and fine grit) - 1 pack, assorted
- Paint or wood stain (optional) - 1 quart
- Drill with drill bits - 1 unit
- Circular saw or table saw - 1 unit
- Measuring tape - 1 unit
- Level - 1 unit
- Square - 1 unit
- Safety goggles - 1 pair
- Work gloves - 1 pair

Step-by-Step Guide:

1. **Measure and Plan**: Determine the desired dimensions for the shelving unit, ensuring it fits the intended space.
2. **Cut Plywood**: Using a circular saw, cut the plywood sheets into shelves measuring 3 feet x 1.5 feet. Aim for four shelves.
3. **Cut 2x4s**: Cut six 2x4 pieces to a length of 6 feet each for vertical supports and six additional pieces to 3 feet for horizontal supports.
4. **Assemble Frame**: Create a rectangular frame for the base using four 2x4s. Secure the corners with wood screws, ensuring they are flush.
5. **Attach Vertical Supports**: Position two vertical 2x4s at each corner of the frame and secure them with wood screws. Ensure they are vertical using a level.
6. **Install Horizontal Supports**: Attach two horizontal 2x4s between the vertical supports at the desired height for the shelves. Use a square to ensure corners are right angles.
7. **Repeat for Upper Levels**: Repeat the process to build upper levels of the shelving unit, spacing the horizontal supports evenly for shelf placement.
8. **Secure Shelves**: Place the cut plywood shelves on top of the horizontal supports. Secure each shelf with wood screws through the top into the supports.
9. **Sand Surfaces**: Smooth all edges and surfaces of the shelving unit using medium and fine-grit sandpaper to prevent splinters.
10. **Finish with Paint/Stain**: (Optional) Apply paint or wood stain to the shelving unit for protection and aesthetics. Allow to dry completely.
11. **Check Stability**: After assembly, ensure the unit is stable and level. Make adjustments as necessary for a secure fit.

Maintenance:

- **Monthly**: Inspect the shelving unit for any signs of warping or loosening screws. Tighten screws as necessary to maintain stability.

- **Yearly**: Re-sand and re-stain or repaint the shelves if wear becomes evident. This protects the wood and extends the life of the shelving unit.

Complexity:

The complexity of building DIY shelving units is moderate. Basic woodworking skills are required, including measuring, cutting, and assembly techniques. Challenges may arise in ensuring accurate measurements and stable construction, but these can be managed with careful planning and attention to detail.

Estimated Time:

- **Planning and Measuring**: 1 hour for measuring and designing the shelving unit.

- **Cutting Materials**: 2 hours to cut plywood and lumber to the specified dimensions.

- **Assembly**: 2-3 hours to construct the frame, attach supports, and secure shelves.

- **Sanding and Finishing**: 1 hour for sanding surfaces and applying paint or stain.

- **Total Estimated Time**: 6-7 hours, allowing flexibility for individual pacing and skill level.

5. First Aid, Hygiene and Health

5.1 Introduction

Basic first aid and wound care are fundamental skills that everyone stepping into a no-grid lifestyle must have. Knowing how to properly clean a cut, bandage a wound, or even set a splint can make a significant difference in an emergency situation. The essentials of a first aid kit should include sterile gauze, adhesive bandages of various sizes, antiseptic wipes or solutions, medical tape, scissors, tweezers, and pain relievers. Familiarize yourself with the use of each item and keep your kit easily accessible and regularly replenished.

Natural remedies and herbalism offer a sustainable complement to your first aid kit, utilizing plants and herbs that can be foraged or grown in your own garden. Many common ailments, such as headaches, digestive issues, and skin irritations, can be effectively managed with natural remedies. For instance, willow bark contains salicin, a compound similar to aspirin, and can be used to relieve pain and reduce fever. Lavender, known for its calming properties, can be applied to help with sleep or alleviate stress. It's important, however, to approach herbalism with caution, ensuring proper identification and understanding of each plant's uses and potential side effects.

Creating a no-grid medical kit extends beyond the basics, incorporating affordable supplies that can address a wider range of health issues. Items such as a manual blood pressure cuff, stethoscope, and basic dental repair kits can be invaluable in situations where professional medical care is not immediately available. Training in basic medical procedures, such as suturing wounds or identifying signs of infection, can further enhance your preparedness.

DIY sanitation and hygiene systems are critical for maintaining health off the grid. A composting toilet, for example, offers a sustainable solution to waste management, converting human waste into compost that can be used to enrich soil. Handwashing stations, easily constructed using repurposed containers and simple pumps, promote cleanliness and help prevent the spread of disease. Greywater recycling systems, which reuse water from sinks and showers for irrigation, can significantly reduce water consumption and minimize waste.

Mental health and wellness are as important as physical health, especially in the potentially isolating environment of off-grid living. Practices such as mindfulness, meditation, and regular physical exercise can greatly contribute to emotional well-being. Establishing a routine that includes activities you enjoy, connecting with nature, and maintaining social contacts, even in a limited form, can help mitigate feelings of isolation or stress.

DIY homemade soap and toothpaste not only reduce reliance on commercial products but also allow for customization to suit personal preferences and avoid harmful chemicals. Soap can be made using basic ingredients like lye, water, and fats or oils, with options to add natural scents or exfoliants. Toothpaste recipes often include baking soda, coconut oil, and essential oils, providing an effective and natural alternative to store-bought versions.

In adopting these practices, it's crucial to approach with a willingness to learn and adapt. Start small, focusing on one or two skills or projects at a time, and gradually build your knowledge and capabilities. Remember, self-sufficiency is a journey, not a destination, and every step you take towards independence and resilience not only enhances your own life but also contributes to a stronger, more sustainable community.

5.2 Basic First Aid and Wound Care Techniques

Basic first aid and wound care techniques are essential skills for anyone, especially for those living a no-grid lifestyle where medical help may not be immediately accessible. The first step in managing minor injuries, such as cuts and scrapes, is to ensure that the area around the wound is clean. Use clean water to gently wash the skin around the injury. Avoid getting soap directly in the wound to prevent irritation. For a deeper cut or scrape, running water can help to remove debris and bacteria from inside the wound itself.

After cleaning, stopping the bleeding is the next priority. Gentle pressure with a clean cloth or sterile gauze for a few minutes should suffice for minor wounds. Elevating the injured area above the heart can also help slow bleeding. It's important not to remove the cloth or gauze to check if the bleeding has stopped as this could disrupt the clotting process. If the bleeding doesn't stop, continue applying pressure and seek medical attention if necessary.

Once the bleeding has ceased, applying an antibiotic ointment can help prevent infection. Then, cover the wound with a sterile bandage or gauze and adhesive tape. This dressing should be kept clean and dry, and changed daily to monitor the healing process and ensure that no infection develops. Signs of infection include increased pain, redness, swelling, or a pus-like discharge. If you notice any of these signs, it's important to seek medical advice.

For more significant injuries, such as deep cuts that may require stitches, immobilizing the affected area and seeking medical help immediately is crucial. While waiting for medical assistance, keep the wound clean and covered to reduce the risk of infection.

In the case of burns, the severity of the burn determines the care needed. For minor burns, running cool (not cold) water over the burn for several minutes can help alleviate pain and reduce damage. Covering the burn with a sterile, non-adhesive bandage or clean cloth can protect the burned skin. Avoid applying ice, butter, or other home remedies to burns as these can cause further damage.

Understanding how to recognize and treat shock is also vital. Symptoms of shock include pale, cold, clammy skin, rapid breathing or pulse, weakness, or dizziness. If someone is in shock, lay them down with their feet elevated and cover them with a blanket to keep them warm. Do not give them anything to eat or drink and seek medical help immediately.

Remember, the goal of first aid is to provide temporary assistance until professional medical treatment can be obtained. Regularly refreshing your knowledge of first aid techniques and keeping a well-stocked first aid kit are proactive steps you can take to ensure you're prepared for any situation. This not only helps in providing care when needed but also in maintaining a sense of calm and control during emergencies. Being prepared and knowing what to do can make all the difference in managing minor injuries and preventing them from becoming major issues.

5.2.1 BASIC FIRST AID KIT

Assembling a basic first aid kit is a fundamental project for anyone, especially those embracing off-grid living or DIY lifestyles. A well-stocked first aid kit empowers individuals to respond effectively to minor injuries, ailments, and emergencies, promoting self-sufficiency and peace of mind. In remote or wilderness settings, access to medical facilities can be limited, making the ability to provide immediate care crucial. This kit should address common injuries such as cuts, scrapes, burns, and allergic reactions. By preparing a first aid kit, individuals ensure they have the necessary tools and supplies on hand, allowing them to manage injuries promptly and confidently. Furthermore, a comprehensive kit can prevent minor issues from escalating into serious health concerns, fostering a safer living environment.

Materials and Tools:

- Durable container (plastic or metal) - 1 unit - medium-sized (12-18 quarts)
- Adhesive bandages (various sizes) - 30 units
- Sterile gauze pads (4x4 inches) - 10 units
- Adhesive tape (medical) - 1 roll
- Antiseptic wipes - 20 units
- Antibiotic ointment (e.g., Neosporin) - 1 tube - 1 ounce
- Hydrocortisone cream (1%) - 1 tube - 1 ounce
- Tweezers - 1 unit
- Scissors (blunt-tipped) - 1 unit

- Disposable gloves (nitrile or latex) - 10 units

- Instant cold packs - 2 units

- Pain relievers (e.g., ibuprofen, acetaminophen) - 1 bottle - 100 tablets

- Thermometer (digital) - 1 unit

- First aid manual or guide - 1 unit

- Elastic bandage (e.g., Ace bandage) - 1 unit - 3 inches wide

- Emergency blanket (space blanket) - 1 unit

- Safety pins - 10 units

- Alcohol pads - 20 units

- Oral rehydration salts - 1 packet

- Eye wash or saline solution - 1 bottle - 4 ounces

Step-by-Step Guide:

1. **Select a Container**: Choose a durable container that is medium-sized (12-18 quarts) to house all first aid supplies.

2. **Clean the Container**: Wipe the inside of the container with a disinfectant to ensure a sterile environment for the supplies.

3. **Gather Supplies**: Collect all materials listed above, ensuring you have the specified quantities and sizes.

4. **Organize Items**: Sort items into categories such as wound care, medications, and tools. Use small, resealable bags or dividers to keep items organized within the container.

5. **Place Wound Care Items**: In one section, place adhesive bandages, sterile gauze pads, adhesive tape, antiseptic wipes, and antibiotic ointment.

6. **Arrange Tools**: In another section, store tweezers, scissors, disposable gloves, and safety pins for easy access.

7. **Add Medications**: Allocate space for pain relievers, hydrocortisone cream, oral rehydration salts, and the thermometer.

8. **Include Cold and Heat Packs**: Place instant cold packs and the emergency blanket in a designated area to handle swelling or shock.

9. **Store Reference Material**: Keep the first aid manual or guide in the container for quick reference during emergencies.

10. **Seal the Container**: Close the container securely and label it clearly as "First Aid Kit" for easy identification.

11. **Check Supplies**: Regularly review the kit to ensure supplies are stocked and medications are not expired. Replace items as necessary.

12. **Maintain Cleanliness**: After each use, wipe down any used items and restock supplies to keep the kit in optimal condition.

Maintenance:

- **Monthly**: Inspect the first aid kit for expired medications or supplies and replace as necessary. Check that all items are in good condition, with no damage to packaging.

- **Annually**: Conduct a thorough inventory of the kit to ensure all necessary items are present. Refresh the antiseptic wipes, alcohol pads, and any perishable items.

Complexity:

The project is low in complexity, suitable for individuals of all skill levels. Basic organizational skills are necessary to sort and categorize supplies effectively. Knowledge of basic first aid principles enhances the kit's effectiveness and allows users to respond confidently to emergencies.

Estimated Time:

Setup: 1-2 hours to gather materials, clean the container, organize supplies, and label everything.

Ongoing maintenance: 15-30 minutes monthly for inspections and restocking.

Annual review: 1 hour for a comprehensive inventory and update of the kit.

5.2.2 BASIC WOUND CARE TECHNIQUES

Basic wound care techniques are essential skills for anyone, particularly those pursuing off-grid living or self-sufficiency. This project focuses on how to properly assess, clean, and dress various types of wounds, from minor cuts to abrasions. Understanding these techniques not only enhances personal safety but also fosters confidence in handling emergencies when professional medical help is not readily available. In remote settings, knowledge of wound care becomes critical; minor injuries can quickly escalate without proper attention. Mastering these techniques empowers individuals to provide immediate care, reduces the risk of infection, and promotes faster healing. The goal of this project is to equip readers with the fundamental skills and knowledge necessary to manage wounds effectively and safely.

Materials and Tools:

- Sterile gauze pads (various sizes) - 10 units
- Adhesive bandages (various sizes) - 30 units
- Antiseptic wipes - 20 units
- Antibiotic ointment (e.g., Neosporin) - 1 tube - 1 ounce
- Adhesive tape (medical) - 1 roll
- Disposable gloves (nitrile or latex) - 10 units
- Tweezers - 1 unit
- Scissors (blunt-tipped) - 1 unit
- Instant cold pack - 1 unit
- Pain relievers (e.g., ibuprofen, acetaminophen) - 1 bottle - 100 tablets
- First aid manual or guide - 1 unit

Step-by-Step Guide:

1. **Assess the Wound**: Examine the injury to determine its severity. Check for foreign objects, excessive bleeding, or signs of infection such as redness or swelling.

2. **Wash Hands**: Before any treatment, thoroughly wash hands with soap and water or use an alcohol-based hand sanitizer.

3. **Put on Gloves**: Wear disposable gloves to prevent contamination and protect yourself from potential infections.

4. **Stop Bleeding**: Apply direct pressure to the wound with a clean cloth or sterile gauze pad. If bleeding persists, elevate the wound above the heart.

5. **Clean the Wound**: Once bleeding stops, rinse the wound under clean, running water for 5-10 minutes. Avoid using soap directly in the wound to prevent irritation.

6. **Disinfect the Wound**: After cleaning, use an antiseptic wipe to gently clean around the wound, ensuring to cover the surrounding skin to reduce infection risk.

7. **Apply Antibiotic Ointment**: Use a clean applicator or your gloved finger to apply a thin layer of antibiotic ointment over the wound.

8. **Cover the Wound**: Choose an appropriate dressing, such as a sterile gauze pad or adhesive bandage. If using gauze, secure it with adhesive tape to keep it in place.

9. **Monitor for Infection**: Keep an eye on the wound over the next few days. Look for signs of increased redness, swelling, or pus. Change the dressing daily or whenever it becomes wet or dirty.

10. **Manage Pain and Swelling**: If necessary, take pain relievers as directed to manage discomfort. Apply an instant cold pack to reduce swelling if applicable.

11. **Remove Gloves**: Carefully remove and dispose of gloves after the procedure. Wash hands thoroughly again after removal.

12. **Document the Injury**: Record the date, time, and details of the injury and treatment in a first aid log for future reference.

Maintenance:

- **Daily**: Inspect the wound for signs of infection. Change the dressing as needed, especially if it becomes wet or soiled.

- **Weekly**: Evaluate the healing progress. Ensure that the wound is closing properly and no new symptoms arise.

- **Annually**: Review first aid supplies to restock any used items, especially gauze pads, bandages, and antiseptics. Refresh knowledge of basic wound care techniques through training or reading.

Complexity:

The complexity of basic wound care techniques is low, making it accessible to individuals of all skill levels. Key challenges include recognizing the severity of the wound and ensuring proper cleaning to prevent infection. Some prior knowledge of anatomy and infection signs enhances the effectiveness of care, but most techniques can be learned quickly through practice and instruction.

Estimated Time:

- **Initial assessment and treatment**: 15-30 minutes, depending on the wound's severity.

- **Ongoing monitoring**: 5-10 minutes daily to check the wound and change dressings.

- **Weekly evaluations**: 10-15 minutes to assess healing and adjust care as needed.

5.3 AFFORDABLE HERBAL REMEDIES

Turning to nature for healing and wellness, we find a wealth of resources in the plants and herbs that grow around us, many of which have been used for centuries to treat a variety of ailments. The beauty of using plants and herbs as natural remedies lies in their accessibility and affordability, making it possible for anyone to harness their healing properties with just a bit of knowledge and preparation.

Starting with some of the most common and easily identifiable plants, consider the dandelion. Often dismissed as a weed, every part of the dandelion has medicinal properties. The leaves are rich in vitamins and can be used to make a detoxifying tea, the roots can be dried and ground into a powder that supports liver function, and the flowers have antioxidant properties. Similarly, plantain, another ubiquitous plant, can be found in yards and along paths. Its leaves are excellent for soothing insect bites and skin irritations when crushed and applied topically.

Aloe vera is well-known for its skin-healing properties, particularly for burns and sunburns. Keeping an aloe plant in your home allows for the immediate application of its soothing gel to affected areas. For those dealing with regular stress or trouble sleeping, chamomile and lavender can be cultivated in a garden or pots. Both herbs are renowned for their calming and sleep-inducing effects, making them perfect for a relaxing tea before bed.

Peppermint is another versatile herb that's easy to grow and has a myriad of uses. A tea made from peppermint leaves can alleviate digestive issues, reduce headaches, and even soothe a sore throat. For respiratory issues, eucalyptus leaves can be steeped in hot water to create a steam inhalation treatment that helps clear congestion.

When cultivating your own medicinal garden, it's essential to remember that the quality of the soil and the absence of chemical pesticides or herbicides directly impact the potency and purity of your herbal remedies. Organic practices ensure that you're getting the full benefit of each plant's medicinal properties without harmful additives.

Harvesting your herbs and plants at the right time is also crucial for maximizing their healing potential. Generally, leaves are best harvested before the plant flowers when the concentration of beneficial oils is highest. Flowers should be picked just as they fully open, and roots are typically dug up in fall when the plant's energy has returned to the earth. Drying and storing your herbs properly—away from direct sunlight and in airtight containers—will preserve their potency for use throughout the year.

Incorporating these natural remedies into your daily life not only empowers you to take charge of your health in a more holistic way but also deepens your connection to the natural world. With a little effort and learning, you can transform common plants and herbs into powerful allies for your health and well-being. Remember, while herbal remedies can offer significant benefits, they should complement traditional medicine, especially in serious or chronic conditions. Always consult with a healthcare professional before starting any new treatment, particularly if you are pregnant, nursing, or taking prescription medications, to ensure it's safe and appropriate for your specific health needs.

5.3.1 YARROW WOUND POULTICE

Creating a yarrow wound poultice offers a natural, effective solution for treating minor cuts, scrapes, and bruises. Yarrow (Achillea millefolium) is a perennial herb known for its potent healing properties, particularly its ability to stop bleeding and promote tissue regeneration. This project not only fosters self-sufficiency by reducing reliance on commercial antiseptics and bandages but also connects you to traditional herbal practices. By preparing a yarrow poultice, you can access a readily available resource for first aid that minimizes chemical exposure and promotes healing through nature's own remedies.

Materials and Tools:

- Fresh yarrow leaves and flowers - 1 cup

- Mortar and pestle or food processor - 1 unit

- Clean cloth or gauze - 1 piece (approximately 6 inches x 6 inches)

- Water - As needed

- Sterile jar or container - 1 unit

- Tweezers (optional, for handling small plant parts) - 1 unit

- Knife (for cutting larger leaves, if necessary) - 1 unit

Step-by-Step Guide:

1. **Harvest Yarrow**: Identify yarrow plants in your area. Harvest fresh leaves and flowers, aiming for 1 cup in total. Use clean scissors or a knife to cut the stems, ensuring not to damage the plant.

2. **Wash the Plant Material**: Rinse the harvested yarrow under cool running water to remove dirt and debris. Pat dry gently with a clean cloth.

3. **Prepare the Poultice**: Using a mortar and pestle or a food processor, crush the yarrow leaves and flowers until they form a paste. This should take about 5-10 minutes. The goal is to release the plant's juices.

4. **Add Water**: If the mixture appears too dry, add a few drops of clean water to achieve a thicker, more spreadable consistency. Avoid making it too watery, as this will dilute the active compounds.

5. **Apply the Poultice**: Take a clean cloth or gauze and place a generous amount of the yarrow paste in the center. Fold the cloth over the mixture to create a poultice.

6. **Position the Poultice**: Gently place the poultice directly on the wound or affected area. Ensure it covers the entire area needing treatment.

7. **Secure the Poultice**: Use medical tape or another piece of cloth to secure the poultice in place, ensuring it stays put while providing maximum contact with the skin.

8. **Leave the Poultice On**: Allow the poultice to remain on the wound for 1-2 hours. Monitor the area for any signs of irritation or allergic reaction.

9. **Remove and Clean**: After the recommended time, carefully remove the poultice. Dispose of any leftover plant material and gently clean the wound with clean water.

10. **Store Remaining Poultice**: If there's any unused yarrow paste, store it in a sterile jar or container in the refrigerator for up to 24 hours. Discard any leftovers after this period.

Maintenance:

- **Weekly**: Check for any new injuries or wounds that may require treatment. Always use fresh yarrow for new poultices to ensure maximum effectiveness.

- **As Needed**: If using yarrow from a home garden, ensure the plants remain healthy by watering and weeding regularly. Avoid chemical pesticides to maintain the integrity of the herbal remedy.

Complexity:

The project is low in complexity and suitable for beginners. It requires basic skills such as harvesting plants and preparing a paste. Potential challenges include accurately identifying yarrow and ensuring that the plant material is fresh and uncontaminated.

Estimated Time:

- **Harvesting and preparing yarrow**: 15-20 minutes.

- **Applying the poultice**: 5 minutes.

- **Waiting time for the poultice to act**: 1-2 hours (not included in active working time).

- **Cleaning and disposing of materials**: 5 minutes.

5.3.2 PLANTAIN LEAF SALVE

Crafting a plantain leaf salve provides a natural remedy for skin irritations, minor cuts, and insect bites. Plantain (Plantago major) is a common herb with remarkable healing properties. Its leaves contain anti-inflammatory and antimicrobial compounds that soothe skin and promote healing. It reduces reliance on commercial ointments and fosters self-sufficiency. By harnessing the power of this readily available plant, you can create an effective solution for everyday skin issues, ensuring you are prepared for minor emergencies without reaching for synthetic alternatives.

Materials and Tools:

- Fresh plantain leaves - 2 cups (packed)

- Olive oil - 1 cup

- Beeswax - 1 ounce

- Double boiler or heatproof bowl - 1 unit

- Cheesecloth or fine strainer - 1 unit

- Glass jar with lid (4-ounce) - 1 unit

- Spoon (for stirring) - 1 unit

- Measuring cup - 1 unit

- Knife (for chopping leaves) - 1 unit

Step-by-Step Guide:

1. **Harvest Plantain Leaves**: Collect fresh plantain leaves from a clean area, ensuring they are free from pesticides or contaminants. Aim for 2 cups packed, roughly 15-20 leaves.

2. **Wash the Leaves**: Rinse the harvested leaves under cool running water to remove dirt and debris. Pat dry with a clean towel to eliminate excess moisture.

3. **Chop the Leaves**: Use a knife to chop the plantain leaves into small pieces, enhancing their surface area for infusion into the oil.

4. **Prepare Double Boiler**: Fill the bottom pot of a double boiler with water, ensuring it does not touch the upper pot. Place it on the stove over low heat.

5. **Add Olive Oil**: Pour 1 cup of olive oil into the top pot of the double boiler. The oil will serve as the base for the salve and help extract the medicinal properties from the leaves.

6. **Infuse the Oil**: Add the chopped plantain leaves to the olive oil in the double boiler. Allow the mixture to heat gently for 1-2 hours, stirring occasionally. Ensure the oil does not reach a boil to prevent damaging the plant's beneficial compounds.

7. **Strain the Mixture**: After infusing, remove the double boiler from heat. Place cheesecloth or a fine strainer over a bowl, and carefully pour the oil-leaf mixture through it to separate the leaves from the infused oil. Squeeze the cheesecloth to extract as much oil as possible.

8. **Add Beeswax**: Return the infused oil to the double boiler and add 1 ounce of beeswax. Stir continuously until the beeswax completely melts and blends with the oil.

9. **Pour into Jar**: Once the beeswax is fully melted, remove the pot from heat. Carefully pour the warm salve mixture into a clean glass jar. Allow it to cool at room temperature until solidified.

10. **Label the Jar**: After the salve cools and hardens, label the jar with the contents and the date of preparation. This helps track the salve's shelf life, which typically lasts up to one year when stored in a cool, dark place.

Maintenance:

- **Monthly**: Check the salve for any signs of spoilage, such as off smells or discoloration. If any changes are detected, discard the salve immediately.

- **Annually**: Prepare a fresh batch of plantain salve to ensure optimal effectiveness. As herbal remedies lose potency over time, an annual refresh keeps the medicine cabinet stocked with effective treatments.

Complexity:

The project is low in complexity and suitable for beginners. The primary skills required include basic chopping and an understanding of how to operate a double boiler. Potential challenges may include ensuring the oil does not overheat and the beeswax is fully melted, but these can be easily managed with attention to detail.

Estimated Time:

- **Harvesting and preparing plantain leaves**: 20 minutes.

- **Infusing the oil**: 1-2 hours (not included in active working time).

- **Straining and mixing**: 15 minutes.

- **Cooling and labeling**: 30 minutes.

5.3.3 PINE NEEDLE TEA

Pine needle tea offers a simple yet powerful way to harness the nutritional benefits of pine trees, making it an essential project for off-grid living and DIY herbal remedies. This aromatic tea contains high levels of vitamin C, antioxidants, and anti-inflammatory compounds, promoting overall health and well-being. If you rely on your surroundings for sustenance, learning to make pine needle tea serves multiple purposes: it enhances the diet, reduces dependence on commercial products, and connects you with nature. This empowers you to utilize readily available resources while enjoying a soothing beverage that can aid in digestion, boost immunity, and alleviate respiratory issues.

Materials and Tools:

- Fresh pine needles - 1 cup (loosely packed)

- Water - 4 cups

- Saucepan - 1 unit

- Fine mesh strainer or cheesecloth - 1 unit

- Glass or ceramic mug - 1 unit

- Knife (for cutting needles) - 1 unit

- Cutting board - 1 unit

Step-by-Step Guide:

1. **Harvest Pine Needles**: Select fresh pine needles from a healthy pine tree, avoiding yellow or brown needles. Aim for 1 cup of needles, loosely packed.

2. **Rinse the Needles**: Rinse the harvested pine needles under cool running water to remove any dirt or insects.

3. **Chop the Needles**: Use a knife to chop the pine needles into smaller pieces, about 1-inch long. This increases the surface area for better infusion.

4. **Boil Water**: Pour 4 cups of water into a saucepan and place it on the stove. Heat the water until it reaches a rolling boil.

5. **Add Pine Needles**: Once the water boils, add the chopped pine needles to the saucepan. Stir gently to ensure the needles are fully submerged.

6. **Simmer the Mixture**: Reduce the heat to low and let the mixture simmer for 10-15 minutes. This allows the essential oils and nutrients to infuse into the water.

7. **Strain the Tea**: After simmering, remove the saucepan from heat. Place a fine mesh strainer or cheesecloth over a glass or ceramic mug, and carefully pour the tea through the strainer to separate the liquid from the pine needles.

8. **Cool and Enjoy**: Allow the tea to cool slightly before sipping. Pine needle tea can be enjoyed plain or sweetened with honey or lemon, depending on personal preference.

Maintenance:

- **Weekly**: If storing fresh pine needles, check for any signs of wilting or spoilage. Use within one week for optimal flavor and nutrient content.

- **Monthly**: Consider foraging for fresh pine needles monthly to maintain a steady supply of this herbal remedy. Clean the saucepan and strainer thoroughly after each use to prevent any buildup.

Complexity:

The project is low in complexity and suitable for beginners. It requires basic skills such as foraging and boiling water. Potential challenges include identifying the correct type of pine tree and ensuring the needles are fresh and free from contaminants, but these can be easily addressed with careful attention to detail.

Estimated Time:

- **Harvesting and rinsing pine needles**: 10-15 minutes.

- **Chopping needles**: 5 minutes.

- **Boiling water and simmering tea**: 15-20 minutes.

- **Straining and cooling**: 5 minutes.

5.3.4 WILLOW BARK PAIN RELIEF

Willow bark, derived from the Salix tree species, has a long history of medicinal use, particularly for pain relief. It contains salicin, a compound that the body converts into salicylic acid, the active ingredient in aspirin. This demonstrates how to create willow bark extract for pain management, making it essential for off-grid living or DIY herbal remedies. By utilizing readily available resources, such as willow bark, you can address pain effectively while minimizing dependency on commercial medications.

Materials and Tools:

- Fresh willow bark - 1 pound

- Clean glass jar with lid - 1 unit, 16 ounces

- Vodka or high-proof alcohol - 1 cup

- Cheesecloth or fine strainer - 1 unit

- Small saucepan - 1 unit

- Water - 2 cups

- Measuring cup - 1 unit

- Stirring utensil - 1 unit

- Labels and marker - 1 set

Step-by-Step Guide:

1. **Harvest Willow Bark**: Identify a healthy willow tree. Use a sharp knife to carefully peel 1 pound of bark from the branches, avoiding damage to the tree.

2. **Prepare the Bark**: Cut the harvested willow bark into small pieces, approximately 1-inch in length. This increases the surface area for extraction.

3. **Create the Extract**: Place the chopped willow bark into a clean glass jar. Pour 1 cup of vodka or high-proof alcohol over the bark, ensuring it is fully submerged.

4. **Seal the Jar**: Secure the lid tightly on the jar to prevent evaporation and contamination.

5. **Infuse the Mixture**: Store the jar in a cool, dark place for 4-6 weeks. Shake the jar gently once a week to help with the extraction process.

6. **Prepare for Straining**: After the infusion period, set up a small saucepan and place the cheesecloth or fine strainer over it.

7. **Strain the Extract**: Pour the infused liquid through the cheesecloth or strainer into the saucepan, separating the solid bark from the liquid extract. Squeeze the cheesecloth to extract as much liquid as possible.

8. **Store the Extract**: Transfer the strained liquid back into the clean glass jar. Label the jar with the date and contents, ensuring it is clearly marked.

9. **Use the Extract**: To relieve pain, dilute 1-2 teaspoons of the willow bark extract in water and consume it. Adjust dosage based on individual tolerance and needs.

Maintenance:

- **Weekly**: Monitor the jar during the infusion process, checking for any signs of mold or contamination. Shake the jar weekly to enhance extraction.

- **Monthly**: Inspect the storage conditions of the final extract. Ensure it remains in a cool, dark place to preserve potency.

- **Annually**: Review and refresh the stock of willow bark extract. If necessary, prepare a new batch to maintain an effective supply for pain relief.

Complexity:

This project is moderately complex, requiring basic skills in herbal preparation and knowledge of safe harvesting practices. Challenges may arise in accurately identifying the willow tree and managing the extraction process, but with careful attention, these hurdles are easily navigable. Patience is essential during the infusion period, as the effectiveness of the extract relies on proper time and technique.

Estimated Time:

- **Harvesting willow bark**: 1 hour

- **Preparing and sealing the extract**: 30 minutes

- **Infusion period**: 4-6 weeks (passive time)

- **Straining and storing the extract**: 1 hour

5.3.5 ELDERBERRY SYRUP

Elderberry syrup, made from the berries of the Sambucus tree, is a powerful natural remedy known for its immune-boosting properties. Rich in antioxidants, vitamins, and minerals, elderberry syrup is especially beneficial for fighting colds and flu, making it a staple for off-grid living and DIY herbal remedies. By preparing elderberry syrup at home, you gain control over ingredients, ensuring a pure and potent remedy.

Materials and Tools:

- Dried elderberries - 1 cup

- Water - 4 cups

- Honey (raw or local) - 1 cup

- Saucepan - 1 unit

- Fine mesh strainer or cheesecloth - 1 unit

- Clean glass jar with lid - 1 unit, 16 ounces

- Measuring cups - 1 set

- Spoon for stirring - 1 unit

- Funnel - 1 unit (optional, for bottling)

Step-by-Step Guide:

1. **Combine Ingredients**: In a saucepan, add 1 cup of dried elderberries and 4 cups of water.

2. **Boil the Mixture**: Place the saucepan over medium heat and bring the mixture to a boil, stirring occasionally.

3. **Simmer the Mixture**: Once boiling, reduce heat to low and let it simmer for 30-45 minutes, until the liquid reduces by half.

4. **Mash the Berries**: After simmering, remove the saucepan from heat. Use a spoon to mash the berries against the side of the pan, extracting more juice.

5. **Strain the Liquid**: Set a fine mesh strainer or cheesecloth over a bowl or another saucepan. Pour the elderberry mixture through the strainer, allowing the liquid to drain completely.

6. **Add Honey**: Measure 1 cup of honey and stir it into the strained liquid while it is still warm. Mix until fully dissolved.

7. **Cool the Syrup**: Allow the syrup to cool to room temperature before transferring it to a jar.

8. **Store the Syrup**: Use a funnel to pour the cooled syrup into a clean glass jar with a lid. Seal tightly and label with the date and contents.

9. **Dosage and Use**: To boost immunity or relieve symptoms, take 1 tablespoon of elderberry syrup daily for prevention or every 2-3 hours when feeling unwell.

Maintenance:

- **Weekly**: Check the syrup for any signs of fermentation or spoilage. If the syrup develops an off smell or bubbles, discard it immediately.

- **Monthly**: Ensure the syrup remains sealed tightly in its jar to maintain freshness. If stored in the refrigerator, it can last up to 3 months.

- **Yearly**: Reassess your elderberry supply and prepare a new batch if necessary, as the syrup's potency decreases over time.

Complexity:

The project is relatively simple, suitable for beginners with basic cooking skills. The main challenge lies in ensuring proper berry identification if foraging. Diligence is necessary to avoid confusion with toxic species, such as the red elderberry. Following the recipe accurately will yield a potent and beneficial syrup.

Estimated Time:

- **Preparation and gathering materials**: 30 minutes

- **Cooking and simmering**: 1 hour

- **Cooling and bottling**: 30 minutes

- **Total estimated time**: 2 hours for initial preparation and production, with ongoing use depending on personal dosage needs.

5.4 BUDGET OFF-GRID MEDICAL KIT

5.4.1 OVER-THE-COUNTER MEDICATIONS KIT

Creating an Over-the-Counter (OTC) Medications Kit is essential for anyone living off-grid or seeking self-sufficiency. This project enables you to stockpile common medications that can effectively treat minor ailments, ensuring you are prepared for everyday health issues without relying on pharmacies. In an off-grid setting, access to commercial healthcare can be limited or delayed, making it crucial to have a comprehensive kit on hand. This

OTC kit not only promotes personal wellness but also provides peace of mind, allowing you to manage minor health concerns confidently. By assembling this kit, you gain the ability to address headaches, allergies, colds, and digestive issues promptly, minimizing disruptions to your off-grid lifestyle.

Materials and Tools:

- Clear plastic storage bin with a lid - 1 unit - 18 quarts

- Label maker or permanent markers - 1 unit

- Pill organizer - 1 unit

- Assorted over-the-counter medications (see specific quantities below):

- Acetaminophen (Tylenol) - 100 tablets

- Ibuprofen (Advil) - 100 tablets

- Antihistamines (Benadryl) - 50 tablets

- Cold and flu relief (DayQuil/NyQuil) - 20 capsules each

- Loperamide (Imodium) - 24 capsules

- Aspirin - 100 tablets

- Antacid tablets (Tums) - 60 tablets

- Cough syrup - 1 bottle - 4 ounces

- Electrolyte powder packets - 10 packets

- First aid supplies (band-aids, antiseptic wipes, gauze) - 1 small kit

- Ziplock bags - 5 units - quart size

- Small scissors - 1 unit

Step-by-Step Guide:

1. **Select a Bin**: Choose a clear plastic storage bin with a lid that holds at least 18 quarts to ensure all items fit comfortably.

2. **Prepare the Bin**: Clean the bin thoroughly with soap and water, then dry it completely to avoid moisture buildup.

3. **Label the Bin**: Use a label maker or permanent markers to clearly label the bin as "OTC Medications Kit." Place the label on the front for easy identification.

4. **Organize Medications**: Gather all over-the-counter medications and separate them by category (pain relief, cold and flu, digestive aids, etc.).

5. **Fill Ziplock Bags**: For each category, place the medications into quart-sized Ziplock bags. Label each bag with its contents and expiration date to maintain organization.

6. **Add a Pill Organizer**: Include a pill organizer for daily doses of medications like acetaminophen or ibuprofen, ensuring you have a quick reference for dosage.

7. **Include First Aid Supplies**: Place a small first aid kit inside the bin to address minor injuries alongside the OTC medications.

8. **Store Cough Syrup**: Securely close the cough syrup bottle and place it upright in the bin to prevent spills.

9. **Add Electrolyte Powder**: Include electrolyte powder packets in a separate Ziplock bag, labeling it clearly for quick access.

10. **Check Expiration Dates**: Review all medications and supplies for expiration dates. Replace any expired items immediately to ensure efficacy.

11. **Seal the Bin**: Once everything is organized and labeled, close the bin securely. Store it in a cool, dry location, easily accessible for emergencies.

Maintenance:

- **Monthly**: Check expiration dates on all medications and replace any that are expired. Inspect the contents for signs of moisture or damage, and ensure the lid is sealed tightly.

- **Quarterly**: Review the overall organization of the kit, ensuring medications are correctly categorized and easily accessible. Restock any frequently used items to maintain readiness.

- **Yearly**: Conduct a complete inventory of the OTC medications kit. Replace items that are outdated and reassess the contents based on changing health needs.

Complexity:

The project is straightforward, requiring minimal skills. Challenges may arise in selecting the right medications or ensuring proper storage conditions. It is vital to be aware of individual health needs and consult with a healthcare provider if uncertain about specific medications or dosages.

Estimated Time:

- **Preparation and gathering materials**: 30 minutes

- **Organizing and labeling medications**: 30 minutes

- **Final assembly and storage**: 15 minutes

- **Total estimated time**: 1 hour and 15 minutes to complete the OTC Medications Kit.

5.4.2 DIY SPLINT AND BANDAGE KIT

Creating a DIY Splint and Bandage Kit is crucial for anyone engaged in off-grid living or outdoor activities. Injuries can happen unexpectedly, and having a well-equipped kit allows you to respond quickly and effectively to minor accidents. This project empowers you to manage sprains, fractures, and cuts, reducing the need for professional medical intervention in remote settings. The kit includes essential materials for immobilizing injuries and dressing wounds, ensuring you can maintain your health and safety in the wilderness. With this self-sufficient approach, you gain the confidence to handle emergencies, promoting a sustainable and independent lifestyle. Ultimately, assembling a splint and bandage kit not only addresses immediate medical needs but also enhances your preparedness for unforeseen situations.

Materials and Tools:

- Sturdy plastic storage bin with a lid - 1 unit - 10 quarts

- Rolled gauze - 2 rolls - 4 inches wide

- Elastic bandages (ACE bandages) - 2 units - 3 inches wide

- Splint material (wooden or plastic) - 2 pieces - 24 inches long

- Medical adhesive tape - 1 roll - 1 inch wide

- Sterile adhesive bandages (various sizes) - 50 units

- Antiseptic wipes - 20 packets

- Disposable gloves - 10 pairs

- Triangular bandages - 2 units

- Cold pack (instant) - 2 units

- Scissors - 1 unit

- First aid manual - 1 unit

Step-by-Step Guide:

1. **Select a Bin**: Choose a sturdy plastic storage bin with a lid that has a capacity of at least 10 quarts to accommodate all materials.

2. **Prepare the Bin**: Clean the bin thoroughly with soap and water, then dry it completely to prevent contamination.

3. **Label the Bin**: Use a permanent marker to label the bin as "Splint and Bandage Kit" for easy identification.

4. **Organize Materials**: Gather all materials and organize them by type (bandages, splint materials, antiseptics) to streamline access.

5. **Pack Gauze Rolls**: Place the two rolls of gauze in the bin, ensuring they are easily accessible for wound dressing.

6. **Add Elastic Bandages**: Store the two elastic bandages alongside the gauze, ready for use on sprains or strains.

7. **Prepare Splint Materials**: Cut two pieces of wooden or plastic splint material to 24 inches long, ensuring they are smooth and free from splinters.

8. **Include Adhesive Tape**: Roll the medical adhesive tape neatly and place it in the bin, ensuring it remains clean and ready for use.

9. **Sort Adhesive Bandages**: Open the box of adhesive bandages and separate them by size. Place them in a resealable bag to keep them organized.

10. **Pack Antiseptic Wipes**: Place the 20 packets of antiseptic wipes in a designated section of the bin for quick access during wound cleaning.

11. **Include Disposable Gloves**: Store the 10 pairs of disposable gloves in a small bag within the bin to maintain hygiene while treating injuries.

12. **Add Triangular Bandages**: Fold the two triangular bandages neatly and place them in the bin, as they can be used for various types of injuries.

13. **Include Cold Packs**: Store the two instant cold packs in the bin, ensuring they are sealed to prevent leakage.

14. **Pack Scissors**: Include a pair of scissors in the bin for cutting gauze, tape, or clothing if necessary.

15. **Add First Aid Manual**: Place the first aid manual in the bin to provide guidance on treating injuries effectively.

16. **Seal the Bin**: Once all materials are organized, close the bin securely. Store it in a cool, dry location for easy access during emergencies.

Maintenance:

- **Monthly**: Check the contents of the kit for any expired items, especially antiseptic wipes and adhesive bandages. Replace as needed. Ensure all items are in good condition, with no damage to bandages, splints, or tools.

- **Yearly**: Conduct a complete inventory of the splint and bandage kit, restocking any frequently used or expired items. Review the first aid manual to stay updated on best practices for treating injuries.

Complexity:

The project is straightforward, requiring minimal skills. Challenges may arise in ensuring all necessary materials are included and properly organized. It is vital to understand the basic principles of first aid, so familiarity with the first aid manual can enhance preparedness.

Estimated Time:

- **Preparation and gathering materials**: 30 minutes

- **Organizing and packing the kit**: 30 minutes

- **Total estimated time**: 1 hour to complete the DIY Splint and Bandage Kit.

5.4.3 PORTABLE MEDICAL SUPPLIES KIT

As the call for self-sufficiency rises, creating a Portable Medical Supplies Kit becomes a vital project for those embracing off-grid living. This kit acts as a compact, all-in-one solution for managing health emergencies, ensuring that you are prepared for injuries or illnesses that can arise in remote settings. By having essential medical supplies on hand, you minimize the risk of complications and promote a proactive approach to health care. A well-organized kit not only addresses immediate medical needs but also fosters confidence in your ability to handle emergencies independently. In an off-grid lifestyle, where access to professional medical services may be limited, this project empowers you to take charge of your health, ensuring that you can provide immediate care for yourself and others.

Materials and Tools:

- Sturdy backpack or duffel bag - 1 unit

- First aid manual - 1 unit

- Adhesive bandages (various sizes) - 50 units

- Sterile gauze pads (4x4 inches) - 10 units

- Medical adhesive tape - 1 roll - 1 inch wide

- Antiseptic wipes - 20 packets

- Disposable gloves - 10 pairs

- Elastic bandages (ACE bandages) - 2 units - 3 inches wide

- Instant cold packs - 2 units

- Splint material (plastic or wooden) - 2 pieces - 24 inches long

- Pain relief medication (ibuprofen or acetaminophen) - 1 bottle - 100 tablets

- Antibiotic ointment - 1 tube - 1 ounce

- Thermometer - 1 unit

- Scissors - 1 unit

- Tweezers - 1 unit

- Safety pins - 10 units

- Oral rehydration salts - 1 packet

Step-by-Step Guide:

1. **Select a Bag**: Choose a sturdy backpack or duffel bag that can comfortably carry all medical supplies and fit your needs for portability.

2. **Prepare the Bag**: Ensure the bag is clean and free from debris before packing. Check for any existing compartments to facilitate organization.

3. **Gather Essential Items**: Collect all materials listed, ensuring you have the correct quantities and sizes for each item.

4. **Pack Adhesive Bandages**: Place 50 adhesive bandages of various sizes in a resealable plastic bag for easy access.

5. **Store Sterile Gauze Pads**: Pack 10 sterile gauze pads (4x4 inches) in a separate resealable bag to keep them sterile and organized.

6. **Include Medical Tape**: Roll the medical adhesive tape and secure it in a designated compartment of the bag to keep it easily accessible.

7. **Add Antiseptic Wipes**: Store 20 packets of antiseptic wipes together, ensuring they are easy to reach when needed for cleaning wounds.

8. **Pack Disposable Gloves**: Place 10 pairs of disposable gloves in a small bag within the kit, ensuring they remain clean and dry.

9. **Include Elastic Bandages**: Add two elastic bandages (ACE bandages) to provide support for sprains or strains, storing them flat to save space.

10. **Store Instant Cold Packs**: Keep two instant cold packs sealed in the bag to address swelling or injuries effectively.

11. **Prepare Splint Material**: Cut two pieces of splint material to 24 inches long if not pre-cut. Store them flat within the bag.

12. **Add Pain Relief Medication**: Include a bottle of pain relief medication (100 tablets) in the bag, ensuring it is clearly labeled and sealed.

13. **Include Antibiotic Ointment**: Pack a 1-ounce tube of antibiotic ointment in the kit to prevent infection in minor cuts and scrapes.

14. **Add Thermometer**: Place the thermometer in a protective case or wrap it in soft material to prevent breakage during transport.

15. **Pack Scissors**: Include a pair of scissors for cutting tape, gauze, or clothing as needed during an emergency.

16. **Include Tweezers**: Add tweezers to assist with splinter removal or picking up small items.

17. **Store Safety Pins**: Pack 10 safety pins in a small bag for securing bandages or clothing.

18. **Add Oral Rehydration Salts**: Include a packet of oral rehydration salts to help manage dehydration in emergencies.

19. **Seal the Bag**: Once all items are organized and packed, close the bag securely, ensuring it is easy to carry.

Maintenance:

- **Monthly**: Check the contents of the kit for any expired items, especially medications and antiseptic wipes. Replace as needed. Ensure that all items are in good condition, paying special attention to the integrity of packaging.

- **Yearly**: Conduct a complete inventory of the Portable Medical Supplies Kit, restocking any frequently used or expired items. Review the first aid manual to stay updated on best practices for treating injuries.

Complexity:

The project is low in complexity, making it suitable for beginners. The primary challenge lies in ensuring that all necessary materials are included and properly organized. Familiarity with basic first aid practices will enhance your ability to respond effectively to emergencies.

Estimated Time:

- **Preparation and gathering materials**: 30 minutes
- **Organizing and packing the kit**: 30 minutes
- **Total estimated time**: 1 hour to complete the Portable Medical Supplies Kit.

5.5 DIY SANITATION: HANDWASHING

5.5.1 PORTABLE HANDWASHING STATION

A portable handwashing station serves as a practical solution for maintaining hygiene in off-grid living or DIY settings. In environments where running water is not readily available, this project provides a way to promote cleanliness and reduce the spread of germs. A handwashing station allows individuals to wash their hands easily after handling food, using the restroom, or engaging in other activities where cleanliness is essential. This simple yet effective setup can be crucial for health, especially in a self-sufficient lifestyle where access to traditional plumbing may be limited. Building a portable handwashing station enhances personal hygiene practices and demonstrates resourcefulness and ingenuity in off-grid living.

Materials and Tools:

- 5-gallon plastic bucket with lid - 1 unit
- Spigot (1/2 inch) - 1 unit
- 3/4 inch PVC pipe - 1 piece - 2 feet long
- PVC elbow fitting (3/4 inch) - 2 units
- PVC T-fitting (3/4 inch) - 1 unit
- PVC primer and cement - 1 unit - 4 oz
- Small basin or wash tub - 1 unit
- Soap dispenser (manual) - 1 unit
- Paper towel dispenser or holder - 1 unit
- Clean water - As needed
- Sanitizing solution (bleach or similar) - As needed
- Plastic sheeting or tarp (optional) - 1 unit
- Drill with 1/2 inch drill bit - 1 unit
- Screwdriver - 1 unit
- Measuring tape - 1 unit

Step-by-Step Guide:

1. **Prepare the Bucket**: Start with a clean 5-gallon plastic bucket. Remove the lid and set it aside for later use.

2. **Install the Spigot**: Use a drill with a 1/2 inch drill bit to create a hole about 3 inches from the bottom of the bucket. Insert the spigot into the hole, securing it tightly according to the manufacturer's instructions.

3. **Cut the PVC Pipe**: Measure and cut a piece of 3/4 inch PVC pipe to 2 feet long using a saw. This will serve as the drainage pipe for the handwashing station.

4. **Assemble the Drainage System**: Attach one end of the PVC pipe to the spigot, using the PVC elbow fittings to create a downward angle for drainage. Use PVC primer and cement to secure the connections.

5. **Create a Drainage Basin**: Place a small basin or wash tub directly beneath the spigot to catch water from handwashing. Ensure it is stable and positioned correctly to avoid spills.

6. **Add Soap Dispenser**: Install a manual soap dispenser on the side of the bucket or nearby, ensuring it is easily accessible. Fill it with liquid soap for handwashing.

7. **Install Paper Towel Holder**: Attach a paper towel dispenser or holder adjacent to the handwashing station. This provides a sanitary way to dry hands after washing.

8. **Fill with Clean Water**: Pour clean water into the bucket until it is full, ensuring that the spigot is closed to prevent spills.

9. **Sanitize the Setup**: Mix a sanitizing solution according to the instructions and use it to wipe down the handwashing station, ensuring it is clean and ready for use.

10. **Set Up Optional Cover**: If desired, use plastic sheeting or a tarp to create a windbreak or cover for the handwashing station, ensuring that it remains clean and protected from the elements.

11. **Test the System**: Open the spigot to test the flow of water. Adjust the connections if necessary to ensure there are no leaks and that water drains effectively into the basin.

Maintenance:

- **Weekly**: Check the water level in the bucket, refilling with clean water as needed. Inspect the spigot and drainage connections for leaks or blockages.

- **Monthly**: Clean the soap dispenser and refill it with liquid soap. Wipe down the entire handwashing station with a sanitizing solution to maintain cleanliness.

- **Annually**: Disassemble the PVC connections and clean them thoroughly to prevent buildup or clogs. Replace any worn or damaged parts, such as the spigot or soap dispenser, to ensure continued functionality.

Complexity:

The project is low in complexity, making it suitable for beginners. Basic skills required include measuring, cutting PVC pipe, and using a drill. Potential challenges may involve ensuring watertight connections and managing the placement of the drainage basin. However, these challenges can be easily overcome with careful planning and attention to detail.

Estimated Time:

- **Preparation and gathering materials**: 30 minutes

- **Construction of the handwashing station**: 1-2 hours

- **Testing and final adjustments**: 30 minutes

- **Total estimated time**: 2-3 hours to complete the Portable Handwashing Station.

5.5.2 DIY Soap Making

DIY soap making is an essential skill for off-grid living, allowing you to create your own personal care products from natural ingredients. This project empowers you to take control of your hygiene needs while reducing reliance on commercial soaps that may contain harmful chemicals or preservatives. By crafting your own soap, you not only save money but also customize your creations to suit your preferences and skin sensitivities. The process of making soap, known as saponification, involves a chemical reaction between fats and lye, resulting in a versatile product that can cleanse, moisturize, and nourish the skin. Engaging in this project cultivates self-sufficiency, fosters creativity, and enhances your ability to live sustainably.

Materials and Tools:

- Lye (sodium hydroxide) - 4 ounces
- Distilled water - 10 ounces
- Olive oil - 16 ounces
- Coconut oil - 16 ounces
- Palm oil - 16 ounces
- Essential oils (optional, e.g., lavender, peppermint) - 1-2 ounces
- Soap mold (silicone or wooden) - 1 unit
- Digital scale - 1 unit
- Thermometer - 1 unit
- Mixing bowls (heat-resistant) - 2 units
- Stick blender - 1 unit
- Safety goggles - 1 unit
- Rubber gloves - 1 pair
- Measuring spoons - 1 set
- Spatula - 1 unit
- Parchment paper (if using wooden mold) - 1 unit

Step-by-Step Guide:

1. **Prepare Your Workspace**: Clear a designated area for soap making, ensuring it is well-ventilated and free of clutter.

2. **Put on Safety Gear**: Wear safety goggles and rubber gloves to protect against lye burns during the soap-making process.

3. **Measure Ingredients**: Use a digital scale to weigh 4 ounces of lye and 10 ounces of distilled water, keeping these measurements precise.

4. **Mix Lye Solution**: In a heat-resistant mixing bowl, carefully add the lye to the distilled water, stirring gently until fully dissolved. Note: Always add lye to water, never the other way around, to prevent a dangerous reaction.

5. **Let Lye Cool**: Allow the lye solution to cool to around 100°F (38°C) while you prepare the oils.

6. **Measure Oils**: Weigh 16 ounces each of olive oil, coconut oil, and palm oil using the digital scale.

7. **Melt the Oils**: Combine the oils in a heat-resistant mixing bowl and heat gently until the coconut oil is fully melted.

8. **Cool the Oils**: Allow the oil mixture to cool to about 100°F (38°C), matching the temperature of the lye solution.

9. **Combine Lye and Oils**: Once both the lye solution and oils are at the same temperature, slowly pour the lye into the oils while stirring continuously.

10. **Blend the Mixture**: Use a stick blender to mix the soap until it reaches "trace," which means it thickens enough to leave a trail when drizzled over the surface.

11. **Add Essential Oils**: If desired, mix in 1-2 ounces of essential oils at this stage, ensuring even distribution throughout the soap.

12. **Pour into Mold**: Pour the soap mixture into the soap mold, smoothing the top with a spatula.

13. **Insulate the Mold**: Cover the mold with a towel or plastic wrap to keep the heat in and allow saponification to occur over the next 24-48 hours.

14. **Unmold the Soap**: After 24-48 hours, carefully remove the soap from the mold. If using a wooden mold, line it with parchment paper for easier removal.

15. **Cut the Soap**: Slice the soap into bars using a sharp knife, allowing each piece to cure.

16. **Cure the Soap**: Place the soap bars on a drying rack in a cool, dry area, allowing them to cure for 4-6 weeks before use. This process ensures the soap is safe and effective.

Maintenance:

- **Weekly**: Check the curing soap for any signs of mold or moisture. Ensure it remains in a well-ventilated area.

- **Monthly**: Assess the storage area for finished soap bars. Store them in a cool, dry place to maintain quality.

- **Annually**: Evaluate your soap-making supplies. Replace any worn-out tools or ingredients to ensure optimal results in future batches.

Complexity:

This project is moderate in complexity, suitable for those with basic kitchen skills. Challenges may arise when handling lye, which requires careful attention and safety precautions. Familiarity with temperature management and achieving the right trace can take practice, but these skills develop over time.

Estimated Time:

- **Preparation and gathering materials**: 30 minutes

- **Soap making process**: 2-3 hours, including cooling and mixing times

- **Curing time**: 4-6 weeks for soap to fully harden and be safe for use

- **Total estimated time for completion**: 4-6 weeks, with active involvement of about 3 hours.

6. INFRASTRUCTURE

6.1 INTRODUCTION

Building a resilient and self-sufficient homestead requires a strong foundation in infrastructure. This encompasses the essential systems and structures that support your off-grid lifestyle, from sanitation and storage to security and shelter. Each aspect of your infrastructure must be carefully planned and executed to ensure your home is not only sustainable but also comfortable and secure.

DIY fencing and property security measures are crucial for protecting your homestead, livestock, and garden. Using locally sourced materials, you can construct fences that deter wildlife and unauthorized access. Additionally, simple security enhancements like motion-sensor lights and secure locks can be implemented to safeguard your property without relying on external power sources.

Insulation and weatherproofing your home are key to maintaining comfort and reducing energy needs. Techniques like adding extra layers of insulation, sealing gaps, and installing thermal curtains can significantly improve your home's ability to retain heat in winter and stay cool in summer. Many of these improvements can be made with recycled or repurposed materials, making them both cost-effective and environmentally friendly.

Each of these components contributes to a robust infrastructure that supports a sustainable, self-sufficient lifestyle. By taking a hands-on approach and leveraging your skills and resources, you can build an off-grid homestead that meets your needs and aligns with your values of independence and environmental stewardship.

6.1.1 DIY FENCING AND PROPERTY SECURITY MEASURES

Constructing a secure fence is a fundamental step in establishing property boundaries and enhancing safety, particularly for those pursuing off-grid living or DIY projects. A well-built fence serves multiple purposes: it deters intruders, contains livestock, protects gardens from wildlife, and provides privacy. Additionally, it creates a defined space that fosters a sense of ownership and security. The scope of this project encompasses the design and construction of a sturdy wooden or wire fence tailored to the specific needs of the property. By investing time and resources into fencing, individuals can significantly enhance their homesteading experience, promoting self-sufficiency and peace of mind. This guide provides detailed instructions for building a reliable fence, ensuring that readers are equipped with the knowledge to tackle this essential DIY project confidently.

Materials and Tools:

- Wooden fence posts (4x4 inches) - 10 units, 8 feet long
- Wooden fence boards (1x6 inches) - 50 units, 6 feet long
- Concrete mix - 4 bags, 50 pounds each
- Galvanized nails (3-inch) - 1 box, 1 pound
- Gravel - 1 cubic yard
- Gate kit (hinges and latch) - 1 unit
- Wire fencing (if applicable) - 100 feet
- Fence staples - 1 box, 1 pound
- Tape measure - 1 unit
- Level - 1 unit
- Drill with drill bits - 1 unit
- Hammer - 1 unit
- Post hole digger - 1 unit

- Saw (hand saw or circular saw) - 1 unit

- Safety goggles - 1 pair

- Work gloves - 1 pair

Step-by-Step Guide:

1. **Select Fence Location**: Determine the boundaries of the property and choose a straight line for the fence installation. Mark the corners with stakes.

2. **Measure and Mark Post Locations**: Using a tape measure, mark the positions for the fence posts, spacing them 6-8 feet apart. Use stakes to indicate these points.

3. **Dig Post Holes**: Employ a post hole digger to excavate holes at least 2 feet deep for each fence post, ensuring they are wide enough to accommodate the posts.

4. **Prepare Concrete Mix**: In a wheelbarrow, mix concrete according to the manufacturer's instructions until it reaches a thick, workable consistency.

5. **Set Fence Posts**: Place the first wooden post in the hole, ensuring it is vertical with a level. Fill the hole with concrete mix, packing it tightly around the post.

6. **Allow Concrete to Set**: Follow the manufacturer's instructions for curing time, typically 24-48 hours, before proceeding to ensure posts are securely anchored.

7. **Attach Horizontal Rails**: Cut 1x6 wooden boards to fit horizontally between the posts. Secure the boards using galvanized nails, ensuring they are level and evenly spaced.

8. **Install Wire Fencing (if applicable)**: If using wire fencing, stretch it between the posts and secure it with fence staples, ensuring it is taut to prevent sagging.

9. **Construct the Gate Frame**: Cut two vertical and two horizontal wooden boards to create a rectangular frame for the gate. Use a drill to secure the boards together with screws.

10. **Attach Hinges to Gate**: Install the hinges on one side of the gate frame and secure the other side to the adjacent fence post.

11. **Install the Latch**: Attach the latch mechanism to the gate, ensuring it aligns with the corresponding strike plate on the fence post.

12. **Add Gravel for Drainage**: Place gravel around the base of the posts, particularly in areas prone to moisture, to facilitate drainage and prevent rot.

13. **Finish with Protective Coating**: Optionally, apply a weather-resistant sealant to the wooden boards and posts to enhance longevity and durability against the elements.

Maintenance:

- **Monthly**: Inspect the fence for any loose boards or damaged sections. Tighten nails or replace damaged boards as needed. Check the gate for proper functionality, ensuring hinges and latches operate smoothly.

- **Seasonally**: Clear vegetation and debris around the fence line to prevent overgrowth that may compromise the fence's integrity. Reapply sealant to the wooden components to maintain weather resistance.

- **Annually**: Evaluate the structural condition of the fence and posts, replacing any that show signs of rot or decay. Tighten or replace wire fencing as necessary, ensuring it remains taut and effective.

Complexity:

The complexity of constructing a fence is moderate, requiring basic carpentry skills and physical effort. Challenges may arise from uneven terrain, which can complicate post placement and leveling. Additionally, the proper selection of materials is crucial; using untreated wood may lead to premature decay. Ensuring the posts are set securely in concrete requires attention to detail and patience. However, with careful planning and execution, even novice DIYers can successfully complete this project.

Estimated Time:

- **Planning and Preparation**: 2-3 hours for site evaluation and material gathering.

- **Digging Post Holes**: 4-6 hours, depending on soil conditions and terrain.

- **Setting Posts**: 2-3 hours for placing and securing posts in concrete.

- **Constructing the Fence**: 6-8 hours to attach rails, boards, or wire fencing.

- **Installing the Gate**: 1-2 hours for constructing and attaching the gate.

- **Total Estimated Time**: 15-22 hours spread over a weekend or two days, allowing for drying time of concrete.

6.1.2 DIY INSULATION AND WEATHERPROOFING TECHNIQUES

DIY insulation and weatherproofing techniques serve as essential strategies for maintaining a comfortable and energy-efficient living space, particularly for those embracing off-grid lifestyles. Effective insulation minimizes heat loss in winter and keeps interiors cool in summer, resulting in significant energy savings and reduced reliance on external heating and cooling systems. This project aims to equip individuals with the knowledge to insulate their homes using sustainable materials and methods, ensuring optimal energy efficiency while enhancing indoor comfort. Proper weatherproofing further safeguards structures from moisture, pests, and air leaks, ultimately prolonging the lifespan of buildings and minimizing maintenance costs. By mastering these techniques, individuals cultivate self-sufficiency and contribute to a more sustainable way of living.

Materials and Tools:

- Fiberglass insulation batts (R-13) - 10 units, 15 inches x 93 inches

- Foam board insulation - 4 sheets, 2 feet x 8 feet

- Weather stripping (adhesive) - 1 roll, 10 feet

- Caulk (silicone or acrylic) - 2 tubes, 10 ounces each

- Spray foam insulation - 1 can, 12 ounces

- Plastic sheeting (6-mil) - 1 roll, 10 feet x 100 feet

- Utility knife - 1 unit

- Tape measure - 1 unit

- Straight edge or carpenter's square - 1 unit

- Caulk gun - 1 unit

- Safety goggles - 1 pair

- Work gloves - 1 pair

- Dust mask - 1 unit

Step-by-Step Guide:

1. **Assess Insulation Needs**: Identify areas requiring insulation, such as walls, attics, and basements, by checking for drafts or cold spots.

2. **Measure Areas**: Use a tape measure to determine the dimensions of the walls or ceilings where insulation will be installed. Record measurements for accuracy.

3. **Cut Insulation Batts**: Using a utility knife, cut fiberglass insulation batts to fit snugly between wall studs or joists. Ensure a tight fit to minimize air gaps.

4. **Install Insulation Batts**: Place the cut batts between the studs with the paper facing the interior space. Push the batts firmly into place to ensure contact with the studs.

5. **Seal Gaps with Caulk**: Apply caulk around edges and seams of the insulation to prevent air leaks. Use a caulk gun for precision and ensure an even bead.

6. **Install Foam Board Insulation**: Cut foam board sheets to fit around windows, doors, or other irregularly shaped areas. Use a utility knife for clean edges.

7. **Secure Foam Board**: Adhere foam board insulation to surfaces using construction adhesive or mechanical fasteners. Ensure edges align properly for a tight seal.

8. **Weatherstrip Doors and Windows**: Measure and cut weather stripping to fit the perimeter of doors and windows. Remove the adhesive backing and press firmly into place.

9. **Apply Spray Foam**: Use spray foam insulation to fill small gaps, cracks, or holes in walls, around pipes, and between windows. Allow foam to expand and cure as per manufacturer instructions.

10. **Cover with Plastic Sheeting**: If applicable, cover insulated areas with plastic sheeting to provide an additional moisture barrier. Use a utility knife to trim excess.

11. **Inspect and Test**: Conduct a thorough inspection of the installed insulation and weatherproofing measures. Test for drafts or moisture accumulation.

12. **Maintain Temperature Control**: Monitor indoor temperatures after installation to ensure desired comfort levels are achieved. Adjust heating or cooling systems as necessary.

Maintenance:

- **Monthly**: Inspect weather stripping for wear and replace as needed. Ensure that no gaps have developed in the caulking around windows and doors.

- **Seasonally**: Check for any signs of moisture damage or pest infiltration in insulated areas. Repair any damaged insulation or weatherproofing materials immediately.

- **Annually**: Evaluate overall insulation effectiveness by conducting a thermal imaging inspection or energy audit. Make adjustments or upgrades as necessary to maintain efficiency.

Complexity:

The complexity of this project is moderate, suitable for individuals with basic DIY skills. Key challenges include ensuring accurate measurements and achieving a tight fit with insulation materials. Attention to detail during the sealing process is crucial to prevent air leaks and moisture issues. Those unfamiliar with handling fiberglass insulation may require additional precautions to avoid irritation. With proper planning and adherence to safety guidelines, anyone can successfully undertake this project.

Estimated Time:

- **Assessing Needs**: 1 hour to evaluate areas and determine insulation requirements.

- **Preparation**: 1-2 hours to gather materials and tools, measure spaces, and cut insulation.

- **Installation**: 4-6 hours to install insulation batts, foam boards, weather stripping, and caulk.

- **Final Inspection**: 1 hour for a thorough check of completed work and any necessary adjustments.

- **Total Estimated Time**: 7-10 hours, ideally completed over a weekend or two days, allowing for any interruptions.

7. COMMUNICATION AND SAFETY

7.1 INTRODUCTION

Creating reliable DIY communication systems is a cornerstone of safety and security in a no-grid environment. The ability to communicate effectively can significantly impact your ability to respond to emergencies, coordinate with family or community members, and access or provide assistance when needed. One of the simplest yet most effective communication tools you can set up is a system of walkie-talkies or two-way radios. These devices, which do not rely on cell phone networks, can be invaluable during power outages or in areas where cell service is unreliable. When selecting walkie-talkies, consider range, battery life, and durability to ensure they meet your needs. It's also wise to have a method for recharging batteries without relying on the grid, such as solar chargers or hand-crank chargers.

In addition to walkie-talkies, setting up a Baofeng radio system can offer a broader range of communication capabilities, including access to emergency frequencies and the ability to communicate over longer distances. Programming a Baofeng radio may seem daunting at first, but with some basic knowledge and practice, it can become a powerful tool in your no-grid communication arsenal. Remember, the legal requirements for operating on certain frequencies vary, so it's important to familiarize yourself with these regulations to ensure you're using your equipment legally and ethically.

DIY safety equipment, such as whistles, flares, and reflective vests, should be included in your no-grid survival kit. These items can be lifesavers in situations where visibility is low or when trying to attract attention during a rescue operation. Making your own reflective vests from high-visibility materials or repurposing items to create signal devices can be simple and effective ways to enhance your preparedness.

Creating a no-grid emergency response plan is another critical aspect of communication and safety. This plan should include designated meeting points, a list of emergency contacts, and a clear outline of roles and responsibilities for each family or community member. Ensure everyone is familiar with the plan and practices it regularly. Including non-electronic forms of communication, such as signal flares or even a simple whistle system, can provide backup options should electronic devices fail.

Self-defense techniques and strategies form an essential part of personal and community safety in a no-grid lifestyle. While the hope is never to encounter a situation where they are needed, being prepared can offer peace of mind and a greater sense of security. Focus on learning basic self-defense moves that can be effectively used regardless of strength or size. Additionally, consider the strategic placement of simple tools or weapons that can be used for defense. These tools should be accessible to those trained to use them but stored securely to prevent accidents.

Building a no-grid community through networking and cooperation can significantly enhance your safety and security. A well-connected community can share resources, information, and assistance, creating a more resilient and supportive environment for everyone involved. Organize regular meetings to discuss safety, emergency preparedness, and other relevant topics. Cooperation can also extend to shared projects, such as community gardens or collective water purification systems, which not only improve sustainability but also foster a sense of unity and mutual reliance.

By focusing on these key areas of communication and safety, you can build a solid foundation for living off the grid. The ability to communicate effectively, respond to emergencies, and ensure personal and community safety are all critical components of a successful no-grid lifestyle. With the right tools, knowledge, and preparation, you can create a secure and resilient environment that supports your independence and self-sufficiency goals.

7.1.1 BAOFENG RADIOS

Using and configuring Baofeng radios is an essential skill for individuals pursuing off-grid living, outdoor adventures, or emergency preparedness. These compact, handheld two-way radios provide reliable communication in areas lacking cellular service, making them invaluable for homesteaders, hikers, and survivalists. The ability to communicate over long distances without reliance on external infrastructure fosters independence and safety. Baofeng radios, specifically the UV-5R model, are versatile, cost-effective, and user-friendly, making them accessible for both beginners and seasoned radio operators. This guide aims to equip users with the knowledge to effectively set up and operate Baofeng radios, ensuring they can confidently communicate in any situation.

Materials and Tools:

- Baofeng UV-5R radio - 1 unit

- Li-ion battery pack - 1 unit

- Charger for battery pack - 1 unit

- Earpiece with microphone (optional) - 1 unit

- Programming cable (optional) - 1 unit

- Computer with programming software (optional) - 1 unit

- User manual - 1 unit (provided with the radio)

Step-by-Step Guide:

1. **Charge the Battery**: Connect the Li-ion battery pack to the charger and plug it into a power source. Charge until the indicator light turns green, typically 4-6 hours.

2. **Attach the Antenna**: Screw the antenna onto the top of the radio. Ensure it is tightly secured for optimal signal reception.

3. **Install the Battery**: Align the battery pack with the grooves on the back of the radio and slide it down until it clicks into place.

4. **Power On the Radio**: Press and hold the power button located on the top of the radio until the screen lights up.

5. **Set the Frequency**: Rotate the knob on the top left of the radio to select the desired frequency band (VHF or UHF).

6. **Adjust the Volume**: Use the volume knob on the top right of the radio to set your preferred listening level.

7. **Select a Channel**: Press the "VFO/MR" button to toggle between VFO (variable frequency) and MR (memory channel) modes. Use the keypad to input the desired channel number.

8. **Program a Channel (Optional)**: If using the programming cable, connect the radio to a computer. Open the programming software, load the radio settings, and input the desired frequencies and settings. Save and upload to the radio.

9. **Test Communication**: Press the push-to-talk (PTT) button on the side of the radio and speak into the microphone. Release the button to listen for a response.

10. **Store the Radio**: Place the radio in a protective case or holster when not in use to prevent damage.

Maintenance:

- **Weekly**: Check battery charge levels and recharge if necessary. Inspect the antenna for damage or wear.

- **Monthly**: Clean the radio's exterior with a soft, damp cloth to remove dirt and dust. Ensure all buttons and knobs function correctly.

- **Yearly**: Review and update programmed frequencies, ensuring they align with current communication needs. Replace the battery pack if performance declines.

Complexity:

This project is low to moderate in complexity. Basic familiarity with electronic devices is helpful, but no advanced skills are required. Challenges may arise during programming, particularly if using the software for the first time. However, clear instructions and user manuals alleviate most difficulties.

Estimated Time:

- **Setup**: 1 hour to charge the battery, attach the antenna, install the battery, and power on the radio.

- **Programming (optional)**: 1-2 hours to familiarize with the software and input desired frequencies.

- **Ongoing use**: 10-15 minutes to perform weekly checks and maintain the radio.

- **Total time for initial setup and basic use**: Approximately 2-3 hours, depending on programming preferences.

7.2 MAKING DIY SAFETY GEAR: WHISTLES, FLARES, VESTS

Creating your own safety equipment such as whistles, flares, and reflective vests is not just a cost-effective approach but also a proactive step towards enhancing your preparedness for emergencies. These items are essential for signaling for help, making yourself visible in low-light conditions, and ensuring you can be found should you become lost or face danger. Let's delve into how you can craft these critical safety tools with readily available materials and simple techniques.

For a DIY whistle, you can use aluminum or tin cans. Cut a rectangular piece from the can, fold it into a narrow rectangle, and curve it into a whistle shape. Small holes punched at one end allow air to flow through, creating the whistle sound when blown. This lightweight and durable whistle can be attached to a keychain, ensuring it's always within reach.

Flares are more complex to DIY safely and effectively, so instead of creating traditional chemical flares, focus on electronic flares which are reusable and environmentally friendly. Using LED lights, you can construct a distress signal device. Secure a bright LED to a small circuit board powered by a battery. Encase this setup in a waterproof, transparent container. Adding a switch allows you to activate the light in emergencies, and the bright LED can be seen from a distance, especially at night.

Reflective vests are crucial for visibility, particularly if you're moving around at night. You can make a simple yet effective vest using a bright-colored mesh fabric or even an old shirt as the base. Sew on reflective tape in strips across the chest, back, and shoulders. This tape is inexpensive and can be found at most craft or hardware stores. The key is to cover enough area on the vest so that light from any direction will be reflected, making you highly visible to rescuers or vehicles.

Remember, the goal of these DIY safety items is not to replace professional-grade equipment but to supplement your emergency kit with items that can be made quickly, affordably, and customized to your specific needs. Each of these projects not only adds an essential layer of safety to your off-grid living setup but also empowers you with the knowledge and skills to protect yourself and your loved ones in various situations. Whether you're hiking, camping, or simply working late at your off-grid homestead, these DIY safety tools ensure that you're prepared to signal for help, navigate safely, and be seen when it matters most.

7.2.1 DIY SAFETY GEAR: WHISTLES

Creating a DIY whistle serves multiple purposes, particularly for individuals living off-grid or those focused on self-sufficiency. A whistle is a crucial signaling device that can be used in emergencies to attract attention or communicate distress. In outdoor scenarios, such as hiking or camping, having a reliable means to signal for help can be life-saving. Whistles are compact, lightweight, and easy to carry, making them ideal for those who prioritize preparedness. The ability to produce a loud sound with minimal effort ensures that help can be summoned quickly in critical situations. This project not only provides a practical tool but also fosters resourcefulness and creativity in using everyday materials.

Materials and Tools:

- Aluminum or tin can - 1 unit (any standard size, such as a soda can)

- Scissors or sharp utility knife - 1 unit

- Drill with 1/8 inch drill bit - 1 unit

- Small rubber or silicone grommet - 1 unit (optional for added durability)

- Sandpaper - 1 piece (medium grit)

- String or lanyard - 1 unit (for attaching the whistle)

- Ruler - 1 unit

- Marker or pen - 1 unit

Step-by-Step Guide:

1. **Choose the Can**: Select an empty aluminum or tin can. A soda can works well due to its manageable size and thin material.

2. **Clean the Can**: Rinse the can thoroughly to remove any residue, ensuring it's safe to handle.

3. **Measure and Mark**: Use a ruler to measure 2 inches from the bottom of the can. Mark this point with a marker.

4. **Cut the Can**: Using scissors or a sharp utility knife, carefully cut the can just above the marked line, creating a cylinder that is 2 inches tall.

5. **Shape the Whistle**: Take the remaining piece of the can and cut it into a rectangular strip approximately 1 inch wide and 3 inches long.

6. **Create the Whistle Body**: Fold the rectangular strip into a U-shape, pinching the ends together to form a small opening at the bottom.

7. **Drill Air Holes**: Use a drill with a 1/8 inch drill bit to create a hole at the top of the whistle body. This hole allows air to flow through when blown.

8. **Smooth Edges**: Sand the edges of the cut can and the whistle body to remove any sharp edges that could cause injury.

9. **Insert Grommet (Optional)**: If using a rubber or silicone grommet, insert it into the drilled hole to reinforce the structure and prevent wear over time.

10. **Attach String**: Cut a length of string or lanyard, approximately 18 inches long. Tie one end securely to the whistle for easy carrying.

11. **Test the Whistle**: Blow into the whistle to test its sound. Adjust the positioning of the whistle body if necessary to enhance the sound quality.

12. **Customize (Optional)**: Paint or decorate the whistle with waterproof materials to personalize it and improve visibility.

Maintenance:

- **Weekly**: Inspect the whistle for any signs of damage or wear. Ensure that the air hole remains clear and unobstructed.

- **Monthly**: Clean the whistle with warm, soapy water to remove any dirt or debris that may accumulate, ensuring it remains functional.

- **Yearly**: Replace the whistle if it shows significant wear or if the sound quality diminishes. Consider making a new whistle using the same process.

Complexity:

The project is classified as low complexity, making it suitable for beginners. Basic skills required include measuring, cutting, and drilling. Challenges may arise when handling sharp tools, so caution is necessary. Ensuring a clean cut and proper shaping of the whistle body is crucial for optimal performance.

Estimated Time:

- **Setup**: 30 minutes to gather materials and tools.

- **Construction**: 30-45 minutes to complete the whistle.

- **Testing and customization**: 15 minutes to test sound quality and add any personal touches.

7.2.2 DIY SAFETY GEAR: FLARES

Creating DIY flares offers a vital signaling tool for emergencies, particularly for those engaged in off-grid living or outdoor activities. Flares provide a bright, visible signal that can be seen from great distances, making them essential for attracting attention during distress situations. Unlike conventional flares, which may require special handling or storage, DIY flares can be crafted from readily available materials, enhancing self-sufficiency and preparedness. This project not only fosters resourcefulness but also empowers individuals to take control of their safety measures in remote environments. With a focus on practicality, DIY flares serve as a cost-effective solution to ensure visibility when it matters most. By following this guide, anyone can create reliable flares that increase their safety in outdoor settings.

Materials and Tools:

- Candle wax - 1 pound

- Cotton wick - 3 units (6 inches long each)

- Metal containers (such as empty soup cans) - 3 units

- Flashing LED lights - 3 units (battery-operated)

- Matches or lighter - 1 unit

- Duct tape - 1 roll

- Old newspapers or cardboard - As needed (for creating a base)

- Pliers - 1 unit

- Scissors - 1 unit

- Heat source (stove or campfire) - 1 unit

Step-by-Step Guide:

1. **Prepare the Workspace**: Set up a clean, flat workspace with adequate ventilation, ensuring safety while working with wax and heat.

2. **Melt the Wax**: Place the candle wax into a metal container. Heat the container over a stove or campfire until the wax melts completely, stirring occasionally.

3. **Cut Wicks**: Using scissors, cut three cotton wicks to a length of 6 inches each. Ensure they are uniform for even burning.

4. **Insert Wicks**: While the wax is still liquid, carefully place one cotton wick into each of the three metal containers. Ensure that the wick stands upright and is centered.

5. **Fill Containers**: Pour the melted wax into each container, filling them to about 1 inch from the top. Allow some space for the wax to expand when it cools.

6. **Cool the Waxes**: Set the filled containers aside and let the wax cool completely. This process may take about 30-60 minutes.

7. **Attach LED Lights**: Once the wax has solidified, take the flashing LED lights and attach them securely to the top of each flare using duct tape. Position the lights so they are easily activated.

8. **Create a Base**: Cut pieces of old newspapers or cardboard into squares, approximately 6 inches by 6 inches. These will serve as bases to prevent the flares from tipping over.

9. **Secure the Flares**: Place each flare on a cardboard base, ensuring they stand upright. Use duct tape to secure the base to the flare if necessary.

10. **Test the Flares**: To ensure functionality, light a wick on one flare using matches or a lighter. Monitor the flame and LED light for effectiveness.

11. **Store Safely**: Store the completed flares in a cool, dry place away from direct sunlight and heat sources. Consider placing them in a sealed container to protect from moisture.

Maintenance:

- **Weekly**: Check the condition of the flares for any signs of damage or wear. Ensure the wicks remain intact and the LED lights are functioning properly.

- **Monthly**: Inspect the storage area for humidity or heat sources that could affect the flares' performance. Replace any flares that show significant wear or damage.

- **Yearly**: Review the overall inventory of flares. Refresh the stock by creating new flares to ensure an adequate supply is always available for emergencies.

Complexity:

This project is classified as low to moderate complexity. It requires basic skills such as melting wax, cutting wicks, and assembling components. Challenges may include ensuring safety when working with heat and maintaining stability during the cooling process. Proper precautions, such as using heat-resistant gloves and ensuring good ventilation, help mitigate these risks.

Estimated Time:

- **Setup**: 15-30 minutes to gather materials and prepare the workspace.

- **Wax preparation**: 30-45 minutes for melting and pouring the wax into containers.

- **Cooling time**: 30-60 minutes for the wax to solidify.

- **Assembly and testing**: 15-20 minutes to attach LED lights and test the flares.

7.2.3 DIY SAFETY GEAR: VESTS

Creating a DIY safety vest is a vital project for individuals pursuing off-grid living or engaging in DIY activities. Safety vests provide essential visibility and protection during outdoor tasks, whether working in low-light conditions, participating in community events, or navigating hazardous environments. By crafting their own safety vests, individuals gain control over materials and designs, ensuring they meet personal safety standards and fit specific needs. This project fosters self-sufficiency, allowing one to utilize available resources creatively while ensuring that safety remains a priority. Ultimately, a DIY safety vest enhances visibility, boosts confidence, and equips individuals with a practical tool for safe outdoor activities.

Materials and Tools:

- Reflective safety fabric - 1 yard
- High-visibility fluorescent fabric - 1 yard
- Heavy-duty sewing machine - 1 unit
- Thread (matching color) - 1 spool

- Scissors - 1 unit

- Measuring tape - 1 unit

- Safety pins - 5 units

- Fabric chalk or marker - 1 unit

- Velcro strips (hook and loop) - 2 pairs (for closures)

- Lining fabric (optional) - 1 yard

- Sewing pins - 10 units

- Iron - 1 unit

- Cutting mat - 1 unit

- Rotary cutter - 1 unit

Step-by-Step Guide:

1. **Measure the Body**: Measure the chest, waist, and desired length of the vest using a measuring tape, recording each measurement.

2. **Cut the Fabric**: Cut one piece of high-visibility fluorescent fabric to the recorded measurements, adding an extra inch for seam allowances. Cut another piece of reflective fabric the same size.

3. **Create Vest Shape**: Fold the fabric in half lengthwise. Use fabric chalk to mark an armhole shape, ensuring it's wide enough for comfortable movement.

4. **Cut Armholes**: Cut along the marked armhole shapes on both the fluorescent and reflective fabric pieces.

5. **Sew the Armholes**: Place the two fabric pieces together, right sides facing each other. Sew around the armholes with a straight stitch, ensuring to leave the bottom open.

6. **Create Side Seams**: Fold the fabric inward at the sides to form the vest shape. Pin the sides in place and sew from the bottom hem to the armhole, securing both fabric pieces together.

7. **Add Lining (Optional)**: If using lining fabric, cut it to the same size as the vest pieces. Pin and sew it to the inside of the vest for added comfort and durability.

8. **Hem the Bottom**: Fold the bottom edge of the vest inward by one inch, pin it in place, and sew a straight stitch to create a clean hem.

9. **Attach Velcro Strips**: Cut Velcro strips to desired lengths and sew them onto the front of the vest for secure closures, ensuring one side is on the fluorescent fabric and the other on the reflective fabric.

10. **Final Touches**: Inspect the vest for any loose threads or uneven seams. Iron the vest to smooth out any wrinkles and ensure a professional finish.

11. **Test the Fit**: Try on the vest to ensure it fits comfortably and allows for easy movement. Adjust the side seams if necessary for a better fit.

Maintenance:

- **Weekly**: Inspect the vest for any signs of wear or damage. Check Velcro closures for effectiveness and cleanliness.

- **Monthly**: Wash the vest according to fabric care instructions, ensuring the reflective material retains its visibility. Repair any loose seams or threads.

- **Yearly**: Review the vest for overall durability. Replace any worn-out materials or consider creating a new vest if significant wear is observed.

Complexity:

This project falls under moderate complexity. It requires basic sewing skills, familiarity with using a sewing machine, and attention to detail when measuring and cutting fabric. Challenges may arise in achieving a proper fit and ensuring all seams are secure, but these can be addressed with careful measurements and adjustments.

Estimated Time:

- **Setup**: 30 minutes to gather materials and prepare the workspace.

- **Cutting and sewing**: 2-3 hours to cut fabric, sew seams, and attach closures.

- **Final adjustments**: 15-30 minutes for fitting and making any necessary modifications.

7.3 CREATING A NO-GRID EMERGENCY RESPONSE PLAN

Creating a No-Grid Emergency Response Plan is essential for anyone looking to live a self-sufficient, off-grid lifestyle. Emergencies and disasters can strike without warning, making it critical to have a plan in place that ensures your safety and the safety of those around you. This plan should be comprehensive, covering all aspects of your off-grid living situation, from water and food supply to communication and shelter.

First, assess the potential risks specific to your area and lifestyle. Are you in a region prone to natural disasters such as hurricanes, floods, or wildfires? Understanding these risks is the first step in developing a plan that addresses them directly. Next, inventory your resources. Do you have enough food, water, and medical supplies to last at least two weeks? Are your energy sources reliable and sustainable in the event of a prolonged power outage?

Communication is a cornerstone of any emergency response plan. In a no-grid scenario, traditional communication methods may not be available. Consider alternative communication tools such as two-way radios or satellite phones, which can be crucial for staying in contact with the outside world or for reaching out for help. Ensure that all family members or group members are familiar with these tools and understand how to use them.

Water and food supply strategies must be robust and capable of sustaining you through an emergency period. This could involve having a rainwater collection system in place, as well as a stockpile of non-perishable food items. Additionally, knowing how to purify water and having the tools on hand to do so is vital.

Shelter and warmth are also critical components of your emergency plan. Ensure your living space is fortified against potential threats and that you have adequate insulation and heating methods that do not rely on external power sources. This might mean having a wood stove and a supply of firewood or alternative heating solutions that are sustainable and efficient.

First aid and medical care cannot be overlooked. A well-stocked first aid kit, knowledge of basic first aid procedures, and an understanding of how to use natural remedies for various ailments are all important. Consider taking a basic first aid course to enhance your skills and confidence in providing care during emergencies.

Finally, practice your emergency response plan regularly. This ensures that everyone knows what to do and where to go when an emergency strikes. It also allows you to identify any gaps in your plan that need addressing. Remember, the goal is not just to survive but to thrive, even in the face of unexpected challenges. By taking the time to create and refine your no-grid emergency response plan, you're taking a significant step towards achieving self-sufficiency and ensuring the safety and well-being of yourself and your loved ones.

7.4 BUDGET-FRIENDLY SELF-DEFENSE TECHNIQUES

Self-defense is a critical skill for anyone embracing a no-grid lifestyle, where professional help may not always be readily available. The good news is that effective self-defense doesn't require expensive equipment or years of martial arts training. Instead, it's about awareness, strategy, and the intelligent use of everyday items to protect oneself. Let's delve into practical, budget-friendly techniques and strategies that can be lifesavers in emergency situations.

First and foremost, situational awareness is your best defense. Always be mindful of your surroundings and the people around you. This doesn't mean living in a state of paranoia but rather in a state of preparedness, knowing who is nearby and what's happening around you. This awareness can give you precious seconds to react in case of an unexpected threat.

One of the simplest and most accessible self-defense tools is a flashlight. Not only is it useful for illumination, but a sturdy flashlight can also serve as a striking tool. Aim for vulnerable points such as the eyes, throat, or groin. The sudden burst of light can also disorient an attacker, giving you a chance to escape. Keep a flashlight handy, especially when moving around in poorly lit areas.

Another everyday item that can be repurposed for self-defense is a pen. A tactical pen, designed for such scenarios, is ideal, but even a regular pen can be effective when used with precision. Target pressure points or soft tissue areas like the side of the neck or the back of the hand. The goal is to cause enough pain or discomfort to your attacker, allowing you to get away.

Keys are something everyone carries, and they can be turned into a makeshift weapon in a pinch. Holding a key firmly between your fingers with the pointed end sticking out can enhance the impact of your punch. However, this technique requires close proximity to the attacker, so it should be used with caution and as a last resort.

Pepper spray is a more traditional self-defense tool that's both affordable and easy to carry. It can incapacitate an attacker long enough for you to escape. Ensure you're familiar with how to use it, and keep it in an easily accessible place, not buried at the bottom of a bag.

When it comes to self-defense strategies, the emphasis should always be on escape. Your primary goal is to put distance between yourself and the threat. This might mean running towards populated areas, yelling for help to attract attention, or using barriers like doors or furniture to slow down an attacker.

Training is also invaluable. Consider taking a basic self-defense class to learn proper techniques for striking, escaping holds, and using everyday items as weapons. These skills can boost your confidence and effectiveness in defending yourself.

Remember, the essence of self-defense lies not in the strength or the weapon but in the will to survive and the wisdom to use what's at hand. By adopting these strategies and incorporating everyday tools into your self-defense repertoire, you're taking proactive steps to ensure your safety and well-being, regardless of the challenges you might face while living off the grid.

8. Waste Management and Recycling

8.1 Introduction

Effective waste management and recycling are crucial components of living a sustainable, no-grid lifestyle. By adopting efficient practices, you can significantly reduce your environmental footprint and contribute to a healthier planet. This chapter provides practical guidance on creating and maintaining a comprehensive waste management system that includes composting, recycling, and reducing waste.

Composting is a natural process that transforms organic waste into valuable fertilizer for your garden, reducing the need for chemical fertilizers and enhancing soil health. Start by setting up a compost bin or pile in your backyard. You can compost kitchen scraps, yard trimmings, and even paper products. The key to successful composting is maintaining a balance between 'greens' such as vegetable scraps, which provide nitrogen, and 'browns' like dried leaves, which supply carbon. Regularly turning your compost pile accelerates the decomposition process, and within a few months, you'll have rich compost to nourish your plants.

DIY composting systems can range from simple piles to more sophisticated tumbler systems. For those with limited space, worm composting or vermicomposting is an effective alternative. This involves using red wiggler worms to break down food scraps and paper into compost. A worm composting bin can be easily set up indoors or outdoors, providing a continuous supply of compost without requiring a large space.

Recycling is another pillar of waste management. While off-grid living may limit access to municipal recycling services, you can still implement a robust recycling system. Start by reducing the amount of waste you produce. Choose reusable products over disposable ones, repair broken items instead of discarding them, and repurpose materials whenever possible. For the waste that cannot be avoided, sort it into categories such as glass, metals, plastics, and paper. Many communities offer drop-off locations for recyclables, or you can explore local businesses that may accept certain materials for recycling.

Creating a no-grid recycling system also involves thinking creatively about how to reuse materials. Glass jars can be repurposed for storage, metal cans can be turned into planters, and scrap wood can be used for a variety of DIY projects. By viewing waste as a resource, you can find innovative ways to minimize your impact on the environment.

DIY cleaning products offer a way to reduce household waste and avoid the harmful chemicals found in many commercial cleaners. Ingredients like vinegar, baking soda, and lemon juice can be used to make effective all-purpose cleaners, window sprays, and disinfectants. Not only do these homemade cleaners reduce the need for plastic packaging, but they also contribute to a healthier home environment.

Living minimalism is a lifestyle choice that complements waste management and recycling efforts. By focusing on what is truly necessary and avoiding excess, you can significantly reduce the amount of waste you generate. This approach not only benefits the environment but also leads to a simpler, more focused life.

Incorporating these waste management and recycling practices into your no-grid lifestyle requires commitment and creativity. However, the rewards are substantial, including reduced environmental impact, improved soil health, and a more sustainable way of living. By taking responsibility for the waste we produce and making conscious choices about how to handle it, we can make a positive difference for the planet and future generations.

8.2 Composting System Project

8.2.1 DIY Worm Composting Bin Project

Creating a worm composting bin, also known as vermicomposting, allows individuals to turn kitchen scraps into nutrient-rich compost. This project holds significant importance for those pursuing off-grid living or DIY sustainability. Worm composting reduces waste and fosters self-sufficiency by providing a constant supply of organic fertilizer for gardens and plants. The process employs red wiggler worms, which efficiently break down food waste and create compost that enhances soil health. Engaging in this project not only benefits personal gardens but also contributes to environmental stewardship by minimizing landfill waste. With minimal space and resources, anyone can establish a worm composting system, making it an accessible solution for achieving a sustainable lifestyle.

Materials and Tools:

- Plastic storage bin - 1 unit - 18 gallons
- Drill with ¼ inch drill bit - 1 unit
- Shredded newspaper - 1 bag - 10 pounds
- Red wiggler worms (Eisenia fetida) – 1 pound
- Organic kitchen scraps (vegetable and fruit waste) - As needed
- Water - As needed
- Burlap sack or old cotton cloth - 1 unit
- Spray bottle - 1 unit

Step-by-Step Guide:

1. **Choose a Bin**: Select a plastic storage bin with a lid that has a capacity of at least 18 gallons. The bin should be opaque to protect worms from light.
2. **Drill Holes**: Use a drill with a ¼ inch drill bit to create ventilation holes in the lid and along the sides of the bin, spaced about 6 inches apart. This ensures proper airflow for the worms.
3. **Prepare Bedding**: Shred newspaper into strips and soak it in water until moist but not soggy. Wring out excess water and fill the bin with 2-3 inches of this bedding material.
4. **Add Worms**: Sprinkle 1 pound of red wiggler worms over the prepared bedding. They will burrow into the bedding to acclimate to their new environment.
5. **Feed the Worms**: Start adding organic kitchen scraps to the bin, burying them under the bedding to prevent odors and pests. Limit food scraps to small quantities, roughly a handful every few days.
6. **Maintain Moisture**: Monitor the moisture level inside the bin. Use a spray bottle to mist the bedding if it appears dry. The bedding should feel like a wrung-out sponge.
7. **Cover the Bin**: Place the lid on the bin to keep out light and pests. Use the burlap sack or old cotton cloth to cover the top for added ventilation while still blocking light.
8. **Monitor Conditions**: Check the bin weekly for moisture and food levels. If the bedding becomes too wet, add dry shredded newspaper to balance it out.
9. **Harvest Compost**: After 3-6 months, check the bottom of the bin for dark, crumbly compost. Move the bedding to one side of the bin and add new bedding and food scraps to the other side. Over time, the worms will migrate to the fresh food, allowing you to collect the finished compost.
10. **Store the Compost**: Collect the compost from the side of the bin and store it in a container for use in the garden. This rich compost will enhance soil fertility and plant health.

Maintenance:

- **Weekly**: Check moisture levels in the bin, adding water or dry bedding as needed. Ensure that the food scraps are buried to prevent odors.
- **Monthly**: Inspect the worms and bedding for signs of pests or imbalance. Adjust the feeding schedule if food remains uneaten for extended periods.
- **Annually**: Harvest compost every 3-6 months. Clean the bin and refresh bedding to ensure a healthy environment for the worms.

Complexity:

The project is low in complexity, suitable for beginners. It requires basic skills such as drilling and monitoring moisture levels. Challenges may include maintaining the right balance of moisture and food, but these can be easily managed with attention and care.

Estimated Time:

- **Setup**: 1-2 hours to gather materials, drill holes, prepare bedding, and introduce worms.
- **Ongoing maintenance**: 10-15 minutes weekly for checking moisture, adding food, and monitoring conditions.
- **Compost harvesting**: 1-2 hours every 3-6 months to separate worms from compost and clean the bin.

8.3 NO-GRID WASTE SORTING & PROCESSING

Creating a no-grid recycling system begins with a commitment to reducing your environmental footprint by managing waste responsibly. This process involves sorting and processing waste materials in a way that repurposes them for new uses, thereby minimizing the amount sent to landfills. The first step is to identify the types of waste commonly produced in your household or off-grid community. These can include glass, paper, plastics, metals, and organic materials. Each type of waste requires a different approach for recycling or repurposing.

For glass and metals, cleaning and sorting by type and color are essential. These materials can often be taken to local recycling centers or scrap metal dealers. However, if access to such facilities is limited, consider creative repurposing within the community. Glass jars can serve as storage containers, candle holders, or small planters. Metals can be crafted into tools, decorative items, or even components for DIY projects.

Paper and cardboard are among the easiest materials to recycle. They can be reprocessed into new paper products, used as mulch or weed barrier in the garden, or shredded and added to compost as a carbon source. When recycling paper, remove any plastic coatings and ensure it is dry and free from food contamination to maintain its quality.

Plastics pose a greater challenge due to the variety of types and the specific recycling processes they require. Start by identifying the recycling codes on plastic items to sort them correctly. Some plastics can be melted down and remolded, but this often requires specialized equipment. For a no-grid approach, focus on reusing plastic containers for storage, as planters, or for crafting. Engage with local initiatives or businesses that collect specific types of plastic for recycling or repurposing.

Organic waste, including food scraps and yard trimmings, is a valuable resource in a no-grid recycling system. Through composting, this waste is transformed into nutrient-rich soil amendment for gardening, reducing the need for chemical fertilizers and enhancing soil health. Vermicomposting, or worm composting, is an efficient method for processing organic waste in smaller spaces, producing both compost and liquid fertilizer.

The success of a no-grid recycling system relies on community participation and education. Hosting workshops or sharing resources on waste sorting, recycling processes, and creative repurposing can foster a culture of sustainability. Establishing a communal space for collecting and processing recyclable materials encourages collective responsibility for waste management.

Implementing a no-grid recycling system is a proactive step towards sustainability, requiring creativity, commitment, and community collaboration. By sorting and processing waste thoughtfully, we can significantly reduce our environmental impact, conserve resources, and contribute to a healthier planet. This approach not only addresses the practical aspects of waste management but also promotes a mindset of resourcefulness and respect for the environment, essential values for thriving in a no-grid lifestyle.

8.4 EASY DIY HOMEMADE CLEANERS

8.4.1 DIY ALL-PURPOSE CLEANER

Creating a DIY all-purpose cleaner empowers individuals to maintain a clean and safe living environment while embracing a sustainable lifestyle. This project is particularly valuable for those pursuing off-grid living or DIY self-sufficiency. Commercial cleaners often contain harsh chemicals that can harm the environment and human health. By making an all-purpose cleaner at home, individuals reduce reliance on store-bought products, minimize plastic waste, and save money. This cleaner can effectively tackle various surfaces, from kitchen counters to bathroom fixtures, providing a natural alternative that is safe for families and pets. The project focuses on using readily available ingredients, ensuring affordability and ease of preparation, which are essential for a resourceful lifestyle.

Materials and Tools:

- Distilled white vinegar - 2 cups

- Water - 2 cups

- Essential oils (e.g., lemon, tea tree, or lavender) - 10-20 drops

- Spray bottle (preferably glass or BPA-free plastic) - 1 unit - 16 ounces

- Funnel - 1 unit

- Measuring cup - 1 unit

- Mixing spoon - 1 unit

Step-by-Step Guide:

1. **Gather Ingredients**: Collect 2 cups of distilled white vinegar, 2 cups of water, and your choice of essential oils.

2. **Measure Vinegar**: Use a measuring cup to pour 2 cups of distilled white vinegar into the spray bottle.

3. **Add Water**: Measure and add 2 cups of water to the spray bottle using the same measuring cup.

4. **Incorporate Essential Oils**: Add 10-20 drops of your selected essential oils into the mixture. For a fresh scent, lemon is ideal; for antibacterial properties, use tea tree oil.

5. **Mix the Solution**: Use a mixing spoon to gently stir the contents of the spray bottle, ensuring that the oils blend with the vinegar and water.

6. **Secure the Spray Nozzle**: Attach the spray nozzle to the bottle, ensuring a tight seal to prevent leaks.

7. **Label the Bottle**: Use a permanent marker or label maker to mark the bottle as "All-Purpose Cleaner" for easy identification.

8. **Test the Cleaner**: Spray a small amount on a hidden area of the surface you intend to clean to ensure compatibility and avoid damage.

9. **Store Properly**: Keep the all-purpose cleaner in a cool, dark place to preserve the efficacy of the essential oils and vinegar.

Maintenance:

- **Weekly**: Check the cleaner for any signs of separation. If separation occurs, shake the bottle before use to mix the ingredients thoroughly.

- **Monthly**: Inspect the spray nozzle for clogs. Clean it with warm water and vinegar if necessary to ensure a fine mist.

- **Annually**: Replace essential oils as needed to maintain scent potency and effectiveness, especially if the cleaner sits unused for an extended period.

Complexity:

This project is low in complexity and suitable for beginners.

Estimated Time:

- **Setup**: 15-20 minutes to gather materials, measure ingredients, and mix the solution.

- **Ongoing maintenance**: 5 minutes weekly for checking the mixture and cleaning the spray nozzle.

- **Essential oil replacement**: 5 minutes annually to select and add new oils as needed.

8.4.2 DIY GLASS CLEANER

Creating a DIY glass cleaner provides an effective solution for achieving streak-free, crystal-clear windows and surfaces. This project is essential for off-grid living or DIY enthusiasts who seek to maintain cleanliness without relying on commercial products laden with harmful chemicals. A homemade glass cleaner offers several benefits: it is budget-friendly, environmentally safe, and straightforward to prepare using common household ingredients. This cleaner tackles tough smudges, dirt, and grime without leaving behind toxic residues, making it safe for use around children and pets. By opting for a natural approach, individuals not only promote a healthier living space but also contribute to sustainability by reducing plastic waste from store-bought cleaners. This guide details how to create an effective glass cleaner that can be used on mirrors, windows, and glass surfaces throughout the home.

Materials and Tools:

- Distilled water - 2 cups

- Rubbing alcohol (isopropyl alcohol) - 1 cup

- Cornstarch - 2 tablespoons

- Essential oil (optional, e.g., lemon or lavender) - 10 drops

- Spray bottle (preferably glass or BPA-free plastic) - 1 unit - 16 ounces

- Funnel - 1 unit

- Measuring cup - 1 unit

- Mixing spoon - 1 unit

Step-by-Step Guide:

1. **Gather Ingredients**: Collect 2 cups of distilled water, 1 cup of rubbing alcohol, 2 tablespoons of cornstarch, and optional essential oil for fragrance.

2. **Prepare the Spray Bottle**: Rinse the spray bottle with warm water to ensure it is clean and free from previous contents.

3. **Measure Distilled Water**: Using a measuring cup, pour 2 cups of distilled water into the spray bottle.

4. **Add Rubbing Alcohol**: Measure and add 1 cup of rubbing alcohol to the spray bottle. This ingredient enhances the cleaning power and helps the solution evaporate quickly, reducing streaks.

5. **Incorporate Cornstarch**: Measure 2 tablespoons of cornstarch and add it to the spray bottle. Cornstarch acts as a natural cleaning agent that aids in achieving a streak-free finish.

6. **Include Essential Oil**: If desired, add 10 drops of essential oil to the mixture for a pleasant scent. This step is optional but can enhance the cleaning experience.

7. **Mix the Solution**: Use a mixing spoon to stir the ingredients gently inside the spray bottle, ensuring the cornstarch dissolves fully and integrates with the other components.

8. **Secure the Spray Nozzle**: Attach the spray nozzle to the bottle, ensuring it is tightly sealed to prevent leaks.

9. **Label the Bottle**: Clearly label the bottle as "Glass Cleaner" for easy identification and to avoid any mix-up with other household products.

10. **Test the Cleaner**: Spray a small amount on a hidden area of the glass surface to test for compatibility. Wait a moment and check for any adverse reactions.

11. **Store Properly**: Store the glass cleaner in a cool, dark place to maintain its effectiveness. Shake well before each use to re-mix any settled cornstarch.

Maintenance:

- **Weekly**: Check the glass cleaner for any signs of separation. Shake the bottle to ensure the cornstarch is evenly distributed before each use.

- **Monthly**: Inspect the spray nozzle for clogs. Clean it with warm water if necessary to maintain an even spray pattern.

- **Annually**: Replace the ingredients as needed, particularly the rubbing alcohol and essential oils, to ensure the solution remains effective.

Complexity:

This project is low in complexity, making it accessible for beginners. If the cornstarch does not dissolve properly, leading to clogs in the spray nozzle, try to mitigate it thorough mixing and consider straining the solution through a fine mesh if needed.

Estimated Time:

- **Setup**: 15-20 minutes to gather materials, measure ingredients, and mix the solution.

- **Ongoing maintenance**: 5 minutes weekly for checking the mixture and cleaning the spray nozzle.

- **Ingredient replacement**: 5 minutes annually to refresh supplies as necessary.

8.4.3 DIY FLOOR CLEANER

Creating a DIY floor cleaner is a practical and effective way to maintain clean and sanitary floors while minimizing environmental impact. This project is particularly important for individuals living off-grid or those seeking to adopt a sustainable lifestyle. The DIY floor cleaner utilizes simple, budget-friendly ingredients like water, vinegar, dish soap, and rubbing alcohol. These components not only provide excellent cleaning power but also avoid the harsh chemicals found in many commercial cleaners. By making a floor cleaner at home, individuals reduce plastic waste from packaging and control the ingredients, ensuring a safer environment for their families and pets. The homemade cleaner effectively cuts through grease, grime, and dirt, leaving floors spotless without the risk of harmful residues. This guide outlines the steps to create an efficient and economical floor cleaner, ensuring that anyone can tackle this project with ease.

Materials and Tools:

- Water - 2 cups

- White vinegar - 1 cup

- Dish soap - 1 tablespoon

- Rubbing alcohol (isopropyl alcohol) - 1 cup

- Spray bottle (preferably glass or BPA-free plastic) - 1 unit - 32 ounces

- Funnel - 1 unit

- Measuring cup - 1 unit

- Mixing spoon - 1 unit

- Cleaning cloth or mop - 1 unit

Step-by-Step Guide:

1. **Gather Ingredients**: Collect 2 cups of water, 1 cup of white vinegar, 1 tablespoon of dish soap, and 1 cup of rubbing alcohol.

2. **Prepare the Spray Bottle**: Rinse the spray bottle with warm water to remove any residues from previous cleaners.

3. **Measure Water**: Using a measuring cup, pour 2 cups of water into the spray bottle.

4. **Add Vinegar**: Measure and add 1 cup of white vinegar to the spray bottle. Vinegar serves as a natural disinfectant and deodorizer.

5. **Incorporate Dish Soap**: Measure 1 tablespoon of dish soap and add it to the mixture. The dish soap helps lift dirt and grease from surfaces.

6. **Include Rubbing Alcohol**: Measure 1 cup of rubbing alcohol and pour it into the spray bottle. This ingredient enhances cleaning power and promotes fast drying.

7. **Mix the Solution**: Use a mixing spoon to stir the ingredients gently inside the spray bottle, ensuring the soap blends well with the liquids.

8. **Secure the Spray Nozzle**: Attach the spray nozzle to the bottle, ensuring it is tightly sealed to prevent leaks.

9. **Label the Bottle**: Clearly label the bottle as "Floor Cleaner" to avoid confusion with other household products.

10. **Test the Cleaner**: Spray a small amount on a hidden area of the floor to test for compatibility. Wait a moment and check for any adverse reactions.

11. **Clean the Floors**: Spray the cleaner directly onto the floor surface or onto a cleaning cloth/mop. Wipe the area clean, focusing on any stubborn spots.

12. **Store Properly**: Store the floor cleaner in a cool, dark place to maintain its effectiveness. Shake well before each use to ensure the mixture is properly combined.

Maintenance:

- **Weekly**: Inspect the spray bottle for any signs of leaks. Check the solution level and refill as needed.
- **Monthly**: Clean the spray nozzle with warm water to prevent clogs. Ensure that the mixture is still effective; replace ingredients if the cleaner starts to lose potency.
- **Annually**: Refresh the ingredients in the cleaner. Replace the spray bottle if it shows signs of wear or damage to ensure continued functionality.

Complexity:

This project is low in complexity, making it suitable for beginners.

Estimated Time:

- **Setup**: 15-20 minutes to gather materials, measure ingredients, and mix the solution.
- **Ongoing maintenance**: 5 minutes weekly for checking the solution level and cleaning the spray nozzle.
- **Ingredient replacement**: 5 minutes annually to refresh supplies as necessary.

8.4.4 DIY BATHROOM CLEANER

Creating a DIY bathroom cleaner empowers individuals to maintain a clean, sanitary space without resorting to harsh chemicals. This project is particularly vital for those embracing off-grid living or pursuing a sustainable lifestyle. The bathroom often becomes a breeding ground for bacteria, mold, and mildew, making effective cleaning essential. This homemade cleaner not only tackles grime but also minimizes environmental impact, as it uses natural, biodegradable ingredients. By opting for a DIY solution, individuals save money, reduce plastic waste, and ensure safety for their families. The project aims to produce a powerful cleaner using liquid castile soap, baking soda, and water. This simple formula effectively cleans surfaces, disinfects, and leaves bathrooms fresh without the harsh odors or residues associated with commercial cleaners. With easy-to-find materials and straightforward instructions, anyone can create a budget-friendly bathroom cleaner.

Materials and Tools:

- Liquid castile soap - 2 tablespoons

- Baking soda - 1 tablespoon

- Water - 2 cups

- Spray bottle (preferably glass or BPA-free plastic) - 1 unit - 16 ounces

- Funnel - 1 unit

- Measuring spoons - 1 unit

- Mixing spoon - 1 unit

- Cleaning cloth or sponge - 1 unit

Step-by-Step Guide:

1. **Gather Ingredients**: Collect 2 tablespoons of liquid castile soap, 1 tablespoon of baking soda, and 2 cups of water.

2. **Prepare the Spray Bottle**: Rinse the spray bottle with warm water to eliminate any residues from previous cleaning solutions.

3. **Measure Water**: Using a measuring cup, pour 2 cups of water into the spray bottle.

4. **Add Castile Soap**: Measure and add 2 tablespoons of liquid castile soap to the water. This soap serves as a natural surfactant that cuts through dirt and grime.

5. **Incorporate Baking Soda**: Measure 1 tablespoon of baking soda and add it to the mixture. Baking soda acts as a gentle abrasive and deodorizer.

6. **Mix the Solution**: Use a mixing spoon to stir the ingredients gently inside the spray bottle. Ensure the baking soda dissolves completely to prevent clumping.

7. **Secure the Spray Nozzle**: Attach the spray nozzle to the bottle tightly to prevent leaks during use.

8. **Label the Bottle**: Clearly label the spray bottle as "Bathroom Cleaner" to avoid confusion with other household products.

9. **Test the Cleaner**: Spray a small amount on a hidden area, such as behind the toilet, to check for any adverse reactions with the surface material.

10. **Clean the Bathroom**: Spray the cleaner directly onto bathroom surfaces such as countertops, sinks, and tiles. Allow it to sit for a few minutes to break down dirt and grime.

11. **Wipe Clean**: Use a cleaning cloth or sponge to wipe the surfaces clean. Focus on areas with stubborn stains or buildup, applying additional pressure if necessary.

12. **Store Properly**: Store the bathroom cleaner in a cool, dark place to maintain its effectiveness. Shake well before each use to ensure proper mixing.

Maintenance:

- **Weekly**: Inspect the spray bottle for leaks. Ensure the solution level is adequate and refill as needed. Clean the spray nozzle with warm water to prevent clogs and ensure even spraying.

- **Monthly**: Check the effectiveness of the cleaner. If odors or residues remain after cleaning, consider refreshing the solution by replacing the castile soap or baking soda.

- **Annually**: Clean the spray bottle thoroughly. Replace it if it shows signs of wear or damage to maintain functionality.

Complexity:

This project is low in complexity, making it suitable for beginners. Ensure proper mixing to avoid clumping of baking soda.

Estimated Time:

- **Setup**: 15-20 minutes to gather materials, measure ingredients, and mix the solution.

- **Ongoing maintenance**: 5 minutes weekly for checking the solution level and cleaning the spray nozzle.

- **Ingredient replacement**: 5 minutes annually to refresh supplies as necessary.

8.4.5 DIY KITCHEN DEGREASER

Creating a DIY kitchen degreaser offers an effective, budget-friendly solution for tackling stubborn grease and grime that accumulates in cooking spaces. This project is particularly essential for those pursuing off-grid living or sustainable DIY practices, as it minimizes reliance on commercial cleaning products filled with harsh chemicals. A homemade degreaser not only cleans effectively but also contributes to a healthier home environment. The ingredients for this degreaser are simple and inexpensive, making it accessible for everyone. Using vinegar, water, and dish soap, this mixture breaks down grease, deodorizes surfaces, and leaves kitchens sparkling clean. With this DIY solution, individuals can confidently maintain a clean kitchen while reducing their environmental footprint. The project aims to empower individuals to create their own cleaning solutions that are safe, effective, and easy to make.

Materials and Tools:

- White vinegar - ½ cup

- Water - 1 cup

- Liquid dish soap - 1 tablespoon

- Spray bottle (preferably glass or BPA-free plastic) - 1 unit - 16 ounces

- Funnel - 1 unit

- Measuring cups - 1 unit

- Measuring spoons - 1 unit

- Mixing spoon - 1 unit

Step-by-Step Guide:

1. **Gather Ingredients**: Collect ½ cup of white vinegar, 1 cup of water, and 1 tablespoon of liquid dish soap.

2. **Prepare the Spray Bottle**: Rinse the spray bottle with warm water to remove any residues from previous cleaning solutions.

3. **Measure Vinegar**: Using a measuring cup, pour ½ cup of white vinegar into the spray bottle. Vinegar is a natural degreaser that cuts through grease effectively.

4. **Add Water**: Measure and add 1 cup of water to the vinegar in the spray bottle. This dilutes the vinegar, making it safe for various surfaces while maintaining cleaning power.

5. **Incorporate Dish Soap**: Measure 1 tablespoon of liquid dish soap and add it to the mixture. The dish soap acts as a surfactant, helping to lift grease from surfaces.

6. **Mix the Solution**: Use a mixing spoon to stir the ingredients gently inside the spray bottle. Ensure the soap is well incorporated into the vinegar and water mixture.

7. **Secure the Spray Nozzle**: Attach the spray nozzle to the bottle tightly to prevent leaks during use.

8. **Label the Bottle**: Clearly label the spray bottle as "Kitchen Degreaser" to avoid confusion with other household products.

9. **Test the Cleaner**: Spray a small amount on a hidden area, such as a corner of the countertop, to check for any adverse reactions with the surface material.

10. **Clean the Kitchen**: Spray the degreaser directly onto greasy surfaces, such as stovetops, countertops, and backsplashes. Allow it to sit for a few minutes to break down the grease.

11. **Wipe Clean**: Use a cleaning cloth or sponge to wipe the surfaces clean. For tough, baked-on grease, apply additional spray and scrub with more pressure.

12. **Store Properly**: Store the kitchen degreaser in a cool, dark place to maintain its effectiveness. Shake well before each use to ensure proper mixing.

Maintenance:

- **Weekly**: Check the spray bottle for leaks. Ensure the solution level is adequate and refill as needed. Clean the spray nozzle with warm water to prevent clogs and ensure even spraying.

- **Monthly**: Inspect the effectiveness of the degreaser. If it fails to cut through grease, consider refreshing the solution by replacing the vinegar or dish soap.

- **Annually**: Clean the spray bottle thoroughly. Replace it if it shows signs of wear or damage to maintain functionality.

Complexity:

This project is low in complexity, making it suitable for beginners.

Estimated Time:

- **Setup**: 10-15 minutes to gather materials, measure ingredients, and mix the solution.

- **Ongoing maintenance**: 5 minutes weekly for checking the solution level and cleaning the spray nozzle.

- **Ingredient replacement**: 5 minutes annually to refresh supplies as necessary.

8.4.6 DIY FURNITURE POLISH

Creating a DIY furniture polish offers a natural and cost-effective way to maintain and enhance the beauty of wooden furniture. For those living off-grid or pursuing a sustainable lifestyle, this project aligns perfectly with the principles of self-sufficiency and environmental responsibility. Many commercial furniture polishes contain harmful chemicals that can negatively impact indoor air quality and pose risks to health. By crafting a homemade polish using simple, readily available ingredients, individuals can ensure a safe and eco-friendly approach to furniture care. This project utilizes natural oils, such as olive or coconut oil, combined with essential oils for fragrance, providing not only protection but also a pleasant aroma that revitalizes living spaces. The resulting polish nourishes wood, restores shine, and helps to repel dust and dirt, making it an essential addition to any off-grid home.

Materials and Tools:

- Olive oil - ½ cup

- White vinegar - ¼ cup

- Essential oil (lemon or lavender) - 10-15 drops

- Mixing bowl - 1 unit
- Whisk or spoon - 1 unit
- Clean spray bottle (preferably glass) - 1 unit - 16 ounces
- Funnel - 1 unit

Step-by-Step Guide:

1. **Gather Ingredients**: Collect ½ cup of olive oil, ¼ cup of white vinegar, and 10-15 drops of your chosen essential oil.
2. **Prepare Mixing Bowl**: Choose a clean mixing bowl to avoid contamination from previous substances.
3. **Combine Olive Oil and Vinegar**: Pour ½ cup of olive oil into the mixing bowl followed by ¼ cup of white vinegar. The olive oil nourishes the wood, while the vinegar cleans and adds shine.
4. **Add Essential Oil**: Drop 10-15 drops of essential oil into the mixture. Lemon oil provides a fresh scent and enhances cleaning power, while lavender offers a calming aroma.
5. **Mix Thoroughly**: Use a whisk or spoon to blend the ingredients thoroughly. Ensure the oil and vinegar are fully combined for an even application.
6. **Transfer to Spray Bottle**: Position the funnel over the spray bottle's opening and pour the mixture into the bottle. This prevents spills and makes transferring easier.
7. **Seal the Bottle**: Secure the spray nozzle onto the bottle tightly to prevent leaks.
8. **Label the Bottle**: Clearly label the spray bottle as "Furniture Polish" for easy identification.
9. **Test the Polish**: Apply a small amount on an inconspicuous area of the furniture to check for any adverse reactions with the finish.
10. **Polish the Furniture**: Spray a light mist of the polish directly onto the wood surface. Use a soft, lint-free cloth to buff the surface in circular motions, enhancing shine and nourishment.
11. **Store Properly**: Keep the furniture polish in a cool, dark place to preserve its effectiveness. Shake well before each use to ensure the ingredients mix properly.

Maintenance:

- **Weekly**: Check the polish level in the spray bottle. Refill as needed using the same recipe.
- **Monthly**: Inspect the furniture for dust accumulation. Use the polish to clean and maintain shine, applying as needed to prevent buildup.
- **Annually**: Evaluate the effectiveness of the polish. If it seems less effective, consider adjusting the essential oil quantity or refreshing the mixture.

Complexity:

This project is low in complexity, making it accessible for beginners.

Estimated Time:

- **Setup**: 10-15 minutes to gather materials, measure ingredients, and mix the solution.
- **Ongoing maintenance**: 5 minutes weekly for checking the polish level and cleaning surfaces.
- **Refill preparation**: 10 minutes as needed to mix a new batch of furniture polish.

8.4.7 DIY CARPET DEODORIZER

Creating a DIY carpet deodorizer offers a simple, effective way to eliminate unpleasant odors from carpets and rugs. This project holds great significance for those living off-grid or embracing a sustainable lifestyle.

Commercial carpet deodorizers often contain harsh chemicals that can harm indoor air quality and the environment. By crafting a natural deodorizer with accessible ingredients, individuals can ensure a safe, eco-friendly solution to maintain a fresh-smelling home. This DIY project utilizes baking soda, a powerful natural odor absorber, combined with essential oils to provide a pleasant fragrance. The result is a carpet deodorizer that not only neutralizes odors but also contributes to a healthier living environment. This homemade solution is cost-effective, easy to make, and perfect for anyone looking to reduce their reliance on store-bought products.

Materials and Tools:

- Baking soda - 1 cup
- Essential oil (lavender, lemon, or tea tree) - 10-15 drops
- Mixing bowl - 1 unit
- Whisk or spoon - 1 unit
- Glass jar with lid - 1 unit - 16 ounces
- Small measuring cup - 1 unit
- Funnel - 1 unit

Step-by-Step Guide:

1. **Gather Ingredients**: Collect 1 cup of baking soda and 10-15 drops of your chosen essential oil.
2. **Prepare Mixing Bowl**: Choose a clean mixing bowl to ensure no contamination affects the deodorizer.
3. **Combine Baking Soda and Essential Oil**: Pour 1 cup of baking soda into the mixing bowl. Add 10-15 drops of essential oil to the baking soda.
4. **Mix Thoroughly**: Use a whisk or spoon to blend the baking soda and essential oil until evenly combined. The mixture should have a consistent texture without clumps.
5. **Transfer to Glass Jar**: Position the funnel over the glass jar's opening and carefully pour the deodorizer mixture into the jar, minimizing spills.
6. **Seal the Jar**: Secure the lid on the jar tightly to preserve the fragrance and effectiveness of the deodorizer.
7. **Label the Jar**: Clearly label the jar as "Carpet Deodorizer" for easy identification and safe storage.
8. **Apply the Deodorizer**: Shake the jar gently to aerate the mixture. Sprinkle an even layer of the deodorizer over the carpet surface, ensuring complete coverage.
9. **Let it Sit**: Allow the deodorizer to sit on the carpet for at least 15-30 minutes. For stronger odors, extend the time to a few hours or even overnight.
10. **Vacuum the Carpet**: After the deodorizing period, vacuum the carpet thoroughly to remove the baking soda and trapped odors.
11. **Store Properly**: Keep the jar in a cool, dark place to maintain its potency. Shake before each use to ensure the mixture remains evenly distributed.

Maintenance:

- **Weekly**: Check the carpet for any lingering odors. If needed, repeat the deodorizing process using the same steps.
- **Monthly**: Evaluate the effectiveness of the deodorizer. If the fragrance fades, consider adding more essential oil to the mixture.
- **Annually**: Refresh the mixture by preparing a new batch of deodorizer. Store the old jar properly if it still retains effectiveness, or dispose of it responsibly.

Complexity:

This project is low in complexity, making it suitable for all skill levels. Ensure an even distribution of the deodorizer on the carpet for optimal results.

Estimated Time:

- **Setup**: 10-15 minutes to gather materials, measure ingredients, and mix the solution.

- **Application**: 15-30 minutes to sprinkle the deodorizer on the carpet and allow it to sit.

- **Vacuuming**: 10-15 minutes to thoroughly vacuum the carpet after the deodorizer has settled.

8.4.8 DIY LAUNDRY DETERGENT PROJECT

Creating a DIY laundry detergent offers a practical solution for those looking to maintain cleanliness without relying on commercial products laden with harsh chemicals. This project is particularly significant for individuals living off-grid or those committed to a sustainable lifestyle. Store-bought laundry detergents often contain synthetic fragrances, phosphates, and fillers that can harm the environment and irritate sensitive skin. By making a homemade detergent, individuals can control the ingredients, ensuring a gentle yet effective cleaning solution for their clothes.

This DIY laundry detergent not only reduces environmental impact but also saves money. A small investment in a few basic ingredients yields multiple batches of detergent, significantly lowering the cost per load compared to commercial options. Furthermore, crafting a homemade detergent empowers individuals, allowing them to take charge of their cleaning supplies and reduce their dependence on retail products. The end goal of this project is to create an efficient, eco-friendly laundry detergent that provides excellent cleaning power while being budget-friendly.

Materials and Tools:

- Washing soda (sodium carbonate) - 1 box - 55 ounces

- Borax (sodium borate) - 1 box - 76 ounces

- Fels-Naptha soap (or another bar soap) - 1 bar - 5.5 ounces

- Grater or food processor - 1 unit

- Large mixing bowl - 1 unit

- Airtight container for storage - 1 unit - 2-gallon capacity

- Measuring cup - 1 unit

- Spoon or spatula - 1 unit

Step-by-Step Guide:

1. **Gather Ingredients**: Collect 1 box each of washing soda and borax, and 1 bar of Fels-Naptha soap.

2. **Grate the Soap**: Use a grater or food processor to finely grate the bar of soap into small flakes. Aim for a texture similar to coarse sand.

3. **Combine Ingredients**: In a large mixing bowl, add 1 cup of grated soap, 1 cup of washing soda, and 1 cup of borax.

4. **Mix Thoroughly**: Use a spoon or spatula to mix the ingredients together until they are evenly combined. The mixture should appear uniform in texture and colour.

5. **Transfer to Container**: Carefully pour the detergent mixture into an airtight container for storage, ensuring minimal spillage.

6. **Seal the Container**: Tightly seal the container to preserve the detergent's effectiveness and prevent moisture absorption.

7. **Label the Container**: Clearly label the container as "DIY Laundry Detergent" for easy identification.

8. **Determine Usage**: For regular loads, use 2 tablespoons of the detergent per load. For heavily soiled clothes, increase to 4 tablespoons.

9. **Store Properly**: Keep the airtight container in a cool, dry place away from direct sunlight to maintain the detergent's quality.

Maintenance:

- **Weekly**: Check the airtight container for any signs of moisture or clumping. If moisture is detected, consider moving the detergent to a drier location.

- **Monthly**: Inspect the detergent for effectiveness. If it seems less effective, consider refreshing the ingredients by mixing in another batch of grated soap.

- **Yearly**: Review the detergent storage conditions. If the container shows signs of wear or damage, replace it to ensure continued protection against moisture.

Complexity:

This project is low in complexity, making it suitable for beginners. Grating the soap may require a bit of physical effort, but the process is straightforward and manageable.

Estimated Time:

- **Setup**: 15-20 minutes to gather materials, grate the soap, and mix the ingredients.

- **Storage**: 5 minutes to transfer the mixture into an airtight container and label it.

- **Usage**: Each laundry load requires only a few seconds to measure out the detergent.

8.5 REDUCING WASTE AND LIVING MINIMALISM

Reducing waste and embracing a minimalist lifestyle are fundamental steps towards achieving a sustainable, no-grid living environment. This approach not only lessens the impact on the planet but also simplifies life, focusing on what is truly essential and eliminating the unnecessary. The journey to minimalism and waste reduction begins with a conscious decision to evaluate personal and household consumption habits, identifying areas where changes can be made to reduce clutter and waste.

One of the first steps is to adopt the principle of 'reduce, reuse, recycle' as a daily mantra. Reducing consumption means buying less and choosing items that are durable, versatile, and necessary. This not only cuts down on waste but also saves money in the long run. When purchases are necessary, opting for second-hand or high-quality items that last longer can significantly decrease the demand for new products and the resources needed to produce them.

Reusing items extends their life and prevents them from ending up in landfills. Simple practices such as using cloth bags instead of plastic, repurposing glass jars as food storage containers, and repairing rather than discarding damaged items can make a substantial difference. Creativity plays a key role here, as many items can serve multiple purposes before they need to be recycled or disposed of.

Recycling is crucial in managing waste that cannot be reduced or reused. Proper sorting of recyclables, understanding local recycling guidelines, and taking advantage of recycling programs are vital steps. However, recycling should be seen as a last resort after efforts to reduce and reuse have been exhausted, as the process itself consumes energy and resources.

Beyond the 'reduce, reuse, recycle' mantra, living minimalism is about simplifying life and focusing on experiences rather than possessions. This involves decluttering living spaces, which not only makes homes more pleasant and less stressful but also reduces the desire to buy and accumulate more stuff. When decluttering, items that no longer serve a purpose or bring joy can be donated, sold, or given to someone who needs them, ensuring they continue to be used rather than discarded.

Minimalism also encourages mindful consumption, questioning the need for purchases and their impact on the environment and personal well-being. This mindset shift can lead to a more fulfilling life, where value is placed on relationships, experiences, and personal growth rather than material possessions.

Incorporating minimalism and waste reduction into no-grid living enhances self-sufficiency and resilience. It promotes a deeper connection with the environment and a greater appreciation for the resources used daily. By making conscious choices about consumption and waste, individuals can live more sustainably, reduce their environmental footprint, and contribute to a healthier planet for future generations.

Embracing these principles requires patience, commitment, and a willingness to change habits. The benefits, however, extend far beyond personal gain, contributing to a global movement towards sustainability and mindful living. Through reducing waste and living minimalism, individuals can find greater satisfaction in a simpler, more intentional life aligned with the values of no-grid living.

9. TOOLS AND EQUIPMENT

9.1 INTRODUCTION

Crafting your own tools and equipment is not just about saving money; it's about gaining the independence and knowledge to maintain and repair your own gear, ensuring you're always prepared, no matter the situation. The ability to create and modify tools using affordable and accessible materials is a cornerstone of self-sufficiency that empowers you to solve problems with confidence and creativity.

Fishing and hunting are vital skills for food procurement in a no-grid lifestyle, and making your own equipment can be both rewarding and practical. A simple fishing kit can be assembled from line, hooks, and sinkers found or repurposed, while DIY traps and snares for small game can be constructed from wire, string, and natural materials found in your environment.

The ability to communicate and signal for help is critical in remote living or emergency situations. Crafting a solar-powered radio or flashlight can ensure you have access to information and a means of illumination without relying on grid power. Similarly, a DIY emergency signal mirror can be made from polished metal or a compact disc, providing a simple but effective way to signal rescuers.

Incorporating these tools and equipment into your no-grid lifestyle not only enhances your self-reliance but also fosters a deeper connection with your environment. By understanding the materials and resources available to you, and how to craft and maintain your own equipment, you're better prepared to face challenges and embrace the independence that comes with a no-grid lifestyle. This hands-on approach to tools and equipment is not just about survival; it's about thriving in harmony with your surroundings, armed with the knowledge and skills you've developed through your own ingenuity and effort.

9.2 ESSENTIAL OFF-GRID TOOL KIT

9.2.1 DIY FIRE STARTER KIT PROJECT

Creating a DIY Fire Starter Kit is an essential project for anyone pursuing off-grid living or engaging in outdoor activities like camping and hiking. This kit provides a reliable means to ignite fires, crucial for cooking, warmth, and signaling in emergencies. The ability to start a fire can be a lifesaver, especially in survival situations where conventional methods may fail. A well-constructed fire starter kit empowers individuals with the knowledge and resources to create flames quickly and efficiently, regardless of the weather conditions. Additionally, this project allows for customization, enabling users to tailor the kit to their specific needs and preferences. Overall, having a DIY Fire Starter Kit promotes self-sufficiency, safety, and preparedness in various environments.

Materials and Tools:

- Waterproof container - 1 unit (e.g., plastic or metal box with a secure lid)

- Cotton balls - 10 units

- Petroleum jelly - 1 small container (approximately 4 ounces)

- Dryer lint - 1 cup (collected and stored in a bag)

- Magnesium fire starter - 1 unit

- Tinder (e.g., shredded paper or natural materials) - 1 bag

- Strike-anywhere matches - 20 units

- Ziplock bags - 2 units (quart-sized)

- Paracord - 10 feet

- Scissors - 1 unit

- Lighter - 1 unit

Step-by-Step Guide:

1. **Select a Container**: Choose a waterproof container that is durable and has a secure lid, such as a plastic or metal box.

2. **Prepare Cotton Balls**: Take 10 cotton balls and coat them thoroughly with petroleum jelly, ensuring they are well-saturated.

3. **Pack Cotton Balls**: Place the coated cotton balls in one of the quart-sized Ziplock bags, sealing it tightly to keep them dry.

4. **Collect Dryer Lint**: Gather about 1 cup of dryer lint and store it in the second Ziplock bag. This material serves as an excellent fire starter.

5. **Include Tinder**: Add a bag of shredded paper or other natural materials as tinder to the container, ensuring it stays dry.

6. **Add Matches**: Place 20 strike-anywhere matches in the container, either in their original box or securely bundled together.

7. **Insert Magnesium Fire Starter**: Include one magnesium fire starter in the container. This tool allows for sparks to ignite tinder efficiently.

8. **Cut Paracord**: Measure and cut 10 feet of paracord. This multi-purpose cord can be useful for various survival tasks.

9. **Store the Lighter**: Include a lighter in the container for an alternative fire-starting method. Ensure it is functional and sealed against moisture.

10. **Organize Contents**: Arrange all items neatly inside the container, ensuring they are secured and organized for easy access during emergencies.

11. **Seal the Container**: Close the container tightly, ensuring it is waterproof and ready for transport or storage.

Maintenance:

- **Monthly**: Check the contents of the fire starter kit to ensure all items are functional and dry. Replace any used matches or depleted supplies.

- **Annually**: Review the entire kit, refreshing the cotton balls with petroleum jelly if they show signs of drying out. Replace the dryer lint and tinder as needed.

Complexity:

This project is low in complexity and suitable for individuals of all skill levels. The primary challenges involve sourcing the materials and ensuring proper sealing of the kit. Attention to detail is essential to ensure all components remain dry and functional, but the steps are straightforward and manageable.

Estimated Time:

- **Setup**: 30-45 minutes to gather materials, prepare items, and organize the kit.

- **Ongoing maintenance**: 5-10 minutes monthly for checking supplies and functionality.

- **Annual review**: 30 minutes for a comprehensive assessment and replacement of any items as needed.

9.2.2 DIY Emergency Shelter Project

The DIY Emergency Shelter Project equips individuals with the skills to construct a temporary shelter in survival situations. This project holds significant importance for those living off-grid or preparing for emergencies, such as natural disasters or outdoor adventures. An effective emergency shelter can provide protection from harsh weather conditions, ensure safety from wildlife, and create a secure environment for rest and recovery. This project emphasizes practicality, enabling individuals to utilize readily available materials and techniques to create a functional shelter in various environments. Whether stranded in the wilderness or facing an unexpected storm, having the ability to build an emergency shelter empowers individuals to enhance their self-sufficiency and resilience.

Materials and Tools:

- Tarps (heavy-duty, waterproof) - 2 units (10 x 12 feet each)

- Rope or paracord - 100 feet

- Tent stakes - 10 units

- Axe or hatchet - 1 unit

- Folding shovel - 1 unit

- Survival knife - 1 unit

- Insulating materials (e.g., leaves, grass) - As needed

- Bungee cords - 4 units

- Firestarter (matches or lighter) - 1 unit

- Emergency blanket - 1 unit

Step-by-Step Guide:

1. **Select a Location**: Choose a flat, dry area for the shelter, avoiding low-lying spots where water may collect.

2. **Gather Materials**: Collect natural materials like branches, leaves, and grasses to enhance insulation and structure.

3. **Set Up Tarps**: Lay one tarp flat on the ground to serve as the floor of the shelter.

4. **Create a Frame**: Use branches to create a triangular frame by leaning them against a sturdy tree or creating a freestanding structure.

5. **Secure the Frame**: Tie the tops of the frame together using rope or paracord to stabilize it. Ensure the structure is strong enough to withstand wind.

6. **Add Second Tarp**: Drape the second tarp over the frame, leaving one side open for entry. Secure it with tent stakes and bungee cords for added stability.

7. **Insulate the Shelter**: Fill the inside of the shelter with insulating materials like leaves and grass to trap heat and provide comfort.

8. **Secure Entry**: Use additional branches or tarps to create a flap for the entry, allowing for easy access while keeping out wind and rain.

9. **Check for Stability**: Test the shelter by applying pressure to the frame to ensure it can withstand movement and environmental factors.

10. **Build a Fire Outside**: If conditions permit, create a fire pit outside the shelter for warmth and cooking. Ensure it is at a safe distance from the shelter to prevent fire hazards.

11. **Use Emergency Blanket**: Inside the shelter, spread the emergency blanket on the ground for extra warmth and insulation.

12. **Prepare for Weather**: Adjust the tarp positioning based on the wind direction to maximize protection against rain or snow.

13. **Maintain Ventilation**: Leave a small opening at the top of the shelter for airflow, preventing condensation and maintaining a comfortable environment.

Maintenance:

- **Weekly**: Check the shelter for any signs of wear or damage. Replace or repair any compromised components, such as frayed ropes or torn tarps.

- **Seasonal**: Evaluate the shelter's condition at the beginning of each season. Reinforce it against anticipated weather changes, like heavy snow or rain.

Complexity:

This project is moderate in complexity, suitable for individuals with basic outdoor skills. Challenges may arise in selecting the right location, ensuring structural integrity, and adapting to varying weather conditions. Familiarity with knot tying and basic construction techniques is beneficial but not mandatory.

Estimated Time:

- **Setup**: 1-2 hours to gather materials, construct the frame, and secure the tarps.

- **Ongoing maintenance**: 10-15 minutes weekly to inspect and repair as necessary.

- **Seasonal evaluation**: 30 minutes at the beginning of each season to assess the shelter's readiness and make any needed adjustments.

9.2.3 DIY Fishing Kit Project

The DIY Fishing Kit Project provides individuals with the ability to assemble a compact, efficient fishing kit suitable for various environments, particularly for those living off-grid or pursuing self-sufficiency. Fishing serves as a vital skill for survival, offering a reliable source of protein and food security. This project empowers individuals to catch fish using minimal equipment while maximizing resourcefulness. The kit can be easily customized to fit personal preferences and local fishing conditions, ensuring effectiveness whether in freshwater or saltwater. Additionally, building a fishing kit encourages individuals to connect with nature and develop essential outdoor skills. With the right materials and techniques, anyone can create a fishing kit that meets their needs, supporting a sustainable lifestyle and enhancing off-grid living experiences.

Materials and Tools:

- Tackle box - 1 unit - medium-sized, waterproof

- Fishing line - 1 spool - 200 yards, 10-12 lb test

- Hooks - 10 units - size 6 or 8

- Split shot weights - 10 units - assorted sizes

- Bobbers (floaters) - 2 units - 1-inch diameter

- Fishing lures - 5 units - assorted types (spinners, jigs)

- Needle-nose pliers - 1 unit - for hook removal

- Scissors - 1 unit - for cutting line

- Fishing license - 1 unit - as required by local regulations

- Bait container - 1 unit - for live bait storage (optional)

- First aid kit - 1 unit - for minor injuries while fishing

- Multi-tool - 1 unit - for various tasks

- Spare fishing line - 1 spool - 100 yards, 10-12 lb test

Step-by-Step Guide:

1. **Select a Tackle Box**: Choose a medium-sized, waterproof tackle box to house all fishing gear securely.

2. **Gather Fishing Line**: Obtain a spool of fishing line with a test strength of 10-12 lb. This line works well for most freshwater fish.

3. **Attach Fishing Line**: Cut a 3-foot length of fishing line from the spool. Tie one end to the eye of a hook using a secure knot (e.g., improved clinch knot).

4. **Add Weights**: Slide a split shot weight onto the fishing line about 12 inches above the hook. Use your fingers to squeeze the weight closed around the line.

5. **Attach Bobber**: Fix a bobber about 2 feet above the hook on the line, allowing it to float while indicating bites.

6. **Choose Lures**: Select five assorted fishing lures, including spinners and jigs. Store them in the tackle box for easy access.

7. **Organize Tackle Box**: Arrange all components—hooks, weights, bobbers, lures, and pliers—neatly within the tackle box for efficient organization.

8. **Include Multi-Tool**: Add a multi-tool to the tackle box for versatile tasks, including cutting line or removing hooks from fish.

9. **Check Local Regulations**: Obtain a fishing license as required by local laws. Keep it in the tackle box for easy access.

10. **Prepare Bait Container**: If using live bait, include a bait container in the kit for storage and transport. Ensure it has ventilation.

11. **Pack First Aid Kit**: Include a compact first aid kit to address minor injuries while fishing. Store it in the tackle box.

12. **Test the Gear**: Before heading out, test the fishing gear to ensure everything functions properly. Check knots, weights, and bobber placement.

13. **Store Kit**: Store the completed fishing kit in a cool, dry location until ready for use.

Maintenance:

- **Monthly**: Inspect fishing line for frays or weaknesses. Replace any damaged line with a new spool. Clean the tackle box and remove any debris or water to prevent rust or corrosion.

- **Seasonal**: Check the condition of hooks and lures, replacing any that show signs of wear. Review local fishing regulations to ensure compliance and renew fishing licenses if needed.

Complexity:

The DIY Fishing Kit Project is low in complexity, making it accessible for beginners. Basic knot-tying skills are necessary for securing hooks to the line. Potential challenges may arise when selecting the right lures and weights for specific fishing environments, but these can be easily addressed with research and experimentation. Assembling the kit requires minimal tools, primarily scissors and pliers, ensuring that anyone can successfully create a functional fishing kit.

Estimated Time:

- **Setup**: 1-2 hours to gather materials, attach hooks, organize the tackle box, and ensure all components are ready for use.

- **Ongoing maintenance**: 15-20 minutes monthly for inspecting the fishing line and cleaning the tackle box.

- **Seasonal review**: 30 minutes at the start of each fishing season to check the kit's condition and replace any worn-out items.

9.2.4 DIY Hunting Kit Project

Creating a DIY Hunting Kit empowers individuals to become self-sufficient while pursuing off-grid living or sustainable hunting practices. This project focuses on assembling a comprehensive kit that provides essential tools and materials for hunting various game. A well-stocked hunting kit increases chances of success in the field and enhances safety and preparedness. It also fosters a deeper connection to nature and the skills necessary for responsible hunting. By preparing a hunting kit, individuals reduce reliance on commercial gear, allowing them to tailor their equipment to specific needs and environments. This guide details the steps necessary to create an effective hunting kit, ensuring that it meets the demands of both novice and experienced hunters.

Materials and Tools:

- Backpack - 1 unit - medium-sized, waterproof
- Hunting knife - 1 unit - fixed blade, 4-6 inches in length
- Multi-tool - 1 unit - with pliers, knife, and screwdriver
- Rope - 1 spool - 50 feet, 550 paracord
- First aid kit - 1 unit - compact and complete
- Flashlight - 1 unit - LED, with extra batteries
- Compass - 1 unit - for navigation
- Map of hunting area - 1 unit - printed or digital
- Hunting license - 1 unit - as required by local regulations
- Binoculars - 1 unit - 8x42 magnification
- Game bags - 2 units - breathable material for transporting meat
- Water bottle - 1 unit - 1-liter capacity, insulated
- Snacks - 5 units - high-energy, lightweight options (e.g., protein bars)
- Field dressing gloves - 1 pair - disposable, nitrile
- Camouflage gear - 1 set - jacket and pants, appropriate for local terrain

Step-by-Step Guide:

1. **Select a Backpack**: Choose a medium-sized, waterproof backpack that fits comfortably and can hold all hunting kit components.

2. **Obtain a Hunting Knife**: Acquire a fixed blade hunting knife, ideally 4-6 inches in length, ensuring it is sharp and easy to handle.

3. **Choose a Multi-tool**: Purchase a multi-tool featuring pliers, a knife, and a screwdriver to assist with various tasks in the field.

4. **Gather Rope**: Secure a spool of 550 paracord, 50 feet long. This durable rope serves multiple purposes, from securing gear to building shelter.

5. **Assemble a First Aid Kit**: Obtain a compact first aid kit containing bandages, antiseptic wipes, and other essentials to address minor injuries.

6. **Select a Flashlight**: Choose an LED flashlight that provides adequate illumination and includes extra batteries for extended use.

7. **Acquire a Compass**: Purchase a reliable compass for navigation in unfamiliar areas, essential for staying oriented during hunting trips.

8. **Print a Map**: Obtain a map of the hunting area, either printed or digital, to identify trails, water sources, and hunting zones.

9. **Check Local Regulations**: Ensure to acquire a hunting license as required by local laws. Keep the license in the backpack for easy access.

10. **Select Binoculars**: Choose binoculars with 8x42 magnification for spotting game from a distance, enhancing visibility and focus.

11. **Pack Game Bags**: Secure two breathable game bags to transport meat after a successful hunt, preventing spoilage and ensuring proper storage.

12. **Prepare a Water Bottle**: Obtain a 1-liter insulated water bottle to keep beverages cool or warm, essential for hydration during long outings.

13. **Include Snacks**: Pack five high-energy, lightweight snacks, such as protein bars, to maintain energy levels while hunting.

14. **Add Field Dressing Gloves**: Include a pair of disposable nitrile gloves in the kit for hygiene when field dressing game.

15. **Purchase Camouflage Gear**: Acquire a set of camouflage gear, including a jacket and pants, designed for the local terrain to blend into the environment.

16. **Organize the Kit**: Arrange all items neatly within the backpack, ensuring easy access and efficient use of space.

17. **Test the Gear**: Before heading out, check all equipment for functionality, ensuring that the knife is sharp, the flashlight works, and the multi-tool is in good condition.

18. **Store the Kit**: Keep the assembled hunting kit in a cool, dry location until ready for use, ensuring all components remain in good condition.

Maintenance:

- **Monthly**: Inspect the hunting knife for sharpness and maintain the edge as necessary. Use a sharpening stone or honing rod. Check the flashlight batteries and replace them if they show signs of low power. Test the flashlight to ensure it functions correctly.

- **Seasonal**: Review the first aid kit for expired items, replacing any supplies that are outdated. Restock as necessary to maintain readiness. Inspect camouflage gear for wear and tear. Clean or replace items as needed to ensure effectiveness in the field.

- **Annually**: Test the functionality of the compass and replace if it shows inaccuracies. Familiarize oneself with how to use it effectively. Update the hunting map to reflect any changes in the area, such as new trails or closures, ensuring navigation remains accurate.

Complexity:

The DIY Hunting Kit Project is of low to moderate complexity, making it suitable for beginners and experienced hunters alike. Key skills include organization and basic knowledge of hunting equipment. Challenges may arise in selecting the appropriate gear based on individual needs and local regulations. However, thorough research and attention to detail ensure successful assembly.

Estimated Time:

- **Setup**: 2-3 hours to gather materials, assemble the kit, and ensure everything is functional.

- **Ongoing maintenance**: 30 minutes monthly for checking the knife, flashlight, and first aid supplies.

- **Seasonal review**: 1 hour at the beginning of each hunting season to inspect gear and update maps.

9.2.5 DIY SOLAR-POWERED RADIO PROJECT

The DIY Solar-Powered Radio Project transforms sunlight into a reliable source of entertainment and information. In an off-grid living scenario, access to news and communication becomes vital, particularly during emergencies or extended periods away from the grid. This project allows individuals to harness solar energy, making it an essential skill for self-sufficiency. A solar-powered radio provides a sustainable solution for staying connected, enabling users to tune into weather updates, emergency broadcasts, or music while reducing reliance on traditional power sources. By creating this solar-powered device, individuals can ensure they have access to critical information without draining battery resources, making it an indispensable tool in any off-grid toolkit.

Materials and Tools:

- Solar panel - 1 unit - 10 watts

- Solar charge controller - 1 unit - 12V

- Rechargeable battery - 1 unit - 12V, 7Ah

- Portable AM/FM radio kit - 1 unit

- Wire - 1 spool - 16 AWG (American Wire Gauge)

- Soldering iron - 1 unit

- Solder - 1 spool

- Electrical tape - 1 roll

- Diode - 1 unit - 1N4001

- Multimeter - 1 unit

- Mounting brackets - 2 units

- Screwdriver set - 1 unit

- Drill - 1 unit

- Drill bits - 1 set

- Safety glasses - 1 pair

Step-by-Step Guide:

1. **Choose a Location**: Identify a suitable location for the solar panel that receives direct sunlight for most of the day.

2. **Mount the Solar Panel**: Use the mounting brackets to secure the solar panel in place. Ensure it is angled for maximum sun exposure.

3. **Connect the Diode**: Solder the diode to the positive terminal of the solar panel. This prevents reverse current flow, protecting the panel.

4. **Attach Wires**: Cut two lengths of 16 AWG wire, one for positive and one for negative connections. Strip both ends of each wire.

5. **Connect to Charge Controller**: Connect the positive wire from the solar panel to the positive terminal of the solar charge controller. Secure it with a screwdriver.

6. **Connect Negative Wire**: Attach the negative wire from the solar panel to the negative terminal of the charge controller, ensuring a tight connection.

7. **Connect Battery to Charge Controller**: Connect the positive wire from the charge controller to the positive terminal of the rechargeable battery. Repeat this with the negative wire.

8. **Install the Radio Kit**: Follow the instructions provided with the portable AM/FM radio kit. Assemble the radio, ensuring all components are securely in place.

9. **Wire the Radio to the Battery**: Use additional 16 AWG wire to connect the radio's power input to the positive and negative terminals of the rechargeable battery.

10. **Test Connections**: Use a multimeter to check all connections, ensuring voltage levels are correct before powering on the radio.

11. **Power On the Radio**: Once all connections are confirmed, power on the radio to test functionality. Tune into local stations to verify reception.

12. **Secure Loose Wires**: Use electrical tape to secure any loose wires and prevent potential hazards.

13. **Finalize Setup**: Ensure the entire setup is weatherproofed, especially connections exposed to the elements.

14. **Monitor Performance**: Check the solar panel's output regularly, ensuring it charges the battery effectively. Adjust the angle if necessary.

Maintenance:

- **Monthly**: Inspect the solar panel for dirt or debris. Clean with a soft cloth to maintain efficiency. Check all electrical connections for signs of corrosion or wear. Tighten any loose connections.

- **Yearly**: Test the battery's charge capacity with a multimeter. Replace the battery if it shows signs of diminished capacity. Examine the radio components for wear, replacing parts as needed to ensure optimal performance.

Complexity:

This DIY Solar-Powered Radio Project is of moderate complexity. Basic electrical skills, including soldering and wiring, are necessary. Challenges may arise in ensuring all connections are secure and that the solar panel receives adequate sunlight. Attention to detail during assembly is crucial for functionality. While beginners can complete the project, some experience with electronics will simplify the process.

Estimated Time:

- **Setup**: 3-4 hours to gather materials, mount the solar panel, connect all components, and test functionality.

- **Ongoing maintenance**: 15-20 minutes monthly for cleaning the panel and checking connections.

- **Yearly maintenance**: 1-2 hours to test the battery, clean the radio, and inspect components.

9.2.6 DIY Solar-Powered Flashlight Project

Creating a DIY solar-powered flashlight combines functionality and sustainability, making it an essential project for off-grid living enthusiasts. This project allows individuals to harness solar energy, converting it into a portable light source. In a world where access to electricity may be limited, having a reliable flashlight powered by renewable energy becomes invaluable. Not only does it reduce reliance on disposable batteries, but it also minimizes waste and environmental impact. This solar-powered flashlight can illuminate pathways during the night, aid in emergency situations, and serve as a dependable tool for camping or outdoor activities. By undertaking this project, individuals gain the satisfaction of building their own sustainable lighting solution, enhancing their self-sufficiency and resourcefulness.

Materials and Tools:

- Solar panel - 1 unit - 5 watts

- Solar charge controller - 1 unit - 12V

- Rechargeable battery - 1 unit - 6V, 4Ah

- LED flashlight housing - 1 unit - standard size

- LED bulb - 1 unit - 3-5 watts

- Wire - 1 spool - 16 AWG (American Wire Gauge)

- Soldering iron - 1 unit

- Solder - 1 spool

- Electrical tape - 1 roll

- Diode - 1 unit - 1N4001

- Switch - 1 unit - toggle switch

- Mounting brackets - 2 units

- Drill - 1 unit

- Drill bits - 1 set

- Multimeter - 1 unit

- Heat shrink tubing - 1 package

- Safety glasses - 1 pair

Step-by-Step Guide:

1. **Select the Solar Panel**: Choose a 5-watt solar panel suitable for charging a 6V battery. Ensure it has a built-in diode to prevent reverse current flow.

2. **Mount the Solar Panel**: Use mounting brackets to securely attach the solar panel to a location that receives direct sunlight for optimal charging.

3. **Prepare the Battery**: Take the 6V, 4Ah rechargeable battery and ensure it is fully charged before connecting it to the solar charge controller.

4. **Connect the Solar Charge Controller**: Connect the positive wire from the solar panel to the positive terminal of the solar charge controller. Use a soldering iron to secure the connection.

5. **Connect the Negative Wire**: Attach the negative wire from the solar panel to the negative terminal of the charge controller, ensuring a tight fit.

6. **Attach the Battery**: Connect the positive terminal of the battery to the positive output terminal of the solar charge controller. Repeat this with the negative terminal.

7. **Prepare the LED Flashlight Housing**: Obtain a standard-sized LED flashlight housing, ensuring it is suitable for the LED bulb being used.

8. **Install the LED Bulb**: Insert the LED bulb into the flashlight housing, following the manufacturer's instructions for secure placement.

9. **Wire the Switch**: Connect a toggle switch to the positive wire leading from the battery to the LED bulb. This allows for easy control of the flashlight.

10. **Connect the Bulb to the Battery**: Use additional 16 AWG wire to connect the negative terminal of the LED bulb to the negative terminal of the battery.

11. **Check for Short Circuits**: Use a multimeter to test all connections, ensuring there are no short circuits or loose wires that could cause malfunctions.

12. **Seal Connections**: Use heat shrink tubing and electrical tape to cover all exposed wires and connections to prevent moisture intrusion and ensure safety.

13. **Power On the Flashlight**: Once all connections are secure, turn on the toggle switch to test the flashlight. Ensure the LED lights up brightly, indicating successful assembly.

14. **Final Assembly**: Secure the flashlight housing, ensuring that all components are held in place and the unit is compact.

15. **Monitor Solar Charging**: Place the solar panel in direct sunlight, checking periodically to ensure it charges the battery effectively. Adjust its angle as necessary.

Maintenance:

- **Monthly**: Inspect the solar panel for dirt or debris and clean with a soft cloth to maintain efficiency. Check all electrical connections for signs of corrosion or wear. Tighten any loose connections.

- **Yearly**: Test the battery's charge capacity with a multimeter. Replace the battery if it shows signs of diminished capacity. Examine the LED bulb and housing for wear, replacing components as needed to ensure optimal performance.

Complexity:

This DIY Solar-Powered Flashlight Project is of moderate complexity. Basic electrical skills, including soldering and wiring, are essential. Challenges may arise in ensuring all connections are secure and that the solar panel receives adequate sunlight for effective charging. Attention to detail during assembly is crucial. While beginners can complete the project, some experience with electronics will simplify the process.

Estimated Time:

- **Setup**: 2-3 hours to gather materials, mount the solar panel, connect all components, and test functionality.

- **Ongoing maintenance**: 15-20 minutes monthly for cleaning the panel and checking connections.

- **Yearly maintenance**: 1-2 hours to test the battery, clean the flashlight components, and inspect for wear.

9.2.7 DIY EMERGENCY SIGNAL MIRROR PROJECT

Creating a DIY Emergency Signal Mirror provides a crucial tool for off-grid living and emergency preparedness. This project equips individuals with a reliable means of signaling for help in survival situations, such as being lost in the wilderness or during natural disasters. A well-crafted signal mirror can reflect sunlight over great distances, drawing attention from rescuers or nearby individuals. This device serves not only as a practical tool but also fosters a sense of self-sufficiency and readiness. The process is straightforward and requires minimal resources, making it accessible for anyone looking to enhance their survival gear. By engaging in this project, individuals can cultivate confidence in their ability to navigate emergencies and reinforce their commitment to self-reliance.

Materials and Tools:

- Acrylic mirror sheet - 1 unit - 12 inches x 12 inches

- Plastic backing sheet - 1 unit - 12 inches x 12 inches

- Waterproof epoxy - 1 tube

- Reflective tape - 1 roll - 1 inch wide

- Utility knife - 1 unit

- Ruler - 1 unit - 12 inches

- Permanent marker - 1 unit

- Sandpaper - 1 sheet - 120 grit

- Safety glasses - 1 pair
- Clamps - 2 units - adjustable

Step-by-Step Guide:

1. **Select Mirror Material**: Choose a high-quality acrylic mirror sheet measuring 12 inches by 12 inches for optimal reflection.

2. **Cut Plastic Backing**: Using the utility knife, cut the plastic backing sheet to match the dimensions of the mirror sheet, ensuring a snug fit.

3. **Prepare the Surface**: Sand the edges of both the mirror and backing sheets lightly to remove any sharp edges or imperfections.

4. **Mark Center Point**: Place the mirror sheet face down on a flat surface and use the ruler and marker to find and mark the center point.

5. **Apply Adhesive**: Apply a layer of waterproof epoxy adhesive to the center of the plastic backing sheet, ensuring an even spread.

6. **Attach the Mirror**: Carefully position the acrylic mirror sheet onto the adhesive-covered backing, aligning the center point. Press down firmly to ensure a strong bond.

7. **Clamp the Assembly**: Use adjustable clamps to hold the mirror and backing sheets together securely while the adhesive cures. Follow the adhesive manufacturer's instructions for curing time.

8. **Create a Signaling Surface**: Cut a strip of reflective tape, approximately 1 inch wide and 12 inches long, and adhere it to one edge of the mirror. This will enhance visibility when signaling.

9. **Test the Mirror**: After the adhesive has fully cured, take the mirror outside on a sunny day. Hold it at different angles to test its reflective properties and ensure it produces a strong flash of light.

10. **Prepare for Use**: Store the completed signal mirror in a waterproof bag or container to protect it from scratches and environmental damage.

Maintenance:

- **Monthly**: Inspect the signal mirror for any scratches or damage. Clean the surface gently with a soft cloth to maintain optimal reflective quality.

- **Yearly**: Check the integrity of the adhesive bond between the mirror and backing. If any separation is noticed, reapply adhesive and clamp as needed.

Complexity:

The DIY Emergency Signal Mirror project is low to moderate in complexity. Basic skills such as cutting, measuring, and adhering materials are necessary. Challenges may arise in achieving a perfect bond between the mirror and backing, as well as ensuring the reflective surface remains unblemished. Attention to detail is vital, particularly when marking and cutting materials.

Estimated Time:

- **Setup**: 1 hour to gather materials, cut, and prepare the mirror and backing sheets.

- **Curing**: 24 hours for adhesive to set fully, though the mirror can be tested sooner.

- **Ongoing maintenance**: 10-15 minutes monthly for cleaning and inspection.

- **Yearly maintenance**: 30 minutes to check the adhesive bond and perform any necessary repairs.

9.3 DIY EQUIPMENT REPAIR & MAINTENANCE

Maintaining and repairing your equipment is a critical skill for anyone living off the grid. The ability to troubleshoot, fix, and preserve your tools and machinery can save you time, money, and potentially prevent dangerous situations. This section will guide you through some basic yet essential maintenance and repair techniques that are easy to learn and apply, even for those with minimal experience.

First, always start with the user manual. It might seem obvious, but many people overlook the importance of the manual that comes with their equipment. These guides often include maintenance schedules, troubleshooting tips, and instructions for simple repairs. Keeping your equipment clean is another fundamental practice. Dirt, dust, and grime can cause machinery to overheat, parts to wear out faster, and can even lead to malfunctions. Regular cleaning, therefore, not only extends the life of your equipment but also ensures it operates efficiently.

Lubrication is another key aspect of equipment maintenance. Moving parts require lubrication to prevent wear and tear. Identify the lubrication points and understand the type of lubricant required for each part. This information is typically found in the user manual. Simple tools like grease guns or oil cans can be used to apply lubricant, and doing so regularly can significantly reduce the risk of equipment breakdown.

For electrical equipment, understanding basic electrical repair skills such as replacing cords, fixing plugs, and troubleshooting common electrical issues can be invaluable. Always ensure your safety by disconnecting the power source before attempting any repairs. A multimeter can be a handy tool for diagnosing electrical problems, allowing you to check for continuity, voltage, and resistance.

When it comes to more complex repairs, don't hesitate to seek out resources for learning. Online forums, instructional videos, and community classes can provide deeper insights into specific repair techniques. Additionally, building a network with other off-grid enthusiasts can be a great way to share knowledge and sometimes even labor when tackling more challenging projects.

Lastly, always have a well-organized toolkit. Knowing where your tools are and having the right tool for the job can make any repair task more manageable. Regularly check your tools for any signs of wear and tear and replace them as necessary. A well-maintained toolkit is as crucial as the maintenance of the equipment itself.

By adopting these maintenance and repair techniques, you'll not only ensure your equipment lasts longer but also gain a deeper understanding of how your tools and machinery work. This knowledge empowers you to be more self-sufficient, reduces your reliance on external repair services, and enhances your off-grid living experience. Remember, the key to effective equipment maintenance and repair lies in regular care, proper use, and the willingness to learn and apply new skills.

9.4 DIY MATERIAL SOURCING & USE

Sourcing and repurposing materials for DIY projects are essential skills for anyone embracing a no-grid lifestyle. These practices not only save money but also reduce waste, aligning perfectly with the principles of self-sufficiency and environmental stewardship. The key to successful material sourcing is knowing where to look and understanding the potential of items that many would consider waste.

Local classifieds, online marketplaces, and community boards are treasure troves for finding free or low-cost materials. People often give away lumber, bricks, and other building materials that can be used for a variety of projects. Similarly, pallets, often available at local businesses, can be repurposed into furniture, fencing, and even small structures. Before taking pallets, always ask for permission as some businesses return them to suppliers.

Construction and demolition sites are another source of materials. With permission, you can salvage wood, metal, and other items that would otherwise end up in a landfill. However, safety is paramount when sourcing from these sites. Always wear appropriate protective gear and ensure you have permission to be there.

Repurposing materials requires a bit of creativity and vision. An old door can become a table, wine bottles can transform into lamp bases, and fabric scraps can be turned into quilts or clothing. The possibilities are endless. The key is to look at items not for what they are but for what they could be.

In addition to sourcing materials, it's important to have a basic set of tools for modifying and working with what you find. A saw, drill, hammer, and screwdriver are essential. As your skills grow, you may find that additional tools like a planer or a router expand your ability to repurpose materials more effectively.

Remember, the goal of sourcing and repurposing materials is not just about saving money or being eco-friendly. It's also about adding a personal touch to your projects, creating something unique that reflects your individuality and your commitment to a sustainable lifestyle. Each repurposed item has a story, and by incorporating it into your home or project, you're continuing that narrative in a meaningful way.

Finally, always be on the lookout for materials that can be repurposed. Whether you're at a garage sale, thrift store, or just driving by a pile of discarded items on the curb, keep an eye open for materials that can be given a second life. With a bit of imagination and effort, you can turn what others see as trash into a valuable resource for your off-grid projects.

9.5 BUDGET-FRIENDLY DIY FURNITURE PROJECTS

Making and repairing furniture with affordable and accessible materials is a skill that can significantly enhance your self-sufficiency and independence while living off the grid. With a focus on practicality and resourcefulness, this approach allows you to furnish your home without breaking the bank or relying on commercial furniture sources. By utilizing materials such as reclaimed wood, pallets, and scrap metal, you can create durable, functional, and unique pieces that reflect your personal style and the needs of your off-grid lifestyle.

Reclaimed wood is a popular choice for DIY furniture projects due to its character, durability, and the environmental benefits of repurposing existing materials. Pallets, often available for free from local businesses, can be disassembled and reworked into everything from chairs and tables to bed frames and shelving units. The key to working with pallet wood is ensuring the wood is safe and free from harmful chemicals. Look for pallets marked with "HT," which stands for heat-treated, indicating they haven't been treated with chemicals.

Scrap metal, another readily available material, can be transformed into sturdy furniture frames, legs, and decorative elements. Metal can be sourced from old appliances, vehicles, or construction remnants. Working with metal requires some basic tools like a welder and grinder, but learning these skills opens up a wide range of possibilities for creating strong, industrial-style furniture.

In addition to sourcing materials, mastering simple construction techniques is essential. Basic joinery, such as screws and dowels, can be used to assemble most furniture projects. For those new to woodworking or metalworking, numerous online tutorials and community classes can provide guidance and build confidence in your abilities.

When it comes to finishing your furniture, there are several low-cost options that can protect your pieces and add aesthetic appeal. Sanding and staining wood can bring out its natural beauty, while paint can add color and protect the surface. For metal, finishes like paint or clear sealant can prevent rust and wear.

Repairing existing furniture is another valuable skill that can save money and extend the life of your pieces. Simple repairs like tightening loose joints, refinishing surfaces, or replacing hardware can make old furniture look and function like new. Learning upholstery can also revive worn chairs and sofas, with many affordable fabrics available that can withstand the rigors of off-grid living.

The satisfaction of sitting on a chair you built or eating at a table you crafted cannot be overstated. Not only do you get a piece of furniture tailored to your space and needs, but you also gain the invaluable experience and confidence that comes with DIY projects. This journey towards creating and maintaining your furniture fosters a deeper connection to your living environment and enhances your resilience and adaptability.

Embracing DIY furniture making and repair is not just about saving money or being eco-friendly; it's a testament to the power of human creativity and ingenuity. With some basic tools, a willingness to learn, and a bit of effort, you can transform affordable and accessible materials into valuable and cherished possessions that enhance your off-grid lifestyle

9.5.1 RECLAIMED WOOD DINING TABLE

Building a reclaimed wood dining table is a rewarding project that allows individuals to create a stunning centerpiece for their dining area while promoting sustainability. This project emphasizes the importance of reusing materials, which aligns perfectly with off-grid living and DIY principles. A reclaimed wood table not only reduces waste but also provides a unique aesthetic, showcasing the character and history of the wood. Each piece tells a story, making the table a conversation starter during meals with family and friends. This guide aims to equip individuals with the knowledge and steps necessary to construct a beautiful dining table that will serve as a functional and stylish addition to their home.

Materials and Tools:

- Reclaimed wood boards (e.g., pine, oak) - 6 units, each 2x6 inches, 8 feet long
- Reclaimed wood for the tabletop - 1 unit, 4x8 feet, thickness varies
- Wood screws - 50 units, 2.5 inches long
- Wood glue - 1 bottle, 8 ounces
- Sandpaper - 1 pack, various grits (80, 120, 220)
- Wood finish or sealant - 1 gallon
- Table saw - 1 unit
- Drill with ¼ inch drill bit - 1 unit
- Clamps - 4 units
- Measuring tape - 1 unit
- Level - 1 unit
- Paintbrush or roller - 1 unit
- Safety goggles - 1 unit
- Dust mask - 1 unit

Step-by-Step Guide:

1. **Select Wood**: Choose reclaimed wood boards that are free from rot and insect damage. Look for boards with interesting textures and colors to add character.

2. **Measure and Cut**: Measure the desired length of the table. For a standard dining table, aim for 72 inches. Use a table saw to cut the wood boards to length.

3. **Create Tabletop**: Lay the reclaimed wood for the tabletop flat. Arrange the boards side by side until the desired width is achieved. Trim the edges if necessary for a clean fit.

4. **Glue Boards Together**: Apply wood glue along the edges of the boards that will touch each other. Press the boards together tightly and use clamps to secure them while the glue dries.

5. **Drill Pilot Holes**: Once the glue has cured (usually 24 hours), remove the clamps. Drill pilot holes along the seams of the tabletop for wood screws, spacing them about 12 inches apart.

6. **Screw the Boards**: Secure the boards together with 2.5-inch wood screws, ensuring the screws are driven straight and flush with the wood surface.

7. **Sand the Surface**: Start with 80-grit sandpaper to remove rough spots, then progress to 120-grit for a smoother finish. Finish with 220-grit sandpaper for a polished surface.

8. **Cut Table Legs**: Measure and cut four legs from the reclaimed wood, each 30 inches long. Ensure all legs are of equal length for stability.

9. **Attach Legs to Table**: Position each leg at the corners of the table. Drill pilot holes into the tabletop and attach each leg using wood screws. Ensure the legs are perpendicular to the tabletop.

10. **Add Support Braces**: Cut two additional pieces of wood for cross-bracing between the legs, each measuring 36 inches. Attach these braces for added stability.

11. **Level the Table**: Use a level to ensure the table sits evenly. Adjust the legs as necessary to achieve a balanced surface.

12. **Apply Finish**: Choose a wood finish or sealant that complements the wood. Apply evenly using a paintbrush or roller, following the manufacturer's instructions for drying times.

13. **Allow to Cure**: Let the finish cure completely before using the table. This may take several days, depending on the product used.

Maintenance:

- **Monthly**: Inspect the table for any signs of wear or damage. Tighten any loose screws to maintain stability.

- **Every 6 Months**: Clean the surface with a damp cloth. Reapply wood finish or sealant as needed to protect the wood from moisture and wear.

- **Yearly**: Sand any rough spots and refresh the finish to maintain the table's appearance and longevity.

Complexity:

This project is of moderate complexity, suitable for individuals with basic woodworking skills. Key challenges include accurately measuring and cutting wood, ensuring the table legs are level, and applying a finish without streaks. With careful attention to detail, these challenges can be effectively managed.

Estimated Time:

- **Setup and Material Gathering**: 1-2 hours to select and gather materials.

- **Construction**: 4-6 hours for cutting, assembling, and securing the table.

- **Sanding and Finishing**: 2-3 hours for sanding and applying finish, not including drying time.

- **Total Estimated Time**: Approximately 7-11 hours, spread over two or more days to allow for glue and finish drying.

9.5.2 PALLET WOOD SHELVING UNIT

Building a pallet wood shelving unit serves as an ideal project for those pursuing off-grid living or DIY sustainability. Pallet wood is often readily available and inexpensive, making it an excellent material for creating functional and aesthetically pleasing storage solutions. This project emphasizes self-sufficiency by repurposing materials that would otherwise contribute to waste, thus aligning with eco-friendly practices. The shelving unit not only maximizes storage space in a home or workshop but also adds rustic charm to any environment. The scope of this project encompasses the design, construction, and finishing of a versatile shelving unit, catering to diverse storage needs.

Materials and Tools:

- Reclaimed wood pallets - 4 units

- Circular saw - 1 unit

- Drill with ¼ inch drill bit - 1 unit

- Wood screws - 30 units, 2 inches long

- Wood glue - 1 bottle, 8 ounces

- Sandpaper - 1 pack, various grits (80, 120, 220)

- Measuring tape - 1 unit

- Level - 1 unit

- Paintbrush - 1 unit

- Wood finish or sealant - 1 gallon

- Safety goggles - 1 unit

- Dust mask - 1 unit

- Clamps - 4 units

Step-by-Step Guide:

1. **Select Pallets**: Choose four intact reclaimed wood pallets, ensuring they are free from rot and insect damage. Inspect for any broken slats or structural issues.

2. **Disassemble Pallets**: Use a pry bar to carefully dismantle the pallets. Remove nails and screws as you go, ensuring the wood remains in usable condition.

3. **Measure and Cut Wood**: Cut the pallets into desired shelf dimensions using a circular saw. For a standard shelving unit, aim for 48 inches wide by 12 inches deep for each shelf.

4. **Sand Wood Pieces**: Sand all cut edges and surfaces with 80-grit sandpaper to remove splinters. Progress to 120-grit for a smoother finish and finish with 220-grit for a polished look.

5. **Create Side Panels**: Cut two pieces of pallet wood for the side panels, each measuring 72 inches tall by 12 inches wide. Ensure both pieces are of equal length for stability.

6. **Attach Shelves**: Determine the desired spacing between shelves. Mark positions on the side panels. Secure each shelf with wood screws, using two screws per side for strength.

7. **Reinforce with Braces**: Cut additional pallet wood into pieces measuring 36 inches for back support. Attach these diagonally from the bottom corners of the side panels to the midpoint of the shelves, using screws.

8. **Level the Unit**: Use a level to check that the shelving unit is even. Adjust the positioning of the legs if necessary to ensure stability.

9. **Apply Wood Finish**: Choose a wood finish or sealant that enhances the wood grain. Apply evenly with a paintbrush, following the manufacturer's instructions for drying times.

10. **Allow to Cure**: Let the finish cure completely before loading the shelves. This may take several days, depending on the product used.

Maintenance:

- **Monthly**: Inspect the shelving unit for any signs of wear or damage. Tighten any loose screws to maintain stability.

- **Every 6 Months**: Clean the surfaces with a damp cloth. Check for moisture or signs of rot and address any issues promptly.

- **Yearly**: Reapply wood finish or sealant as needed to protect the wood from moisture and wear. Sand any rough spots and refresh the finish to maintain the shelving unit's appearance.

Complexity:

This project is of moderate complexity, suitable for individuals with basic woodworking skills. Key challenges include safely disassembling the pallets without damaging the wood and ensuring the shelves are securely attached and level. Attention to detail is crucial during assembly to avoid structural issues.

Estimated Time:

- **Setup and Material Gathering**: 1-2 hours to select and gather materials.

- **Construction**: 4-6 hours for cutting, assembling, and securing the shelving unit.

- **Sanding and Finishing**: 2-3 hours for sanding and applying finish, not including drying time.

- **Total Estimated Time**: Approximately 7-11 hours, spread over two or more days to allow for glue and finish drying.

9.5.3 SCRAP METAL AND WOOD COFFEE TABLE

Building a scrap metal and wood coffee table represents an excellent opportunity for DIY enthusiasts to blend functionality with artistic expression. This project allows individuals to repurpose leftover materials, making it not only budget-friendly but also a sustainable choice for off-grid living. A coffee table serves as a central piece in any living space, often used for entertaining guests or holding personal items. By constructing a table from scrap materials, individuals contribute to waste reduction while creating a unique piece of furniture that reflects their style and resourcefulness. The project emphasizes creativity, practicality, and self-sufficiency, making it a worthwhile endeavor for anyone looking to enhance their home with handcrafted furniture.

Materials and Tools:

- Reclaimed wood planks - 4 units, each 2 inches thick by 6 inches wide by 48 inches long
- Scrap metal sheet - 1 unit, 48 inches by 24 inches, 1/8 inch thick
- Steel angle brackets - 8 units, 2 inches by 2 inches
- Wood screws - 24 units, 1.5 inches long
- Metal screws - 12 units, 1 inch long
- Wood glue - 1 bottle, 8 ounces
- Drill - 1 unit
- Circular saw - 1 unit
- Measuring tape - 1 unit
- Level - 1 unit
- Sandpaper - 1 pack, various grits (80, 120, 220)
- Safety goggles - 1 unit
- Dust mask - 1 unit
- Paintbrush - 1 unit
- Wood finish or sealant - 1 gallon
- Workbench or sturdy surface - 1 unit
- Clamps - 4 units

Step-by-Step Guide:

1. **Select Wood Planks**: Choose four reclaimed wood planks, ensuring they are in good condition and free from rot.
2. **Cut Metal Sheet**: Use a circular saw to cut the scrap metal sheet into a rectangular top measuring 48 inches by 24 inches.
3. **Sand Wood Planks**: Sand the wood planks using 80-grit sandpaper, then progress to 120-grit and finish with 220-grit for a smooth surface.

4. **Align Wood Planks**: Lay the four wood planks side by side on the workbench, aligning the edges to form a rectangular tabletop.

5. **Secure Planks**: Apply wood glue between the planks, then clamp them together tightly. Allow the glue to dry for at least 30 minutes.

6. **Attach Angle Brackets**: Position steel angle brackets at each corner of the underside of the tabletop. Use metal screws to secure them, ensuring the brackets are flush with the surface.

7. **Position Metal Sheet**: Place the cut metal sheet over the glued wood planks, centering it to create a sleek top.

8. **Secure Metal Sheet**: Attach the metal sheet to the wood planks using additional metal screws, spacing them evenly along the perimeter.

9. **Create Legs**: Cut four wooden pieces to serve as legs, each measuring 30 inches tall by 3 inches wide. Ensure all legs are of equal length for stability.

10. **Attach Legs**: Position the legs at each corner of the underside of the table, using wood screws to secure them to the angle brackets. Ensure each leg is vertical by checking with a level.

11. **Finish Table**: Apply wood finish or sealant with a paintbrush to protect the wood and enhance its appearance. Follow the manufacturer's instructions for drying times.

12. **Allow to Cure**: Let the table cure for at least 24 hours before using it to ensure all materials are securely bonded and finishes are dry.

Maintenance:

*   **Monthly**: Inspect the table for any signs of wear or loose screws. Tighten any screws that may have come loose over time.

*   **Every 6 Months**: Clean the table surface with a damp cloth. Reapply wood finish or sealant as necessary to maintain the wood's protection.

*   **Yearly**: Check for any rust or deterioration on the metal sheet. If needed, sand down any rust spots and reapply metal primer and paint to protect the surface.

Complexity:

This project ranks as moderate in complexity. It requires basic woodworking and metalworking skills, along with the ability to safely operate power tools. Key challenges may include aligning the metal sheet and ensuring the legs are securely attached and level. Attention to detail during assembly is critical to achieving a stable and aesthetically pleasing final product.

Estimated Time:

*   **Setup and Material Gathering**: 1-2 hours to gather materials and prepare the workspace.

*   **Construction**: 4-5 hours for cutting, assembling, and securing the table components.

*   **Sanding and Finishing**: 2-3 hours for sanding and applying the finish, not including drying time.

*   **Total Estimated Time**: Approximately 7-10 hours, spread over two or more days to allow for glue and finish drying.

9.5.4 RECLAIMED WOOD BED FRAME

Constructing a reclaimed wood bed frame offers a sustainable and aesthetically pleasing solution for anyone looking to furnish their bedroom with a unique, handcrafted piece. This project not only champions eco-friendly practices by repurposing discarded wood but also enhances self-sufficiency for those embracing off-grid living. A reclaimed wood bed frame provides numerous benefits, such as durability, character, and a connection to the past, as each piece of wood carries its own story. By undertaking this project, individuals can achieve a functional, sturdy bed frame that serves as the centerpiece of their sleeping area while promoting environmental stewardship and personal craftsmanship.

This guide walks through the entire process, from selecting the right materials to assembly, ensuring that anyone, regardless of experience level, can successfully complete this rewarding project.

Materials and Tools:

- Reclaimed wood planks - 10 units, each 1 inch thick by 6 inches wide by 80 inches long (for the frame)
- Reclaimed wood boards - 6 units, each 1 inch thick by 6 inches wide by 60 inches long (for the slats)
- Wood screws - 40 units, 2.5 inches long
- Wood glue - 1 bottle, 8 ounces
- Sandpaper - 1 pack, various grits (80, 120, 220)
- Drill - 1 unit
- Circular saw - 1 unit
- Measuring tape - 1 unit
- Level - 1 unit
- Safety goggles - 1 unit
- Dust mask - 1 unit
- Wood finish or sealant - 1 gallon
- Clamps - 4 units
- Workbench or sturdy surface - 1 unit

Step-by-Step Guide:

1. **Select Reclaimed Wood**: Choose ten reclaimed wood planks for the bed frame and six boards for the slats, ensuring they are free from rot and structurally sound.

2. **Cut Wood Planks**: Use a circular saw to cut the wood planks to the required lengths. For a queen-size bed frame, cut four planks to 80 inches (side rails) and two planks to 60 inches (head and foot rails).

3. **Sand the Planks**: Sand all edges and surfaces of the cut wood planks starting with 80-grit sandpaper, moving to 120-grit, and finishing with 220-grit for a smooth surface.

4. **Align Side Rails**: Position the two 80-inch planks parallel to each other on the workbench to form the side rails of the bed frame.

5. **Attach Head and Foot Rails**: Position the 60-inch planks at both ends, ensuring the ends of the side rails are flush with the head and foot rails. Use wood screws to secure them, drilling two screws into each joint.

6. **Reinforce Frame**: Apply wood glue at the joints before inserting screws for added strength. Clamp the joints together and allow the glue to dry for at least 30 minutes.

7. **Cut Slats**: Measure and cut the six reclaimed wood boards into slats, each measuring 60 inches in length, using the circular saw.

8. **Position Slats**: Lay the slats evenly across the width of the frame, spacing them approximately 6 inches apart for optimal support.

9. **Secure Slats**: Attach the slats to the side rails using wood screws, placing two screws in each slat to ensure stability.

10. **Finish Frame**: Apply wood finish or sealant to the entire bed frame using a paintbrush, following the manufacturer's instructions for drying times.

11. **Allow to Cure**: Let the bed frame cure for at least 24 hours to ensure all materials are securely bonded and finishes are dry.

12. **Move to Bedroom**: Carefully lift and position the completed bed frame in the desired location within the bedroom.

Maintenance:

- **Monthly**: Inspect all joints and screws for tightness. Tighten any loose screws as needed to maintain stability.

- **Every 6 Months**: Clean the surface of the bed frame with a damp cloth. Reapply wood finish or sealant if the surface shows signs of wear or fading.

- **Yearly**: Check for any signs of wear or damage on the reclaimed wood. Address any issues promptly to prolong the life of the bed frame.

Complexity:

This project ranks as moderate in complexity. It requires basic woodworking skills and familiarity with power tools such as drills and circular saws. Key challenges include ensuring precise measurements and securing joints effectively. Attention to detail during assembly is critical for achieving a sturdy and aesthetically pleasing final product.

Estimated Time:

- **Setup and Material Gathering**: 1-2 hours to gather materials, prepare the workspace, and make necessary cuts.

- **Construction**: 4-6 hours for sanding, assembling the frame, and securing slats.

- **Finishing**: 2-3 hours for applying the finish, not including drying time.

- **Total Estimated Time**: Approximately 7-11 hours, spread over two or more days to allow for glue and finish drying.

9.5.5 PALLET WOOD OUTDOOR BENCH

Building a pallet wood outdoor bench is an excellent way to create functional outdoor seating while practicing sustainability and resourcefulness. This project not only utilizes reclaimed materials but also enhances outdoor living spaces, making them more enjoyable and inviting. A bench constructed from pallets offers versatility, allowing customization in size, style, and finish to suit individual preferences. For those living off-grid or seeking DIY solutions, this bench serves as an essential piece of furniture, encouraging outdoor gatherings and relaxation. It promotes self-sufficiency by providing a cost-effective alternative to store-bought furniture, and its rustic charm fits seamlessly into natural landscapes. The skills developed during this project—such as measuring, cutting, and assembling—translate into other woodworking endeavors, further enhancing one's self-reliance.

Materials and Tools:

- Pallets - 3 units (standard size)

- Wood screws - 40 units, 2.5 inches long

- Wood glue - 1 bottle, 8 ounces

- Sandpaper - 1 pack, various grits (80, 120, 220)

- Circular saw - 1 unit

- Drill - 1 unit

- Measuring tape - 1 unit
- Level - 1 unit
- Safety goggles - 1 unit
- Dust mask - 1 unit
- Outdoor wood finish or sealant - 1 gallon
- Clamps - 4 units
- Workbench or sturdy surface - 1 unit

Step-by-Step Guide:

1. **Select Pallets**: Choose three standard-sized pallets, inspecting them for structural integrity and ensuring they are free from rot or significant damage.
2. **Disassemble Pallets**: Use a pry bar and hammer to carefully disassemble the pallets, separating the slats from the base. Aim to keep the slats intact for easier assembly.
3. **Cut Pallets**: Use a circular saw to cut two slats to 48 inches (for the bench seat) and four slats to 32 inches (for the bench legs).
4. **Sand Slats**: Sand all cut edges and surfaces of the slats using 80-grit sandpaper first, followed by 120-grit and finally 220-grit to achieve a smooth finish.
5. **Assemble Seat Frame**: Position two 48-inch slats parallel to each other on the workbench to form the bench seat frame. Attach two 32-inch slats perpendicular between them to create a rectangle, securing with wood screws at each joint.
6. **Attach Legs**: Position the remaining two 32-inch slats vertically at each corner of the frame to serve as legs. Secure them with wood screws, ensuring they are flush with the bottom of the seat frame.
7. **Reinforce Structure**: Apply wood glue at all joints before securing screws. Use clamps to hold the structure together while the glue dries, ensuring a solid bond.
8. **Prepare for Finish**: Wipe down the assembled bench to remove any dust or debris accumulated during construction.
9. **Apply Wood Finish**: Use a paintbrush to apply an outdoor wood finish or sealant to the entire bench, following the manufacturer's instructions for coverage and drying times.
10. **Allow to Cure**: Let the finish cure for at least 24 hours in a well-ventilated area before using the bench.
11. **Move to Outdoor Area**: Carefully lift and position the completed bench in the desired outdoor location, ensuring it sits level on the ground.

Maintenance:

- **Monthly**: Inspect the bench for any loose screws or joints. Tighten as necessary to maintain stability.
- **Every 6 Months**: Clean the bench with a damp cloth to remove dirt and debris. Reapply wood finish or sealant if the surface shows signs of wear or fading.
- **Yearly**: Check for any signs of rot or damage to the pallets. Address any issues promptly to prolong the life of the bench.

Complexity:

This project ranks as moderate in complexity. It requires basic woodworking skills and familiarity with power tools such as drills and circular saws. The main challenges involve ensuring precise measurements and securing joints effectively. Careful attention to detail during assembly is crucial for achieving a sturdy and visually appealing final product.

Estimated Time:

- **Setup and Material Gathering**: 1-2 hours to gather materials, prepare the workspace, and make necessary cuts.

- **Construction**: 3-5 hours for sanding, assembling the frame, and attaching legs.

- **Finishing**: 2-3 hours for applying the finish, not including drying time.

- **Total Estimated Time**: Approximately 6-10 hours, spread over two or more days to allow for glue and finish drying.

9.5.6 SCRAP METAL CHAIR FRAME WITH UPHOLSTERED SEAT

Creating a scrap metal chair frame with an upholstered seat offers a unique blend of functionality and creativity. This project stands as a testament to resourcefulness, transforming discarded materials into a stylish and sturdy piece of furniture. For those living off-grid or pursuing DIY sustainability, crafting furniture from scrap metal not only reduces waste but also encourages self-sufficiency. The benefits of this project extend beyond aesthetics; it provides a durable seating option that withstands the elements and can be customized to fit any decor style. This chair frame serves as an essential addition to outdoor spaces, gardens, or workshops, promoting both practicality and personal expression. By utilizing scrap materials, individuals can save money while gaining valuable skills in metalworking and upholstery.

Materials and Tools:

- Scrap metal tubing (steel or aluminum) - 10 feet

- Metal corner brackets - 4 units

- Metal screws - 20 units, 1 inch long

- Upholstery foam - 1 piece, 2 inches thick, 24 x 24 inches

- Upholstery fabric - 1 yard

- Heavy-duty staple gun - 1 unit

- Staples - 1 box, ¼ inch

- Angle grinder - 1 unit

- Drill - 1 unit

- ¼ inch drill bit - 1 unit

- Measuring tape - 1 unit

- Safety goggles - 1 unit

- Welding machine (optional) - 1 unit

- Sandpaper - 1 pack, various grits (80, 120, 220)

- Paint or rust inhibitor - 1 can

- Paintbrush - 1 unit

- Level - 1 unit

Step-by-Step Guide:

1. **Measure and Cut Metal Tubing**: Measure and cut four pieces of scrap metal tubing to 24 inches for the chair legs and two pieces to 20 inches for the seat supports.

2. **Assemble Seat Frame**: Lay the two 20-inch pieces parallel on a flat surface. Attach the 24-inch legs to each corner using metal corner brackets, securing them with metal screws.

3. **Add Support Crossbars**: Cut two additional pieces of tubing to 18 inches. Attach these between the legs at the midpoint for added stability.

4. **Sand Edges**: Use sandpaper to smooth all cut edges and surfaces of the metal tubing, ensuring there are no sharp edges that could cause injury.

5. **Weld Frame (Optional)**: If skilled in welding, weld the joints for added strength. If not, ensure all screws are tightly secured to maintain structural integrity.

6. **Prepare Upholstery Foam**: Cut the upholstery foam to fit the seat frame dimensions, ensuring it covers the entire surface for comfort.

7. **Cut Upholstery Fabric**: Cut the upholstery fabric to 2 inches larger than the foam on all sides, allowing enough material to wrap around and secure underneath the frame.

8. **Attach Foam to Frame**: Center the foam on the frame. Use the heavy-duty staple gun to attach the foam securely, stapling every few inches around the perimeter.

9. **Wrap and Secure Fabric**: Lay the fabric over the foam, centering it. Pull the fabric tight and staple it underneath the frame, ensuring there are no wrinkles on the top surface.

10. **Finish with Paint**: Apply paint or rust inhibitor to the metal frame using a paintbrush, ensuring even coverage. Allow the paint to dry completely according to the manufacturer's instructions.

11. **Check for Stability**: Use a level to ensure the chair is stable and all legs are even. Adjust as necessary by sanding or trimming any uneven areas.

12. **Move to Desired Location**: Once dry, move the completed chair to the desired outdoor or indoor location, ensuring it is placed on a flat surface for optimal stability.

Maintenance:

- **Monthly**: Inspect the metal frame for signs of rust or damage. Touch up with paint as necessary to protect against the elements.

- **Every 6 Months**: Check the stability of the screws and brackets. Tighten any loose connections to ensure the chair remains safe and functional.

- **Yearly**: Reassess the upholstery condition. Clean the fabric with a suitable cleaner and reapply any protective coatings if needed.

Complexity:

This project is moderate in complexity, requiring basic skills in metalworking and upholstery. Key challenges include accurately measuring and cutting metal, ensuring stability in assembly, and mastering the upholstery technique. Individuals should be comfortable using power tools and may need assistance with welding, depending on their skill level.

Estimated Time:

- **Setup and Material Gathering**: 1-2 hours to gather materials, prepare the workspace, and measure and cut metal.

- **Construction**: 4-6 hours for assembling the frame, attaching the upholstery, and finishing with paint.

- **Total Estimated Time**: Approximately 5-8 hours, depending on skill level and complexity of the design.

9.5.7 RECLAIMED WOOD AND SCRAP METAL BOOKSHELF

Creating a reclaimed wood and scrap metal bookshelf offers an excellent opportunity for DIY enthusiasts to combine sustainability with functionality. This project not only showcases personal style but also contributes to environmental conservation by repurposing materials that might otherwise end up in a landfill. For those living off-grid or seeking self-sufficiency, this bookshelf serves as a practical storage solution, capable of housing books, plants, or decorative items. The reclaimed wood brings warmth and character to any space, while the scrap metal adds an industrial edge. Together, these materials create a robust, unique piece that enhances the aesthetics of a home while minimizing costs. This guide provides a detailed, step-by-step approach to constructing a stylish and functional bookshelf that aligns with budget-friendly DIY principles.

Materials and Tools:

- Reclaimed wood planks - 6 units, 1x12 inches, 6 feet long
- Scrap metal brackets - 4 units, L-shaped, 2x2 inches
- Wood screws - 32 units, 1.5 inches long
- Wood glue - 1 bottle, 8 ounces
- Sandpaper - 1 pack, various grits (80, 120, 220)
- Drill - 1 unit
- ¼ inch drill bit - 1 unit
- Measuring tape - 1 unit
- Level - 1 unit
- Saw (circular or hand saw) - 1 unit
- Paint or wood finish - 1 can, 1 quart
- Paintbrush - 1 unit
- Safety goggles - 1 unit
- Work gloves - 1 pair

Step-by-Step Guide:

1. **Gather Materials**: Collect all materials listed, ensuring reclaimed wood is free from rot or damage.

2. **Measure and Cut Wood**: Measure and cut four wood planks to 6 feet for the vertical supports. Cut two planks to 4 feet for the top and bottom shelves.

3. **Prepare Shelves**: Sand all edges and surfaces of the cut wood planks, starting with 80-grit sandpaper and finishing with 220-grit for a smooth finish.

4. **Assemble Frame**: Position two vertical 6-foot planks parallel to each other. Attach the 4-foot top plank horizontally at the top using wood screws and wood glue for added strength.

5. **Secure Bottom Shelf**: Attach the 4-foot bottom plank parallel to the top plank, ensuring it is 12 inches above the floor. Use a level to confirm it is straight.

6. **Install Metal Brackets**: Position two scrap metal brackets on each side of the frame at the bottom and top. Secure them with wood screws to reinforce the structure.

7. **Add Additional Shelves**: Cut additional wood planks to the desired shelf height (typically 12 inches apart) and repeat the attachment process, ensuring they are level.

8. **Finish the Wood**: Apply a coat of paint or wood finish to enhance durability and aesthetics. Allow it to dry completely according to the manufacturer's instructions.

9. **Final Assembly**: Once dry, double-check all screws and brackets for tightness. Make any necessary adjustments to ensure stability.

10. **Position the Bookshelf**: Move the completed bookshelf to the desired location, ensuring it is on a level surface to prevent tipping.

Maintenance:

- **Monthly**: Inspect the stability of the bookshelf, tightening any loose screws or brackets as necessary. Dust surfaces regularly to maintain cleanliness and appearance.

- **Yearly**: Check for any signs of wear or damage to the wood or metal. Reapply wood finish or paint as needed to protect against moisture and wear.

Complexity:

This project is rated as moderate complexity. It requires basic woodworking skills, familiarity with power tools, and attention to detail during assembly. Challenges may arise in ensuring the frame is level and stable, particularly if working with uneven reclaimed wood. However, with careful measurement and adjustment, even novice DIYers can successfully complete this bookshelf.

Estimated Time:

- **Setup and Material Gathering**: 1-2 hours to collect materials and prepare the workspace.

- **Construction**: 4-6 hours to cut, assemble, and finish the bookshelf.

- **Total Estimated Time**: Approximately 5-8 hours, depending on individual skill level and available tools.

Made in the USA
Monee, IL
03 March 2025

13329573R00103